The Republic of Ireland

The Republic of Ireland

Its Government and Politics

Morley Ayearst

Professor Emeritus of Government
New York University

New York: New York University Press
London: University of London Press Ltd.
1970

PREFACE

This account of the Government and politics of the Irish Republic is primarily descriptive and only casually analytical and comparative. It is addressed to the reader who would like to know something about the Irish political system—its history and evolution and its relation to the Irish community.

The author would like to convey his thanks to the many in Ireland, of all political persuasions, who received him so warmly and who were so tolerant of his questions and so generous with their time in discussing Irish life and politics. Without their help this study would lack such insight as it may have.

In particular, thanks are due to the librarian of Trinity College, Dublin, for the hospitality of his magnificent library, and to Professors Chubb and Skeffington for their counsel. The author also would like to thank the staff of the Irish Consulate General in New York and Vice Consul James Flavin for his generous assistance. Special gratitude is owed for the penetrating comments of Mr. Michael McInerney, political correspondent of the *Irish Times*, and also for those of Conor Cruise O'Brien, sometime Albert Schweitzer Professor of the Humanities at New York University. The author is grateful, as well, for the thoughtful and valuable suggestions of Dr. Joseph M. Curran of Le Moyne College, Syracuse, New York.

Morley Ayearst

EAST HAMPTON, NEW YORK
MAY, 1969

CONTENTS

The Republic of Ireland

I

IRISH POLITICAL HISTORY TO THE CIVIL WAR

In few countries is the sense of history so strong and all-pervading as in Ireland. No study of Irish politics is comprehensible without reference to this history and to the selective memory of it that often motivates Irish political behavior. The specific task of this essay is a study of the present governmental system and its operation in Ireland but, to begin with, it is necessary to review briefly the history of which the existing political climate and party system is, in part, one of the results.

Like the Welsh and the Scottish tribes of Scotland and those early political refugees, the Bretons, the Irish were a Celtic-speaking people. But unlike most of the others, they were not directly affected by the English invasion of Britain in the late fifth century, A.D. Indeed, this was the period of Ireland's golden age. To use the old cliché, Ireland was then "a land of saints and scholars." In 548 a monastic university was founded at Clonmacnois, where impressive ruins may still be seen. Irish missionaries pushed deep into pagan Europe and established many monasteries, one of the latest at Regensburg in 1090. The Swiss Christian name "Fridolin" is derived from an Irish abbot and saint who founded monasteries in eastern France and Switzerland, probably in the seventh century. St. Gall, who had a Swiss town and canton named after him, was another Irish missionary saint.

But this is not the whole story, even though, for many Irish, nothing must be allowed to dispel the soft, golden haze which wraps "the land of saints and scholars." Ireland was unable to develop and maintain political unity. Despite the fact that the high king held court at Tara perhaps as early as A.D. 200, long before there was a king of England, the petty kings remained independent of his authority most of the time. Before the Norman conquest of England, Irish history was centuries of constant and often senseless intertribal slaughter and of cruel oppression of the peasantry by the bo-aire, the small gentry, as evidenced by the provisions of the ancient Irish law code, the Senchus Mor. The failure to attain an integrated society and an effective national government was a factor in the vulnerability of the Irish coasts to Norse raiders. The pagan Norsemen despoiled the monasteries, one by one, from late in the eighth century onward, and built their own fortified coastal towns. They were checked but not completely expelled by Brian Boru's victory over the Vikings at Clontarf on Dublin Bay in 1014.

It is possible that Ireland's history might have been different had a thorough Norman conquest of Ireland followed the pattern of the Norman conquest of England. A piecemeal invasion began with the expedition of Richard de Clare, Earl of Pembroke, nicknamed "Strongbow," in 1170, but despite the carving out of feudal lordships by De Clare and other Norman barons there was no total displacement by Normans of the Irish kings as the English earls and thanes had been displaced, almost to a man. The Irish kings remained to become earls and to swear fealty to the English king, although the king was never able to make the royal writ effective throughout Ireland. By the fifteenth century, English rule had shrunk to the area around Dublin and Wexford called the Pale. Nor did their feudal oaths prevent the Irish earls from rebelling against the English monarch when circumstances permitted.

Hugh O'Neill, Earl of Tyrone, broke openly with Queen Elizabeth in 1595. After negotiations and desultory fighting, Hugh defeated an English force in August, 1598, and all Ireland began to stir. Although Hugh received some help from Spain, Queen

Elizabeth acted decisively, the rebellion was crushed, and in March, 1603, Hugh submitted. The rebellious Irish chiefs were not harshly treated; they were confirmed in their estates and titles and Hugh's companion-in-arms, Rory O'Donnell, was even given a new title, Earl of Tyrconnel. It seemed that with the conquest of Ulster and this peaceful agreement with the Irish nobles, the domination of Ireland by the British Crown was complete. But as English rule became more obtrusive it became clear to the Irish lords that despite their new titles their old authority was gone. They resented this and when the Earl of Tyrone was summoned to London, he and Tyrconnel with some two hundred followers took ship for the Continent in 1608. This "flight of the earls" gave the British Government the excuse to accuse them of treason and to confiscate their lands, including the counties of Armagh, Cavan, Coleraine (Londonderry), Donegal, Fermanagh and Tyrone, and open them to English and Scottish colonists. Only a small area in each county was set aside for "deserving natives" who might remain on their lands. For the rest, grants were made to English and Scottish proprietors who undertook to bring in settlers to populate and farm the land. It was at this time that the city companies of London formed a joint-stock enterprise to settle part of Ulster, and the town of Derry was renamed Londonderry. A great many lowland Scots settlers came as well, many of them Presbyterian "Covenanters" who had suffered some religious persecution in their native Scotland. These were the ancestors of the Orangemen.

The Protestant Reformation had not affected Ireland. Outside of the Ulster Plantations the vast majority of the inhabitants, whether native Irish or "Old English," as the descendants of Hibernicized medieval English settlers were called, were "recusants." That is, they remained faithful to the Roman Catholic Church and refused to take the legally required Oath of Supremacy to the English monarch. They sided with Charles I in his quarrel with the English Parliament and the Civil War divided Ireland as badly as it did England. There had been bloody battles in Ireland between royalist and parliamentary forces for some nine years before Cromwell arrived in Dublin with his 3,000 Ironsides in

1649. His immediate capture of Drogheda followed by the slaughter of its royalist garrison, along with any Catholic priests that could be found, made a profound impression upon the Irish. The story of this event grew with repetition and gained in horrifying detail. There would seem to be no evidence that the whole population of Drogheda was killed or that the Irish were singled out. The garrison consisted mainly of English royalists. Cromwell next proceeded to subdue most of the southern counties before he left Ireland in 1650. All fighting had ceased and Parliament had triumphed by 1652.

Ireland was then placed under commissioners appointed by the English Parliament. They proceeded to confiscate the lands of Irish "delinquents" in whole or in part and see that they were removed across the Shannon into Connaught, where they were to be given lands equal in value to that part of their old property, if any, which they were allowed to retain. This plan was difficult to administer and actually was not carried out completely although several thousands of the Irish were moved, bag, baggage, and cattle, across the Shannon, and their former lands given to the soldiers who held debentures in lieu of back pay and the Adventurers who held government scrip.

The Restoration of the Monarchy in 1660 did little to reverse the Irish land confiscations. Of course Charles II was constantly importuned by the dispossessed Irish landlords and an Act of Settlement was passed to adjudge their claims. In practice, however, only a small number had their property restored. The Cromwellian beneficiaries of the confiscations were enraged at this reversal of policy and threatened rebellion, but had to give back about one-third of their grants. This was not nearly enough to satisfy the claims of the dispossessed, but King Charles dared go no further. The Cromwellian plan to turn Ireland into a totally Protestant country was not realized but the composition of the population had been altered permanently. Before the Civil War well over half of all the land in Ireland had been owned by Roman Catholics, but after the confiscations and restorations they held little over one-fifth. In addition, they had been pushed out of the towns and had seen almost all Irish business and commerce taken over by Protestants who also dominated the restored Irish Parliament.[1]

The Protestant triumph was soon to be seriously threatened. The accession of King James II led to the domination of the Irish Government by Richard Talbot, the Roman Catholic Earl of Tyrconnel, who purged the army of Protestant officers, appointed Roman Catholic sheriffs, and reorganized local government to permit Catholic control. In many cases the alarmed Protestants fled to England where they helped to turn sentiment against the King. The latter received some assistance from France, trading five Irish regiments for 4,000 French troops which arrived in Ireland in 1690. Simultaneously the Protestant contender for the throne, William of Orange, arrived in the North. The decisive encounter came at the Boyne River where William defeated the army of King James, an event still celebrated by Northern Protestants on July 12 with parades of the Orange Lodges, the beating of enormous drums and, only too often, riotous behavior directed against their Catholic neighbors.[2] Unwilling to accept the fact of defeat, the Irish Parliament, now predominantly Catholic, passed legislation designed to more than reverse the Confiscations and virtually dispossess all the Protestants. In fact, the Battle of the Boyne did not finish the fighting, although it made the end certain. More than that, it left the Protestant and Catholic communities so sharply divided that the victorious Protestants felt themselves to be completely justified in adopting the harshest discrimination against the Catholics and in enforcing to the letter the old penal laws which had usually been overlooked in the past.

The treaty of Limerick, signed in October, 1691, ended the war in Ireland. Under this treaty some Jacobite landowners were left on their estates, but about another million acres were confiscated, reducing Catholic holdings to about one-seventh of all Irish land.[3]

The Government of Ireland was now divided between the English and Irish Parliaments. The latter was completely Protestant as no Roman Catholic could take the oath abjuring Catholic doctrines required of all members by an act of 1691. This Irish Parliament then proceeded to pass several bills which seemed designed to destroy the Roman Catholic religion. Bishops and religious orders were banished. No Roman Catholic might hold any public office, nor buy land, nor inherit land from a Protestant, nor will his land to anyone. Even so, these laws were far less savage than the anti-Protestant laws of France. Ordinary secular clergy (parish priests) were allowed to remain in Ireland and to celebrate mass and perform other religious functions. It is suggested by Professor Beckett that these laws were designed not so much to destroy the Catholic faith as to ensure that Catholics would be kept in an inferior position, economically, politically, and socially. An important provision in this scheme was the refusal of any higher education to the Catholic laity. Very few Catholics could afford to attend a foreign university and a law of 1695 prohibited the sending of children abroad to be educated.

The Irish Parliament, as noted above, was totally unrepresentative of the Irish people. It was the voice of the Anglo-Irish Ascendancy only. Catholics might, indeed, vote for Protestant members down to 1724, but the franchise was removed from them in that year. It was restored to Catholics meeting the ancient forty-shilling-freehold requirement by the Catholic Relief Act of 1793 which Pitt forced the Irish Parliament to accept. This did nothing to destroy the power of the landlords because an Irish tenant leasing a freehold had to vote as directed or face eviction. In Ireland, as in England at the time, there were few genuine electoral contests. Political parties were nonexistent or, at most, inchoate. Insofar as there were any, they consisted of informal groups of members who tended, more or less consistently, to support or oppose the government of the moment. Great landed families had "pocket" constituencies. For generations the Wellesley family had not only a peerage, and therefore a seat in the Irish House of Lords, but also what amounted to an hereditary seat in the House of Commons. But this parliament had very limited powers. It had no authority over the army and no effective control of financial policy. It could and did suggest legislation which, under Poynings' Law, had to be submitted to the English Privy Council for approval, might be amended there, and had then to be accepted or rejected by the Irish Parliament precisely as resubmitted by the

Privy Council. Furthermore, the Lord Lieutenant, who represented the English Government in Dublin, could dissolve the Irish Parliament at will. As a rule the Irish Parliament held a session only once in two years and did not bother to hold a general election except after the death of the monarch.

The Irish Parliament had, as noted, some initiative in proposing legislation but the English Parliament claimed the right, sometimes exercised, to legislate directly for Ireland. It did so in 1699, prohibiting the export of Irish woolens to any foreign country. This ruined the woolen trade, which had been expanding and which was mainly conducted by Protestants. The result was a demand, similar to that made in the American colonies, for the extension of the rights of Englishmen to all subjects of the King. In Ireland this led to a demand that legislative powers in Irish affairs be confined to the Parliament of Ireland. This did not reflect any romantic Irish patriotism on the part of the Protestants but was a pragmatic approach to their economic problems. This claim, amounting to an assertion that Ireland and England were in a state of personal union, sharing a common monarch, but not subordinate one to the other, was stated cogently by Dean Swift in the fourth of his *Drapier's Letters* in 1724. The English Parliament did not accept this argument and continued to legislate for Ireland from time to time.

This was, in all essentials, a colonial situation. Despite the elegance of eighteenth-century Dublin and its impressive buildings, such as the Parliament, Trinity College, the Four Courts, and others, as well as the several squares of graceful Georgian houses surrounding parks, all suitable to a national capital, real authority resided not there, but in Westminster. The Lord Lieutenant in Dublin Castle was merely the voice of his masters in London. Insofar as any Irish interest was represented at Westminster it was that of the Anglo-Irish landlord class. The "colonists" were the Anglo-Irish Ascendancy, who owned most of the land and enjoyed a disproportionate share of its production. Others also battened on Ireland. Irish tax revenues were used to pay pensions to royal favorites to the tune of some £30,000 per annum and sinecures, mostly enjoyed by Englishmen, cost the Irish treasury more than this. Altogether Irish remittances to Great Britain for rents, interest, pensions, salaries, and other payments during the period from 1668 to 1773 amounted to about £1,110,000 a year.[4] The native Irish provided the necessary labor force and their interests were no more considered than were those of the West Indian slaves on the sugar estates. The "mere Irish," as they were called, were not allowed to rise above subordinate positions or to train for a profession. They were denied entry into public posts. In cities such as Dublin and Limerick they were required to leave the city at sundown and sleep in an "Irishtown" outside the walls, an "apartheid" enforced to forestall insurrections as well as crimes against persons and property.

As in the American colonies in the days of the Old Colonial System, the colonial Ascendancy had a voice in government, but final authority rested with the Secretary of State in London or his local representative. Indeed, some West Indian colonial assemblies enjoyed more actual control of the colony's finances than did the Parliament in Dublin. In other respects too, the Irish Parliament suffered in comparison with some colonial assemblies. Its hereditary House of Lords was even more unrepresentative of the Irish people than were the nominated members in the colonies of the general interest of their communities. Its House of Commons was a caricature of an elected body. More than half its members represented "pocket" districts and were the nominees of individual landlords. Corruption was employed by the British Government to insure that only loyal members were elected.[5] The Whigs justified this with the need to ensure that Ireland should not become a beach-head for England's enemies, Spain and, later, France.

The Anglo-Irish Ascendancy and the Ulster Presbyterians were the first Irish "patriots" in eighteenth-century Ireland. They began to identify themselves with Irish interests which were, indeed, their own, and even with the "Irish nation." Many Scots-Irish Presbyterians as well as Catholic Irish had emigrated to the American colonies and when the American war of independence broke out these Irish Americans helped to stimulate sympathy in Ireland for the American cause which closely resembled that of Ireland. Some Irish Protestants were inspired to recruit and train volunteer militia, not only to defend Ireland against a threatened French invasion but to put some muscle behind their claims upon the English Government. Hostility toward Roman Catholics began to diminish and the Irish Parliament reflected this sentiment by moderating the old property restrictions placed upon Catholics. There seemed to be reason to believe that a reconciliation among Christians might come to pass. Under Irish and opposition pressure, the Prime Minister, Lord North, freed Irish trade in 1779–1780. The Irish patriot Grattan continued to demand an independent Irish government. In the end a modified, semi-independence for Ireland was granted although a royal veto on Irish bills was retained. This "Constitution of 1782" also provided for the control of Irish administration by a Lord Lieutenant, appointed by and responsible to the British Government.

The French Revolution was the next international event to have repercussions in Ireland. Although the Catholic clergy were horrified by its excesses and its treatment of the Church, it seemed probable that enthusiasm for reform, partly inspired by the French Revolution, might induce the Ulster Presbyterians to join their Catholic neighbors in working for an extension of popular government and religious equality. An important instrument in this movement was the Society of United Irishmen, a founder of which was Wolfe Tone. But the alliance between the two religious groups was not to endure. Contests for land between Protestant and Catholic farmers in Ulster led to intimidation and violence. One especially bloody affray in County Armagh in 1795 resulted in the defeat of the Catholic fighters and the formation of the Orange Society by the victorious Protestants. There followed violent persecution of Catholics in Ulster, many of whom were forced to take refuge in Connaught.

Despite this setback to religious toleration, the rebellion against British rule did not end. Fighting continued between British troops and the United Irishmen. A brutal and bloody miniature civil war broke out in Wexford in May, 1798. Most unusual was the leadership of the Irish rebels by some local Catholic clergy. This revolt was crushed in a month's time and another outbreak in Ulster was also quickly suppressed. Wolfe Tone managed to bring some French help to the rebels but this did not change the course of events. Tone himself was captured and executed for treason, to become a revolutionary symbol for later generations.

It was under these conditions that Prime Minister Pitt conceived his plan to solve the Irish problem by uniting Ireland with England. If Ireland could be made an integral part of the United Kingdom, as were Wales and Scotland, and if Irish grievances were removed by suitable reforms, surely the disloyal Irish might soon be transformed into loyal Britons.

But first he had to convince the Irish Parliament that union was desirable. Under the Constitution of 1782 the English Parliament could no longer legislate directly for Ireland and Pitt had no easy task in persuading the Irish Parliament to sign its own death warrant. He used a variety of arguments and methods. The Irish masses were indifferent and of course had no voice in the Irish Parliament. Also, their old enemies, the bailiff and the tithe-proctor, would still operate under the Union. The collapse of the 1798 rising had left a residue of bitterness and unrest which had, in turn, stimulated brigandage and terrorism in the countryside. The police and courts could do little because witnesses could not be produced to testify. The Protestant Ascendancy therefore, was open to Pitt's argument that only the Union could save it from being swamped by a Catholic democracy. This argument alone was not enough. A great deal of bribery was necessary as well. Some was used to ensure the election to the Irish House of Commons of members favoring union. Some members of both Commons and Lords were promised United Kingdom peerages. A few were simply given cash bribes.[6] The Roman Catholic bishops and upper- and middle-class Catholics were induced to accept the Union by a promise of Roman Catholic emancipation to be passed by the post-Union British Parliament. Finally, the Ulster Presbyterians, who had fallen out of sympathy with the French Revolution, were resentful of the Irish Parliament because of the measures it had taken after the 1798 rising. They were willing to accept union.

Grattan led a last-ditch fight in the Irish House of Commons to save the Irish Parliament. He failed in this attempt and on August 2, 1800, the five-hundred-year-old institution ceased to function. Unmourned by the great majority of the Irish people it might, under other circumstances, and with more foresight and goodwill on the part of all, have developed into a genuinely national and democratic legislature, as did those of the American colonies.

Ireland was now to be represented in the House of Lords at Westminster by 4 archbishops and bishops of the Church of Ireland and by 28 temporal lords elected for life by the Irish peerage. The House of Commons would have 100 new Irish members. The Churches of Ireland and England were united. With some exceptions, free trade was established between Great Britain and Ireland. The national debts were to remain separate but Ireland was assessed a share of the cost of the combined Government. The amount was fixed at two-seventeenths, an amount which proved too heavy for Ireland in view of the heavy war costs which continued for many years.

At first the Irish members at Westminster did very little. They did not form a political party nor act in unison. In Ireland nothing changed except that Dublin seemed less important—it was no longer a real capital city. The Protestant Ascendancy continued unaltered in its economic and social domination. Ireland now had a viceroy, for no very good reason except that this was felt to be a sop to Irish pride. Irish administration continued to be run from Dublin Castle and the Irish departments were not integrated with their English equivalents.

The Ascendancy, whose members had been very skeptical about the Union to begin with, before long were convinced that it was a good thing. The Irish peers in the House of Lords and their English supporters there were quite capable of preventing any reform measures likely to threaten or even inconvenience the Ascendancy landlords and Protestant businessmen. Previously, political differences had cut across religious lines. Many Protestants had been Irish patriots and had struggled for Irish freedom. Some, like Wolfe Tone, had become martyrs in the struggle. Some

Roman Catholics had been more conservative and had hoped for favorable treatment by demonstrating their loyalty to the British throne. But now Protestants, with almost complete unanimity, were Unionists and nearly all Catholics were against the Union and, in due time, Home Rulers.

One of the principal arguments for union had been the economic prosperity it was supposed to bring to Ireland. This did not happen although the linen industry in Ulster did expand and flourish, so that Ulster Protestants were happy with the Union while Southern Catholics came to regard it as the principal cause of their poverty.

There was much rural distress and many, "a large majority," according to Beckett, had no more than a mud cabin and a potato patch and had to try to keep alive by casual or harvest labor. The population grew apace and the size of the holdings became even smaller. By 1841 there were 8,175,000 inhabitants on an island with scarcely any industry and far from enough farmland to support such a population. In 1815 Peel tried to get the Cabinet to accept a scheme for assisting Irish emigration to Canada, but this was rejected. Some landlords tried to get their excess tenants to emigrate but few tenants could be induced to do so. At the same time there was considerable English emigration to Canada, the United States, and Australia, for hard times had followed the close of the Napoleonic Wars. Only a carefully planned and generously subvented emigration plan could have saved the situation in Ireland and this was not done. It would have run counter to the universally accepted economic principle of laissez-faire. There was no single villain. Had there been no rack-renting, no absentee landlords, nor any tithe-proctors, and even if the Irish peasant had had to pay neither rent nor taxes, disaster would surely have struck as it did unless massive government intervention had prevented it. In fact, almost the only attention paid to Ireland by the British Government was the provision of military force to preserve the peace and suppress crimes and riots. Under these conditions the Irish tenantry sometimes resorted to violence against the landlords and their property. Secret societies were formed to frighten landlords into moderating their demands upon tenants and sometimes these tactics were successful. Naturally such behavior reinforced the English conviction that the Irish were a lawless and treacherous folk.

Irish farmers had discovered that the potato could provide the maximum quantity of food per acre and landlords had found that unemployed farm workers were willing to sell their services in return for a small plot on which to build a cabin and raise potatoes. By 1846 potatoes were the "daily bread" of the Irish people. In that year the potato plants were stricken by a blight that destroyed almost the entire crop. Sir Robert Peel, the Prime Minister, acted vigorously and intelligently. He appointed a scientific committee to find the cause of the disease but the biologists of the time were baffled by it. He instituted relief projects which were not ineffective. Then, in order to make cheaper food grains available, he secured repeal of the Corn Laws which had been enacted to protect British farmers from foreign competition. This was an abandonment of a basic Tory policy. It led to a deep split in his party and the triumph of the Whigs under Lord John Russell. The Whigs were firm believers in laissez-faire principles and held that private enterprise should be left alone to solve the food scarcity in Ireland. Some relief projects might be needed but they would have to be financed out of Irish taxes. Before long the Irish Board of Works was swamped by a flood of unemployed for whom it had no work. An unusually cold winter added to the misery and encouraged the spread of epidemics. Malnutrition was common—even actual starvation. Most of those who could arrange to do so chose to emigrate. By 1851 Ireland's population had shrunk from more than eight million to about six and a half million. About half of the missing millions had died as a result of starvation and disease, and the other half had left Ireland. Thenceforward emigration continued to be the answer to Ireland's surplus labor problem and for more than a century the Irish population continued to shrink steadily, with depressing effects upon the Irish economy and upon the Irish attitude toward their future as a nation. Thenceforward also Irish politics would be influenced by the views and attitudes of the Irish emigrants and the funds they supplied for Irish national movements.

Political leadership within post-Union Ireland had to be found among members of the middle class. Except in Ulster there was hardly any rural middle class. In towns and cities, the middle class, predominantly Protestant, consisted of a relatively few professional men and merchants. This was due to the denial of professional education to Irish Catholics and to the fact that, in part owing to British legal restrictions, Ireland had been by-passed by the Industrial Revolution. The rural landlord class, even that part of it that lived in Ireland and took an interest in the welfare of the peasants, was unlikely to provide leaders for a rebellious tenantry. The Roman Catholic parish clergy might have done so but the Church was mainly concerned with securing its own emancipation and in appeasing the legal authorities in furtherance of this end. In their public utterances, the clergy were loyal to the British connection.

The middle class felt themselves frustrated by the economic shackles which union had not removed. Governed from Westminster, Ireland seemed to be doomed forever to stagnate under a colonial economic system. Naturally, therefore, middle-class politicians could embrace and defend only policies devoted in some degree to Irish emancipation, political and economic. Their following, if numerous, had to come from the depressed classes, rural as well as urban. At the same time, these middle-class nationalists were far from being revolutionaries and their economic and social views were conservative.

The most outstanding of them, and also the first to be of native Irish, Roman Catholic stock, was Daniel O'Connell, the son of a Kerry landowner and one of the first of his faith to be admitted to the bar after Catholics were allowed to train for the law under an act of 1792. For almost a generation preceding his death in 1847 he had the greatest following of any Irish politician. Although the worst of the penal laws had been repealed, Irish Catholics still suffered disabilities. They were barred from the higher posts in government and the civil and armed services and could not be made judges. These disabilities affected only the educated middle class and it was not until O'Connell founded his Catholic Association in 1823 that there was a united movement for repeal of this religious discrimination. But now, for the first time in history, there was a national movement supported by all classes of the Irish people. It had the enthusiastic support of the middle class, the clergy, and the urban workers as well as the tenant farmers who faithfully subscribed their penny or sixpence a month to the "Catholic rent" collected by the parish priests and sent to the Association headquarters in Dublin. By 1825 these subscriptions amounted to about £2,000 a week. In the general election of 1826 a number of members of Parliament who opposed Catholic Emancipation were replaced by men who supported it, although they too were necessarily Protestants. Irish tenant farmers were beginning to vote according to their own opinions and the advice of their parish priests, and not as directed by their landlords, despite the very real danger of eviction for disobedience. In 1828 O'Connell himself, although prevented by the law from taking a seat in Parliament, defeated a popular member by a majority of almost two to one. His supporters marched to the polls marshaled by their parish priests.

By this time the House of Commons was no longer adamantly opposed to Catholic Emancipation. In fact, there may have been a slight majority in favor of it, on the merits of the issue. Accordingly, when the Conservative Prime Minister, the Duke of Wellington, and his Home Secretary, Sir Robert Peel, introduced the Catholic Emancipation Bill, it passed without difficulty and became law in April, 1829. At long last Pitt's promise had been kept. Roman Catholics could now hold any office except that of Lord Lieutenant in Ireland, Lord Chancellor in either England or Ireland and, of course, the monarchy.

Irish farmers were deeply interested in another reform, the abolition of the tithes on arable land which went to support the alien, Protestant Church of Ireland. Almost one-third of the incumbents of these Protestant livings were absentees, their parishes having no communicants and, in many cases, no churches.[7] As far as the Irish were concerned, these livings were nothing more than parasitic sinecures. As a rule, the absentee clergymen never visited Ireland and left tithe collection to "tithe farmers" who worked on commission. The English Conservative rationalization of this system was that every Christian state should have an established church, that the Church of Ireland was the established church there, and that all Irish owed tithes to it whether they belonged to it or not. This view was acceptable even to some Catholic prelates. One bishop placed a chapel under interdiction because some parishioners had posted a notice there denouncing tithes.[8] However, some bishops, such as Dr. Doyle, Bishop of Kildare, held the Church of Ireland tithing system to be immoral and despotic. In 1832 the collection of tithes was made a function of the civil authorities. This only tended to stimulate the disorders that had become a commonplace accompaniment to the enforcement of payment. The Anglican bishops and their allies in the House of Lords were able to block reform for some time but in 1838 the Tithe Commutation Act reduced the tithe by one-quarter and added it to the rent owed by tenants. From the tenants' viewpoint, this was a most unsatisfactory reform.

O'Connell's great victory in the matter of Catholic Emancipation had convinced him that the English Government would give way before peaceful agitation and a clear demonstration of the popular will without any need to employ violent methods. He believed that the Liberal Party was more likely than the Conservative Party to respond to Irish demands and accordingly he supported it in Parliament. When the Liberals were defeated in 1841 and the Conservative leader, Sir Robert Peel, became prime minister, O'Connell thought the time ripe to begin agitation for the repeal of the Act of Union. Repeating the method which had been so successful on the previous occasion, the Repeal Association was founded along the lines of the Catholic Association. Once again the parish clergy were enlisted to collect a "Repeal rent." An important feature of the campaign was the organization of mass meetings of impressive size, designed to impress the British Government with Irish unanimity on the issue. One of these meetings, held at Tara in August, 1843, is said to have attracted an audience of three-quarters of a million people.

In this campaign, O'Connell did not have the unanimous support of the Catholic clergy. The hierarchy in particular, insofar as they concurred with papal policy, may have seen an advantage in maintaining a bloc of Irish Catholic M.P.'s at Westminster, a leaven in the Protestant loaf, rather than in their removal to Catholic Ireland. For this very reason, Cardinal Manning had opposed Gladstone's first Home Rule Bill, calling it a "Catholic and world-wide danger." [9]

But the decisive factor in O'Connell's defeat was not the attitude of the Irish hierarchy but that of the House of Commons. In 1829 the English M.P.'s were at least half convinced that Catholic emancipation was overdue. In 1843 almost all were utterly opposed to repeal of the Act of Union. Sir Robert Peel, who had supported Catholic Emancipation, was prepared to face the possibility of civil war rather than give in to the repeal demand. In this spirit the Government banned the last of O'Connell's series of monster mass meetings, scheduled to be held at Clontarf, outside Dublin, in October, 1843. O'Connell, as a law-abiding subject, called off the meeting. Thereafter the Repeal Association began to lose its impetus and its former supporters to look elsewhere for leadership and inspiration.

For some, this was supplied by a new movement called Young Ireland. Its founder was a Protestant barrister of Dublin named Thomas Davis who hoped for a truly national movement of both Protestants and Catholics. He was joined by Charles Gavan Duffy, editor of *The Nation*, a weekly founded in 1842 to present O'Connell's views. Duffy was the originator of the idea that Irish M.P.'s should refuse to join any British party or accept any government post offered by a British prime minister. This stratagem, put into practice by Parnell, enabled him to exert considerable leverage upon policies. Another influential Young Irelander was John Mitchel, who held out for complete Irish independence and was not averse to the use of physical force to gain it. A frequent contributor to *The Nation* was James Fintan Lalor, who argued that the Irish people in general could be enlisted in the fight for national independence only if this fight were associated with the land question which concerned them so closely. This idea was also fully exploited later by Parnell and Davitt. The Young Irelanders had been forced to the conclusion that their old leader, O'Connell, had become out of date in aims as well as methods. They broke away from him in 1844. Many of them accepted Mitchel's advice and attempted an insurrection in 1848, the "year of revolutions," when several European governments were overthrown. The Irish rising was crushed at once by the prompt action of the Royal Irish Constabulary and the Young Ireland movement collapsed with it. Nevertheless, as already noted, several of the Young Irelanders' ideas were influential later on. Furthermore, they kept alive the ancient Irish tradition of armed rebellion, and veterans of 1848 were among those who revived it in the Fenian rising of 1867 which, in turn, was quickly suppressed by the RIC.[10]

By the middle of the nineteenth century the great majority of the Southern Irish were totally opposed to the Union, while the landlord class and the entire Protestant population of Ulster were determined to maintain it at all costs. To this sizable minority, union meant the protection of their privileges, and for the Ulstermen, the prosperity of an industrial North where the linen industry and shipbuilding were expanding. It was very different in the South. There was no industry there. The loss of population during and after the Great Famine had not eased the tenants' situation, for the competition for land and work remained desperate. More than half the population lived as tenants on estates covering half of Ireland's arable lands. About five-sixths of these tenants were tenants-at-will who could be evicted at the whim of the landlord.[11]

Not all landlords were inconsiderate of their tenants. Indeed, some of the largest landholders were among the best. Some tried to educate their tenants in better methods of farming, supplied them with improved seed, kept their cottages in repair, and postponed or remitted rents in case of a crop failure. The harshest landlords were the absentees [12] and the small landholders, far from rich themselves, who regarded the slightest sign of prosperity among the tenants as an excuse to raise the rent.[13] The absentee landlords were likely to take no interest in the tenants they never saw. Of the five largest absentee proprietors in County Mayo, who held altogether some 369,000 acres and received a total annual income from rents of between £80,000 and £100,000, not one was recorded as having contributed anything to the relief fund which saved the peasantry from starvation in the winter of 1879–1880.[14]

Absenteeism, however, was not the chief obstacle to good landlord–tenant relations. After the Great Famine, the Encumbered Estates Act (1849) was passed to provide a clear title to newly purchased Irish estates. Nine out of ten of the buyers of distressed properties were Irish and many were shrewd speculators interested only in quick profits. They began "rack-renting" at once. It was the general pattern of land-holding in Ireland, the scarcity of good land as compared with the demand for it, and the vagaries of the weather which so affected the crops that created the economic aspects of the Irish land problem.[15]

An attempt to grapple directly with this problem was made by Charles Gavan Duffy, the former Young Irelander, who formed the Tenant Right League in 1850. Its objectives were fair rents, fixed tenure, and the legal right of the tenant to sell his lease. Duffy hoped to gain these objectives by the election to Parliament of enough sympathetic M.P.'s to secure the necessary legislation. The Irish franchise had been enlarged from time to time under the Union and the reformed English Parliament after 1832 was more sympathetic than its predecessors to the idea of popular representation. An act of 1850 more than doubled the Irish electorate and this helped the Tenant Right League to secure the election of forty pledged supporters in the Irish delegation of one hundred and three in the election of 1852. But this marked the high point in the League's fortunes. An important factor in its failure was its lack of clerical support. Duffy had tried to get a working alliance between the Presbyterian tenant farmers of Ulster and the Catholic tenants in the South. To begin with, he had some success and both Presbyterian ministers and Catholic priests were among the early sponsors of the League until the bishops ordered the priests to desist from this "political" activity. Some professed adherents of the League had used it simply as an electioneering device. Two of these, Messrs. Sadlier and Keogh, whose verbal parade of Catholicism had earned them the nickname of "the Pope's brass band," quickly betrayed the principles of the League in return for the prize of minor ministerial posts in the British

Government. No doubt the failure of the League influenced some Irish patriots to turn again to "physical force."

Some of the veterans of the abortive Rising of 1848 had escaped the police net and fled to New York, where they regrouped their forces. The result was the Fenian Brotherhood, founded simultaneously in New York and Dublin in 1858.[16] Its goal remained that of 1848—Irish independence and an Irish republic to be secured by an insurrection to take place when the British arms were engaged elsewhere. Some Fenians, but not all, advocated sabotage and political assassinations while awaiting the insurrection. At this time Irish conspirators were busier in the United States than in Ireland. One reason for this was the greater freedom to meet and plan without danger of arrest by the RIC. Another reason was the generosity with which Irish-Americans supported their cause. It is said that between 1858 and 1866 the Fenians collected about $500,000 in the United States and Canada.[17] Without this financial support the Irish Republican Brotherhood in Ireland, as the Fenians called themselves there, would have been seriously hampered. Its membership was derived largely from the working class and the IRB could count upon neither middle-class nor clerical sympathy or help. Because of its secret, oath-bound nature, its goal of violence and revolution, its republicanisms and its inclusion of non-Catholics, it was unlikely to get the approval of the Catholic Church. In both Ireland and the United States the Fenian oath was one of allegiance to "the Irish Republic, now virtually established. . . ." Soon there were thousands of Fenians in the United States, Great Britain, and Ireland. Possibly because of its religiously mixed membership and its appeal to the working class, some clergy denounced the movement as communist, which it was not. Most of the bishops condemned the Fenians, and one, Bishop Moriarty of Kerry, in a magnificent example of Irish hyperbole, said from the pulpit: "Hell is not hot enough nor eternity long enough to punish the Fenians." [18] This attitude was not shared by all the clergy and there was a widespread feeling of outrage in Ireland when three Fenians were hanged for their part in the attack upon a prison van in Manchester in the course of which a policeman had been shot.

Especially outrageous was the fact that, in accord with normal British practice in the case of convicted murderers, they were buried inside the prison walls in unconsecrated ground. Many masses were said for them in Ireland and the Archbishop of Tuam, Dr. MacHale, assisted at a high mass for them.

The Fenian acts of sporadic violence did accomplish two things: they kept alive the tradition of violent rebellion against the British connection and they forced Gladstone and his Liberal Party to examine Irish grievances. An early result of this examination was the disestablishment of the Church of Ireland in 1869. This was an indirect result of Fenianism and a direct result of a temporary alliance between the Irish Catholic bishops and the Liberal Party in backing this reform. Archbishop Cullen and others of the hierarchy assisted in the founding in 1864 of the National Association of Ireland to provide a constitutional, non-violent means of securing the redress of Irish wrongs.[19] It was hoped that this Church-sponsored movement would counter the spread of Fenianism which was affecting even some of the clergy. The Association lasted only some ten years and had only a modest success in securing the election of members pledged to its objectives. It was of help in securing disestablishment, but once this had been achieved, it had lost a main reason for its existence and differences among its adherents over a number of issues diminished its effectiveness in bringing pressure upon the British Government. Not even all the bishops had supported the National Association and the lower clergy had never embraced it with the enthusiasm they had shown for O'Connell's Catholic Association.

But the National Association was of considerable help in securing the election of Liberals in the general election of 1868. It threw its weight on the Liberal side because nothing could be hoped for from Disraeli and his Tories and because Gladstone had become convinced that disestablishment was the right policy. Cardinal Cullen voted for a Liberal even though this candidate was a Quaker. After disestablishment, Gladstone turned to the land problem, which he realized was a fundamental cause of Ireland's troubles. His first serious attempt to solve this problem took the form of the Landlord and Tenant (Ireland) Act (1870). This conferred upon all tenants the "Ulster tenant-right," an indirect admission of the Irish contention that a tenant had a moral right to keep his land. Under this act he had the right not to be evicted so long as he paid his rent, the right to sell his tenancy, and the right to compensation at the termination of a tenancy for improvements previously made. In addition, the act gave the tenant the right to buy his land outright and to be given a loan by the Board of Works for this purpose.

Even while Parliament was considering Gladstone's proposals, a new attempt to provide a constitutional solution for Ireland's difficulties was being made there. This was the Home Rule movement, founded by a Protestant barrister, Isaac Butt. He wanted the restoration of an Irish parliament but not the republic demanded by the Fenians. At first the movement attracted much support, especially among the middle class. In the general election of 1874 Home Rulers won over half of the Irish seats. Butt's methods in Parliament, however, were ineffective. His patient, low-keyed speeches and unfailing parliamentary courtesy had little effect upon the English M.P.'s. Some of his followers thought that some results might be achieved by more vigorous and even obnoxious behavior. Two Home Rulers of Fenian background began to use procedural technicalities to obstruct the business of the House. In this they were joined by another Irish M.P., Charles Stewart Parnell, a Protestant landowner from County Wicklow. Butt was shocked at these tactics, but even before Butt's death in 1879 Parnell had emerged as the leading figure in the party. Although not an outstanding orator, he proved to have remarkable abilities as a political leader and a remarkable endowment of the quality known as charisma. Even though official Fenian policy condemned parliamentary activity as useless, Parnell soon enjoyed much Fenian support as well as that of Irish nationalists of all classes. Before long Parnell came to enjoy a prestige and popularity hitherto unknown in Ireland. The "uncrowned king of Ireland," as he was called, could secure the nomination of any candidate he chose. Even when corruption in his party had become notorious, his own prestige was hardly affected. Not until the publicity given to the O'Shea divorce proceedings did personal scandal bring about his downfall.

Parnell organized his party in Parliament so that, unlike former Irish delegations, it would act unanimously under his leadership and remain in permanent opposition to all British governments, Whig or Tory.

Gladstone's Landlord and Tenant Act of 1870 did little for the Irish tenantry. Most of them had no lease and could still be evicted, in effect, by rack rents. Landlords were generally able to avoid fair payment for improvements made by the tenant. When an estate or farm was sold, tenants could seldom compete in the bidding against the big speculators. The winter of 1878–79 was so rainy that there were crop failures and, following this, many evictions of tenants who could not pay the rent. This, in turn, led to violence directed against landlords and the farmers who took over the lands of evicted tenants. In the West, conditions almost approached those of the Great Famine and would have done so had it not been for a private charity effort of international dimensions.

The Irish response to continued agrarian distress was the formation of the Land League, which appealed to almost the entire population except the landlords. Its principal founder was Michael Davitt, the son of a poor tenant farmer of Mayo, who had spent seven years in an English jail for Fenian activities and who had been released through the efforts of Parnell. Davitt urged Parnell to accept the leadership of the new movement and Parnell was duly elected president of the Land League in October, 1879. It became almost impossible to secure election to Parliament without the endorsement of the League. Agrarian disorder continued. By the close of 1880, the local magistrates found themselves unable to convict anyone for the murder of landlords, estate agents, or "land-grabbers" because no witnesses could be found to testify for the prosecution. The boycott, a method of bringing pressure to bear upon landowners, which took its name from that of a landlord and estate agent against whom it was first applied, came into wide use. A boycotted person was ostracized. Nobody would work for him; shopkeepers would not serve him; and when he died, no laborer would dig his grave. Anyone who failed to observe the rules of the boycott was in danger of being boycotted as well. Not a few landlords were forced by the boycott to leave Ireland.

In the beginning of the Land League agitation the Catholic clergy were far from unanimous in its support. It was denounced by the Archbishop of Tuam, the (Catholic) Archbishop of Dublin, and the Bishops of Cork, Cloyne, Ross, and Kerry. At the same time, many of the parish clergy sympathized with the League and some bishops, notably Archbishop Croke of Cashel and Bishop Nulty of Meath, supported it, as did a number of Protestant ministers.

As in the case of the Fenian movement, the Land League had wide support in America. By 1881 there were over twelve hundred branches of the League in Canada and the United States. A considerable part of the money that financed Parnell's activities came from the American branches, stimulated by the enthusiasm and zeal of an Irish emigrant, Patrick Ford, editor of the (New York) *Irish World*. According to Arnold Schrier, more than $1,000,000 was sent to the League in Ireland and most of this had been collected between 1880 and 1883.[20]

The general election of 1880 saw Gladstone's return to power and Parnell at the head of the Irish delegation to Parliament. Gladstone's response to the "land war" was the Protecting Life and Property Act (1881) empowering the courts to imprison without trial and so to avoid the necessity to find witnesses. One of the first to be arrested under this law was Davitt. This was the "stick." The "carrot" was a new Irish Land Act (1881) setting up a land court to fix fair rents. The act also allowed a tenant to wipe out arrears of rent by paying one year's rent, an equal amount to be given the landlord from the funds of the Church of Ireland. This was too little and too late to satisfy the Land Leaguers, who issued a manifesto calling upon the tenants to refuse to pay any rent at all. Gladstone's response was the arrest of all the principal Land League leaders—Parnell, Dillon, O'Brien, and others—followed by the suppression of the League in October, 1881. Eventually Parnell and Gladstone came to an agreement, usually called the "Kilmainham treaty" after the jail in which the

Land Leaguers had been held. Both agreed to call a stop to violence and Gladstone agreed to submit further legislation on the land problem. The Land Leaguers were released from jail. But the new era of goodwill was almost ended before it had well begun by the senseless murder in Phoenix Park on May 6, 1882, of the newly appointed Chief Secretary, Lord Frederick Cavendish, and the Under Secretary, T. H. Burke. This was the act of a secret assassination club within the Fenian movement, calling themselves "The Invincibles."

In truth, Gladstone's Land Act of 1881 had rendered the Land League obsolescent. Many tenants had ignored the "No Rent" manifesto, preferring to seek relief from excessive rents by appealing to the Land Court. In the first three years of its operations the Land Court reduced rents by almost twenty percent. But the Land League agitation was not yet over. In 1886, two of its leading figures, William O'Brien and John Dillon, advanced a new solution to the tenant problem which they called "the Plan of Campaign." By this, tenants would set their own rents and give the money to a trustee who would offer it in a lump sum to the landlord. If the landlord would not accept it as payment in full he would get nothing and the money would be given to any tenants who were evicted. The Archbishop of Dublin, Dr. Walsh, supported the plan as did some other clerics, although it was denounced by the Bishop of Limerick, Dr. O'Dwyer, who also condemned its enforcement device, the boycott. At this point an emissary from the Vatican, Monsignor Persico, was sent to report on the Irish situation. His report resulted in the issuance of a papal rescript in 1888 condemning the Plan of Campaign for reasons which seemed, from the Irish standpoint, to be unconvincing. The Irish Catholic members of Parliament held a meeting at which they condemned the rescript.

Parnell himself had not actively supported the Plan of Campaign but he remained the unquestioned leader of the Irish Parliamentary Party. As a united and disciplined group, Parnell and his followers held the balance of power in the House of Commons after the general election of 1885. Gladstone was then induced to adopt the policy of Home Rule for Ireland. But all of Gladstone's

eloquence could not hold his party together on this issue. The
86 members of Parnell's party, the "86 of '86," were insufficient to
counterbalance the 93 Liberal Unionists like Joseph Chamberlain
who voted against the bill on its second reading, when it lost by
30 votes. In fact the bill did not grant anything like complete
home rule and had been accepted by Parnell only with reluctance. It removed Irish representation from both Lords and
Commons in England and set up a single-chamber parliament for
Ireland in which two "Orders" of members were to sit together
unless separate discussion were demanded by either order. The
first order was to consist of the 28 representative peers for Ireland who had previously sat in the House of Lords, plus 75 other
persons meeting a high property qualification and elected by well-
to-do voters (" £25 occupiers") for a 10-year term. The second
order would have 204 members elected for a 5-year term by the
regular parliamentary voters. The Royal Irish Constabulary,
detested as the arm of British imperialism, was not immediately to
fall under the authority of the new Irish Government, presumably
to give its members time to leave the service and avoid possible
reprisals. A key provision of the bill was that the Irish Parliament
should have no authority to alter the status of the Lord Lieutenant,
who therefore would continue, as before, to serve as the head of
the Irish administration and representative of the British Government only.

Having lost on such an important bill, Gladstone had no
choice but to "appeal to the country." The result was a Conservative victory and an administration headed by the Marquess of
Salisbury. The Unionists undoubtedly represented prevailing
British opinion, for this was the hey-day of British imperialism
when Englishmen gloried in the far-flung British Empire and were
strongly averse to its reduction, even by such semiwithdrawal
from British authority as was involved in Irish Home Rule. They
were confirmed in this attitude by their old prejudices about the
Irish, whom they held to be treacherous, savage, and unfit for
self-government. If further confirmation of Unionist attitudes
was needed, it was supplied by Orange Ulster and its spokesmen.

The Unionist Party, a combination of Conservatives and Liberal Unionists, remained in power for the remainder of the century except for the years 1892 to 1895. In 1892 Gladstone was again able to form an administration with a majority of forty, including the Irish Nationalists. This enabled the introduction of his second Home Rule Bill in 1893. This bill, unlike the first one, allowed for continued Irish representation at Westminster, but by 80 instead of 103 members. This provision did not appeal to some Liberal "Home Rulers" who favored Home Rule in part because it would remove the Irish delegation from the House of Commons. Like the previous bill it gave Ireland only a restricted version of Home Rule. Its financial provisions were attacked by some Irish members as "keeping Ireland in bondage." The bill was passed in the Commons by the narrow margin of thirty-four votes but suffered a predictable defeat in the House of Lords. That the British public was still Unionist in sentiment would seem to be proved by the Conservative victory of 1895.

In 1890, before the defeat of the second Home Rule Bill, Parnell had been named co-respondent in a divorce action brought by an Irish M.P. named Captain O'Shea. The resulting scandal shattered the Irish Nationalist movement. Parnell was disowned by both the Protestant Dissenters that made up a considerable section of the Liberal Party and the Irish Catholic clergy. Indeed the bishops issued a manifesto declaring him to be unfit for political leadership. His subsequent marriage to Mrs. O'Shea only "capped the climax of brazen horrors," in the words of Bishop O'Donnell of Raphoe.[21] Those who stood by Parnell and those who repudiated his leadership split his party into bitterly warring factions. The clergy were uncompromising in their hostility toward the Parnellites. Bishop Nulty of Meath wrote in a pastoral: "No man can remain a Catholic as long as he elects to cling to Parnellism." He declared, further, that even to read the *Westmeath Examiner*, a pro-Parnell newspaper, was sinful and if continued despite this warning, would make absolution "null and void." [22] The unprecedented alliance forged by Parnell of middle-class Nationalists, tenant farmers, and urban, working-class ex-Fenians—with the blessing and support of a large part of the clergy—had now been broken beyond repair. No other Irish leader was ever again able to weld such a union. A semblance of unity was restored when John Redmond became party chairman in 1900. Redmond was leader of the Parnellite faction and the party in Parliament never again attained the complete unanimity it had displayed under Parnell. The majority did accept Redmond's leadership and the party still enjoyed American financial support.

Their victory in 1895 gave the Conservatives a chance to try their policy of reform within the Union, "killing Home Rule by kindness." The Land Act of 1896 had provisions favorable to the tenantry including compulsory sale of distressed estate lands to the tenants. The Irish landlords who had worked hard for a Unionist-Conservative victory were not well pleased with the result. The culmination of this line of policy came with Wyndham's Land Purchase Act of 1903, which greatly aided tenants in buying their farms by partial payment of the price from government funds. In many cases, the farmer could buy his farm on terms easier than his previous rent payments. By this reform, Ireland became, as it has remained, a land of peasant proprietors. In effect, the Cromwellian and Williamite confiscations were canceled.

In 1907 the British Government proposed a political reform in Ireland along the lines later employed in Crown Colonies advancing from representative to responsible government. The Irish Council Bill of 1907, applying to all Ireland, North as well as South, provided that eight departments should be handled by an Irish administrative council. This was to be composed of eighty-two elected and twenty-four nominated members. Their responsibilities would include supervision of the Local Government Board, Congested Districts Board, Commissioners of Public Works, Commissioners of National Education, Intermediate Education Board, Reformatory and Industrial Schools, and Registrar General. The Chief Secretary of Ireland would attend meetings and speak but have no vote. The Lord Lieutenant, like a Crown Colony governor, would review decisions of the council and would be free to approve them, veto them, or return them to the council for further study.

Most Irish Nationalists thought this proposal insulting. It fell far short of their aspirations to be given a government suitable for a West Indian Crown Colony not yet considered fully capable of managing its own affairs. The Catholic hierarchy was horrified at the prospect of Irish education in the control of lay boards, many of whose members would be Protestants. Naturally it was opposed by the Ancient Order of Hibernians. This society, initially organized in the United States, had established an Irish branch called the Board of Erin. It was strongest in Ulster, where it constituted a riposte to the Orange lodges. It had begun to exercise some influence in Irish politics and its condemnation of the council plan together with that of the clergy was sufficient to veto the bill before its enactment. Parnell's successor, John Edward Redmond, had at first supported the bill as a step toward Home Rule. In fact, if it had been put into effect, it might have been just that—and possibly would have brought about a working relationship between North and South that would have prevented the partition of Ireland in 1921. A mass meeting at the Mansion House, Dublin, presided over by Redmond, vigorously condemned the proposal. Redmond felt obliged to give way before what seemed to be Irish public opinion and when the bill was introduced, moved its rejection. Campbell-Bannerman, the Prime Minister, then withdrew it.

Such cautious advances as the Council proposal could not now reconcile Irish nationalists to the Union. Even Home Rule, still the preference of the majority, was beginning to lose some of its appeal. A new movement had appeared in 1905 to try to give a new direction to nationalist efforts. This was Sinn Féin (literal translation: "Ourselves"), founded by Arthur Griffith, a Parnellite and editor of the *United Irishman* since it first appeared in 1899. Griffith held the Act of Union to be illegal and Home Rule an insufficient remedy. At first a separatist, he later advocated a "dual monarchy" in which Ireland and Great Britain would have no governmental connection except that of the symbolic Crown. He thought this would have wider appeal in Ireland than a republic. Most Sinn Féiners, however, sympathized with the Irish Republican Brotherhood, even though the IRB was firmly committed to armed rebellion, whereas Sinn Féin favored passive resistance and the withdrawal of Irish M.P.'s from the British Parliament. In the beginning, Sinn Féin gained few converts. Most nationalists were still willing to settle for Home Rule, now within grasp because the Parliament Act of 1911, passed with the help of the Irish delegation, had "drawn the Lords' teeth" by substituting a two-year suspensory veto for their old absolute veto. The third Home Rule Bill had passed the Commons in 1912 and the Liberals, still in power, were prepared to pass it again in 1914.

In Ulster the immanent enactment of Home Rule aroused a violent reaction. Irish Unionists and English Conservatives were united in this. Bonar Law, the Conservative Leader of the Opposition, actually made public statements amounting to approval of armed rebellion by Ulster Protestants if Home Rule were enforced.

Although Parnell was a Protestant and a landlord, most Irish Protestants, especially of the landlord and well-to-do class, had always been bitterly opposed to Home Rule. There were several reasons for this attitude. They feared a weakening of the British connection, a further loss of the social and economic advantages accruing to the Protestant Ascendancy, already sadly diminished, and Roman Catholic domination of an independent Irish government. The commercial and manufacturing interests in Ulster were especially fearful of what might be done to them by a Home Rule parliament. Most Protestants were Unionists. In much of Ireland this meant an opposition to Home Rule by an upper- and middle-class minority. In the Ulster counties, the Protestants included small farmers, laborers, and factory workmen as well. Here, all were united to fight Home Rule and the Orange lodges gave a framework to their organized opposition. With the assistance of the Orange Order, an armed force called the Ulster Volunteers was quickly assembled, as well as a provisional government to take charge in Ulster if Home Rule were to be applied there. Fanatically anti-Catholic, the Ulster Protestants believed implicitly in their slogan, "Home Rule is Rome Rule." As citizens of an all-Ireland state they were sure that they would become a helpless minority, subjected to religious and economic persecution.

The South already had the nucleus of a native militia in the small Irish Citizen Army, enrolled in 1913 by James Connolly, the revolutionary socialist labor leader, for the immediate task of intervening between strikers and the police and the ultimate objective of constituting the vanguard of a socialist revolution. Another paramilitary force in the South was formed with a nationalist rather than a socialist end in view. This was the Irish Volunteers. Its principal founders included Padraic Pearse and Eoin MacNeill as well as Protestant Irish nationalists such as Bulmer Hobson and Sir Roger Casement. Although not formed as a counterbalance to the Ulster Volunteers, it had IRB support and would have taken part in a civil war had one broken out. Both sides began to import arms illegally. The Ulster Volunteers had a smoothly working system whereby arms arrived at night and were whisked away and distributed before the police could interfere. The Irish Volunteers boldly landed arms at Howth, across Dublin Bay, in daylight. A military detachment was sent to intercept them but arrived too late. As the British soldiers marched back along Bachelor's Quai in Dublin they encountered a jeering crowd, some of whom hurled stones at them. No order to fire was given but some soldiers did fire into the crowd and three persons were killed. This seemed, in Irish eyes, to provide clear evidence that there was one law for the Unionists of Ulster and another for Irish nationalists.

The deadlock between Carson and Craig, the Ulster Unionists, and the Home Rule leaders, Redmond and Dillon, was unaffected by a conference called by King George in July, 1914. No doubt civil war would have broken out in Ireland as soon as the Home Rule Bill had become law, but the entire situation changed with the outbreak of World War I in August. Carson at once agreed to stop opposing passage of the Home Rule Bill if Redmond would agree to the addition of a clause postponing its operation until after the war. This was done and both leaders called for full support of the British war effort. Redmond's action was not unpopular with most of his followers, especially after the German invasion of Belgium. He had the support of a majority of the Irish electorate until 1916. A great many young Irishmen volunteered for service in the British armed forces. War prices brought prosperity to Irish agriculture. Some optimists thought that the truce between Carson and Redmond might lead to a peaceful postwar solution and Home Rule for all Ireland.

This was to underestimate the North's intransigence and the depth of anti-British feeling on the part of some nationalists. For the latter, the suspension of Home Rule "for the duration" was another example of British duplicity. They repudiated Redmond's pledge and hoped the war would provide the opportunity for a successful rebellion. The secret IRB and the Irish Volunteers could provide the nucleus for a national rebellion. Among the most aggressive of the leaders was Padraic Pearse, who called for an Irish "blood-sacrifice." He and others began to plan for a rising. Their motto was: "England's enemies are Ireland's friends," and, just as their predecessors had requested and received help from France, they now hoped for German arms and munitions. Sir Roger Casement went to Germany by way of New York to arrange arms shipments. The authorities at Dublin Castle had an effective intelligence system and so the British were kept informed of most of the anti-British activities. However, they regarded the IRB and the amateur soldiers of the Irish Volunteers as impotent fanatics, too few in numbers to create a serious disturbance in peaceful, prosperous Ireland. The Volunteers and the Citizen Army were allowed to parade and to drill with rifles without interference by police or military.

Pearse, MacDonagh, and the other IRB leaders had chosen Easter Sunday, April 23, 1916, as the date of an insurrection to be commenced simultaneously at several places in Ireland. It was timed to occur immediately after a large shipment of German arms had been received. But the arms shipment and the German ship carrying it were intercepted by the British navy. Sir Roger Casement, having landed in Ireland, was taken prisoner. The Rising had been the pet project of the IRB and Connolly's Citizen Army. Eoin MacNeill, the commander of the Irish Volunteers, had been dubious about it from the outset and he now sent messages canceling the "manoeuvres" scheduled for Sunday. The Dublin leaders decided to go ahead anyway, postponing action for one day only. On Easter Monday they occupied the General Post Office on Sackville Street (now O'Connell Street) and Pearse read a proclamation declaring the establishment of the Irish Republic and demanding the allegiance of the Irish people. By Monday evening the insurgents had occupied a number of buildings in Central Dublin, but the military outcome was never in doubt. The British forces struck back and by Saturday all was over. Pearse, as commander, surrendered unconditionally. There was almost no public support for this rising when it took place. Most Irish people denounced it as stupid and useless when it was going on and after the surrender. It seemed that the Easter Rising had set back the cause of Irish nationalism. That the contrary was the case was due to the reaction of the military authorities. Martial law was proclaimed in Ireland and in short order fifteen leaders of the Rising, including all seven signatories of the republican proclamation, had been court-martialed and shot. As the executions of these "traitors" were announced, one after another, popular disapproval of these misguided patriots changed feelings of outrage against the Government. The military authorities were guilty of gross political stupidity. At one stroke they gave the IRB and also the moderate Irish nationalists an entire hagiology of martyrs and turned into potential rebels many Irish people who had resolutely opposed rebellion before the Easter Rising. Although the hierarchy had long ago condemned the IRB and several bishops denounced the Easter Rising in pastoral letters, evidently the episcopate was not unanimous on the point. After all, the Irish clergy were Irishmen and their emotional response to the independence struggle might well be one of strong sympathy—sometimes strong enough to lead them to try to find theological justification for the violence employed against agents of the British Government. Even those who could not, in good conscience, approve this violent adventure may have agreed with the great Irish poet, William Butler Yeats, in seeing "a terrible beauty" in the mad, foredoomed rebellion. At any rate, as noted by Sir James O'Connor, a meeting of the entire Irish episcopate at Maynooth after the Rising did not result in any general pronouncement on it. Instead the bishops issued a manifesto on Irish missions in China.[23] The shift of clerical support away from the Parliamentary Party and toward Sinn Féin was dramatized by the funeral cortege of Thomas Ashe, a hunger-striking Sinn Féiner who died in prison a few hours after he had been forcibly fed. The funeral procession was headed by Eamon de Valera and Bishop Fogarty of Killaloe who, at one time, had been strongly opposed to Sinn Féin. There were many other priests in the procession. Even such a prominent prelate as Archbishop Walsh of Dublin became known as a Sinn Féin sympathizer. A final British move which united the great majority of Irish behind Sinn Féin was the proposal to apply military conscription to Ireland in the final stages of World War I.

Griffith's "dual monarchy" proposal was dropped by Sinn Féin in favor of an independent Irish republic. This policy change gained for Sinn Féin the political support of the IRB and the left-wing followers of Connolly and Larkin. In the 1918 elections Redmond's Parliamentary Party all but disappeared. Only 6 Redmond Nationalists won seats as compared with 26 Unionists, mainly from Ulster, and 73 Sinn Féin candidates.

To the English, the Irish remained an enigma. It was incomprehensible that they should continue to refuse to become British. Old grievances had been eliminated. Ireland no longer suffered under a tyrannical British Government. On a population basis, Ireland was overrepresented at Westminster. Ireland received the benefit of any social welfare legislation passed by Parliament and a series of reforms had given the land of Ireland back to the Irish. Especially outrageous, in English eyes, was an armed revolt while Great Britain was fighting for its life in Europe and for the freedom of the Western World. This attitude may help to explain the savage reaction of the authorities to the Easter Rising.

The newly elected Sinn Féin members, true to their pledge, refused to take their seats at Westminster but instead met in Dublin in January, 1919, organizing themselves into a body they named Dáil Éireann. They declared their independence of Great Britain, reaffirmed the Republic that had been proclaimed by Pearse at the Easter Rising and elected as President of the Republic one of the few surviving senior officers of the Rising, Eamon de Valera. The Irish Republican Army was authorized to make war upon the English "foreign invader" and execute all informers and Irish traitors who served as agents for the English enemy.

This amounted to a declaration of war upon Great Britain, but a war in which the British would not recognize the Irish Republican Army as insurgents entitled to the treatment normally accorded the soldiers of a belligerent enemy, but as ordinary criminals. Thus began the period of "the Troubles," a very mild term indeed for the bitter, vicious guerilla fighting marked by atrocities and counteratrocities that lasted from early in 1919 until 1921.

Conceivably it would have been possible for the British Government, by the use of unlimited military force and numerous concentration camps, to destroy the IRA and clamp Ireland to a stern, military autocracy. Aside from any question of right and justice, such a solution was politically impossible. English liberal opinion would not have tolerated it, as evidenced by the reaction to the British "police action" in the columns of the *Daily News*, *Manchester Guardian*, and *Westminster Gazette* as well as statements by prominent Liberals and Labourites. Also American opinion could hardly be ignored, and this was strongly hostile toward the suppression by force of Irish independence. The attempt to enforce British rule was limited to the activities of the Royal Irish Constabulary and their auxiliaries, nicknamed the Black and Tans.[24] These auxiliaries were mainly demobilized British soldiers and some of them may have been brutalized by their war experiences. There were excesses on both sides and the longer the attempt continued to seek a solution by force, the more remote the solution seemed to be. Certainly a peaceful solution was not furthered by assassinations, raids on police barracks, and houseburnings by the IRA, nor by the burning of villages, the indiscriminate shooting of villagers, and the hasty executions and terror tactics of the police. In a considerable part of Ireland the legal (British) authority could not operate and had been replaced by that of the Republic.

Even while the fighting between the police and the IRA was still going on, Lloyd George made a final attempt to keep Ireland within the United Kingdom by the Home Rule device. The Government of Ireland Act (1920) divided Ireland into Northern Ireland (the six Northeast counties) and Southern Ireland (the remainder). Each was assigned a parliament with powers similar to those granted by the suspended Home Rule Act of 1914. Both parts of divided Ireland would continue to have representation at Westminster and the British Parliament would retain sovereignty over Ireland.

The Irish Republicans regarded this act as derisory but they did make use of the electoral procedure provided by the act to demonstrate their complete domination of Irish politics outside of Northeast Ulster. The election of May, 1921, known as the "partition election," saw the return of 124 unopposed Sinn Féin candidates. Considering the circumstances, it would have been foolhardy for a Unionist candidate to oppose them. In fact, four Unionists were elected but these represented (Protestant) Trinity College, Dublin. They alone appeared at the inauguration of the new parliament for Southern Ireland which soon adjourned. In Northern Ireland the party representation was reversed. The Unionists won forty of the fifty-two seats.

In June, 1921, a truce was arranged, after which Lloyd George invited the Irish Republican leaders to discuss a permanent settlement with him. The invitation was accepted and on July 12 President de Valera went to London accompanied by Arthur Griffith, Austin Stack, R. C. Barton, and Erskine Childers. Lloyd George offered terms, the principal element of which was that Ireland should have the status and powers of a British "dominion" within the British Commonwealth of Nations. De Valera rejected this offer and was supported in the rejection by the Dáil on his return to Dublin. A final series of conferences began in October, but this time President de Valera did not attend, leaving negotiations in the hands of Arthur Griffith, Michael Collins, Eamon J. Duggan, and George Gavan Duffy. The conferences dragged on until December when Lloyd George presented an ultimatum: an agreement must be reached at once or the full resources of Great Britain would be used to crush the Irish rebellion.

The final British offer was a treaty to create an Irish Free State with dominion status. The Lord Lieutenant would be replaced by a Governor General, as in Canada, to represent the Crown. A complicated oath of allegiance was phrased, after much haggling, so as to offer minimum offense to Irish sensibilities (or so it was hoped). The Free State would assume a fair share of the national debt and pay pensions to the civil servants of the old Irish Government. The British navy would continue to have port facilities in Ireland, patrol Irish coastal waters, and maintain certain harbor defenses. Irish armed forces would number no more in relation to the Irish population than British forces to the population of Great Britain. Northern Ireland should be governed under the terms of the 1920 act if it wished, and if it did, a boundary commission should determine the Free State–Northern Ireland border "in accordance with the wishes of the inhabitants." Neither Northern Ireland nor the Free State should endow any religious denomination nor confiscate religious property.

From the Irish point of view this offer was far from satisfactory. It was not the Republic for which they had been fighting. Dominion status was still imprecise of definition. Could the imperial Parliament legislate for Canada, and also, therefore, for the Free State, without the dominion's consent? The vagueness of this status, along with British insistence upon the retention of the royal symbol and refusal to consider an Irish republic, rendered the treaty totally unacceptable to devoted republicans. The partition of Ireland was also unacceptable.

From the British standpoint the offer was remarkably generous. Irish authorities had acknowledged the sovereignty of British monarchs ever since the Middle Ages. Irish grievances had been removed and Irish people now enjoyed full British citizenship. As they wanted a parliament and government of their own, it was hereby offered to them. What more could they ask?

The Irish negotiators in London had to make a hard decision. Little as they liked some of the treaty provisions, they liked even less the probability of renewed armed conflict if it were refused. De Valera would not have signed it had he been there but Griffith, Collins, and their colleagues considered it to be the best bargain obtainable and affixed their signatures. It then had to be ratified by the Dáil and ratification was preceded by long and bitter debate. De Valera, Stack, and Brugha held that the plenipotentiaries had exceeded their authority in signing and that they should have held out for more concessions on the part of Britain. Griffith and his supporters insisted that the treaty gave a large measure of independence and did not preclude further advances. The treaty was approved by the narrow margin of sixty-four votes to fifty-seven. De Valera resigned the presidency at once and Griffith was elected to succeed him.

Had Eamon de Valera chosen to accept the decision of the Dáil at this point it is possible that the civil war might have been averted, but when he organized a new republican government apart from the Dáil and called upon the old IRA to support him, he made war inevitable.

The only Irish force in being in the Free State area was the Irish Republican Army, which had been reorganized and strengthened during the months following the truce. This was no ordinary, politically neutral army, automatically accepting orders from a universally accepted government. Rather it was an armed political movement. For the IRA the big issue was whether or not to accept the treaty. As it turned out the IRA was as much divided on this question as were other Irish citizens. Some of them became the military arm of the new Free State but others, faithful to their ideal of a pure republic, refused to take orders from the Government, which they regarded as an illegal and usurping junta.

Griffith and Collins proceeded to set up a provisional government for the Free State, as required by the treaty. A drafting committee under the chairmanship of Collins was appointed by the Provisional Government to draw up a constitution for the IFS. This was done and presented to the British Government. It was a purely republican scheme of government and made no mention of the king. British draftsmen had to alter it to make it fit the treaty stipulations.

The revised draft was not ready soon enough to permit careful consideration by the electorate before the election of June 16, 1922, but at that election the only issue was acceptance or rejection of the treaty. De Valera had made a pact with Collins in May, 1922, whereby the two sides would present the voters with a joint panel containing pro-treaty and anti-treaty candidates in the same proportion as in the previous Dáil. Nevertheless, there was much disorder during the campaign. Meetings were sabotaged and pro-treaty candidates threatened, but the result was a triumph for the pro-treaty forces, which won a sweeping victory.[25]

The revised draft constitution was duly accepted by the British Parliament and received the royal assent on December 6, 1922. On this same date in Ireland the Provisional Government was superseded by that of the Irish Free State. The Lord Lieutenant ceased to function and Timothy Healy became the first Governor General of the new dominion. The remaining British forces began to leave, and completed the evacuation by December 16. Northern Ireland immediately took the necessary steps to remain outside the Free State as permitted by the treaty.

But the civil war begun by the adamant republicans of Sinn Féin and a part of the IRA, inspired and led by Éamon de Valera, was not yet over. Their original stratagem seems to have been acts of violence directed primarily against the British troops remaining in Ireland, both North and South, so as to provoke a violent reaction and thus a renewal of the Anglo-Irish war.[26] But the British troops did not react nor, for some time, did the National Army of the IFS. The failure to use force against the IRA "irregulars," as they were called, may have been due to a reluctance to attack former comrades and some uncertainty as to the reliability of the national troops in such an encounter. But the situation could not be allowed to last indefinitely and its strong public backing in the June election encouraged the Provisional Government to act against the irregulars. On June 28 the Government ordered the irregulars to give up the building complex of the Four Courts which they had held since March. They refused to do so and artillery was employed to force their surrender. This incident marked the real beginning of the civil war. The Provisional Government and its successor, the IFS Government, were compelled to fight this civil war while trying desperately to set up a national administration, replace the Royal Irish Constabulary with the inexperienced Civic Guard, and reorganize the judiciary. It is little wonder that many of the police-state measures which the British authorities used during the Anglo-Irish "Troubles" were revived. Imprisonment without trial, summary executions, and even the execution of prisoners in reprisal for the acts of others, were all employed. Not until the spring of 1923 did Eamon de Valera, recognizing his failure to win the armed struggle or to win converts to his position, give up and order the irregulars to lay down their arms. Not all of them did so and the IFS Government retained legislation permitting police actions without review by the courts.[27]

Ireland had suffered far more destruction during the civil war than in the period of the "Troubles." Railroads had been sabotaged constantly and rendered inoperable in many places. Several scores of country houses had been burned and many looted. No doubt would-be criminals were quick to take advantage of the absence of effective police supervision; many of these outrages may have had criminal rather than political motivation. There is some evidence too that the new Communist International hoped to take advantage of the chaotic situation in Ireland.[28] One historian has advanced the theory that the civil war was not so much a struggle over the treaty as one between socially conservative nationalists and socially radical republicans. In defending this thesis he mentions the mansion house burnings, the workmen's riots in Wexford and Waterford, and the actual establishment of temporary "Soviets" in some places.[29]

The subsequent history of Sinn Féin and Fianna Fáil make it very clear that the great majority of the antitreaty fighters were neither Communists nor socialists but simply Irish nationalists. They were ardent republicans mainly because of their hatred of the British connection and its symbol, the monarchy.

Notes

1. J. C. Beckett, *The Making of Modern Ireland, 1603–1923* (London, 1966), pp. 120, 121.

   It should be noted that the term "Protestant," as used in Ireland, refers only to the Church of Ireland (the Irish branch of the Church of England) and its communicants, and not the Presbyterian or other nonconformist churches. In this study, however, the usual practice is followed and "Protestant" covers all non-Roman Catholic Christian sects.

2. One of the more printable Orangemen's toasts is this: "To the glorious, pious and immortal memory of William III, Prince of Orange

who saved us all from popery, brass money and wooden shoes." "Brass money" refers to debased coinage issued by James II.

3. Beckett, *op. cit.*, p. 149.

4. W. W. H. Lecky, *A History of Ireland in the Eighteenth Century*, I (1892 edn.), 199, 213. The pound sterling at that time had about eight times its current purchasing power.

   Both George I and George II made lavish use of Irish sinecures and pensions "to provide for their mistresses, their bastards, and their German relations and dependents" (Beckett, *op. cit.*, p. 171).

5. Nicholas Mansergh, *Britain and Ireland* (London, rev. edn., 1946), p. 23. Lecky estimates that 176 of the 300 members of the Irish House of Commons were chosen by individual patrons (Lecky, *op. cit.*, I, 196).

6. Beckett, *op. cit.*, p. 278.

7. R. B. McDowell, *Irish Public Opinion and Government Policy in Ireland, 1801–1846* (London, 1952), pp. 19, 20.

8. The Bishop's letter is quoted in Castlereagh's *Memoirs*, II, 387. It is possible that the Bishop's action was motivated by opposition to civil disobedience rather than simple approval of the tithing system.

9. Sir Shane Leslie, *Henry Edward Manning, His Life and Labours* (London, 1921), p. 415.

10. It should be observed that the Royal Irish Constabulary was a national police force, quartered in barracks, under military discipline. It resembled the French *gendarmerie* and the Italian *carabinieri* rather than a municipal police force. Like its Italian and French counterparts its primary function was not so much the suppression of individual crimes or the apprehension of ordinary criminals as it was the preservation of public order and suppression of public disturbances. It acted also as the eyes and ears of Dublin Castle (the British-directed Government of Ireland). In the view of many Irish Nationalists it represented the vanguard of an army of occupation. This does much to explain the hatred of the RIC and some of the acts of savagery both by and against the police during the "Troubles" of 1918 to 1921.

11. Norman Dunbar Palmer, *The Irish Land League Crisis* (New Haven, 1940), pp. 9, 10.

12. The proportion of absentee landlords has been exaggerated. Among proprietors of more than one hundred acres, residents outnumbered absentees by seven to two (Palmer, *op. cit.*, pp. 27, 28).

13. If a tenant went to church wearing anything better than patched work clothes and hobnailed boots, he might find landlord or agent at his door on Monday morning to announce an increase in the rent.

14. Palmer, *op. cit.*, p. 32.

15. The best study of land tenure down to the 1890's is W. E. Montgomery, *The History of Land Tenure in Ireland* (Cambridge, 1889).

16. The society took its name from the warrior band who had fought under the legendary hero of ancient Ireland, Finn MacCool.

17. Arnold Schrier, *Ireland and the American Emigration 1850–1900* (Minneapolis, 1958), p. 105.

18. Quoted in E. R. Norman, *The Catholic Church and Ireland in the Age of Rebellion* (Ithaca, New York, 1965), p. 117. See Chapter 3, "The Church and Fenianism."
19. *Ibid.*, Chapter 4, "Birth of the National Association, 1864–5."
20. Schrier, *op. cit.*, p. 127.
21. O'Connor, *op. cit.*, II, p. 145.
22. *Ibid.*, II, p. 147.
23. O'Connor, *op. cit.*, II, p. 278 n.
24. So called because of their temporary uniforms, a mixture of military and civilian dress and a reference also to the pack of hounds of a celebrated hunt.
25. "Southern Ireland" General Election, June, 1922:

Pro-treaty Sinn Féin	58
Republican Sinn Féin	36
Labour (mostly pro-treaty)	17
Farmers (mostly pro-treaty)	7
Independents (mostly pro-treaty)	10

26. See W. Alison Phillips, *The Revolution in Ireland 1906–1923* (London, 1923), p. 283.
27. The bitterness engendered by the civil war lasted long and may not yet have disappeared completely. Michael McInerney, political correspondent of the *Irish Times*, reported a "distressing scene" in the Dáil as late as 1964, when there was a heated exchange between Mr. Aiken and General MacEoin, two of the civil war veterans still active in politics. See *Irish Review and Annual, 1964*, p. 18.
28. Phillips, *op. cit.*, p. 289 n., quoting *The Communist International*, May, 1921.
29. See E. Strauss, *Irish Nationalism and British Democracy* (London, 1951). There were two examples of union action in 1920 which might be regarded as revolutionary socialism. Creamery workers at Knock-along, Limerick, after a wage dispute, seized the creamery and continued to operate it with the cooperation of the local dairy farmers. Coal miners at Arigna, Lietrim, seized the mine. These are the only reported instances of such action by unions.

II

POLITICS SINCE THE TREATY

All who participate in a revolution are compelled to work together if the revolution is to be successful. Whatever differences they may have over political objectives or constitutional details must be suppressed for the time being in view of the paramount need to maintain discipline and unity of action until victory has been won. But once the revolution has been accomplished, two political results follow. Those who fought against the revolution must either emigrate or accept defeat and temporarily, at least, withdraw from active politics. The victorious revolutionaries, no longer compressed into a disciplined force by military necessity and by their unifying objective of victory, begin to split apart and regroup to work for their differing policies.

In the Ireland of 1922, this situation was strictly conditioned by the immediate necessity of deciding upon acceptance or rejection of the treaty. The Sinn Féin membership, instead of splitting into a number of groups and parties based upon several ideological or economic interests, had to decide whether they were in favor of the treaty or opposed to it. Whichever stand they took, they were compelled to cooperate with others who had the same attitude on the treaty, even though they might agree upon few other policies.

The Unionists, of course, could no longer exist as a party. Individuals who regretted the separation from Great Britain had either to abstain altogether from political activity or make their peace with the existing situation and support independent candidates who took a moderate or conservative position and were anti-republican.

The old Irish Nationalist Party was in little better case. To Sinn Féin it was "the party of corruption and compromise." Sinn Féin claimed to be a "pure" party of true nationalism, untainted by the jobbery of the Nationalists under Redmond and Dillon. This was true enough, because at this time Sinn Féin had little to offer but a chance to work for Irish national aspirations and certainly no government posts to present to its adherents.

The major parties destined to dominate subsequent political life had to be created out of Sinn Féin itself. When De Valera refused to accept the treaty of 1921 he found himself the leader of all who took a similar stand, including the doctrinaire Republicans and fanatical Irish Nationalists, as well as those who believed that a better compromise with the British Government could be attained.

To be sure, the treaty split did not completely prevent the emergence of minor parties concerned with other issues as well. The Labour Party had existed ever since James Connolly's resolution to form such a party had been accepted by the Irish Trades Union Congress in 1912. This party had virtually submerged its identity in favor of Sinn Féin during the struggle with Britain and had nominated no candidates to oppose those of Sinn Féin in the general elections of 1918 and 1921. Now it sought again to have a separate existence. Now too the farmers' union established its own political arm, the Independent Farmers' Party, created in 1922, and particularly interested in free trade as an aid to agricultural exports. The Farmers' Party supported Cosgrave on the treaty question and, without enthusiasm and with a show of neutrality, so did Labour. But the treaty issue, which divided Sinn Féin into violently opposed sections, remained the overriding consideration to the Irish elector.

To some degree, the split over the treaty was a "natural" one,

in that the less doctrinaire and radical, more pragmatic and conservative Dáil members tended to be pro-treaty, whereas the doctrinaire republicans who attached almost as much value to the
symbols of independence as to its reality, were anti-treaty. The
latter were supported by the socially radical members, if for no
other reason, because the treaty represented a compromise with
the defeated Ascendancy. It may well be that among the reasons
for the persistence of the two-party situation in Ireland is the fact
that, at the start, the treaty question not only induced all politically
active Irish to take one side or the other, but created a split which
corresponded roughly with the universal dichotomy between the
conservative and radical points of view.[1] But more important as a
factor in the persistence of the two major parties is the fact that
their differences in radicalism or conservatism became slight, even
imperceptible, in the course of time. This reflects the situation
among the Irish electorate. Irish extremists usually have been extreme nationalists; rarely are they social revolutionaries, although
there were traces of social revolutionary aims among some of the
anti-treaty forces during the civil war.[2] These were atypical of the
Irish electorate as a whole. As major parties, attempting to make
the widest appeal to the greatest number of voters, both Fianna
Fáil and Fine Gael must approach agreement as to policy goals,
differing only in minor matters. In fact, they have traded policies
at various times. It was Fine Gael which achieved the republican
form of government free of Commonwealth ties. On the other
hand, it was Fianna Fáil which concluded a trade reciprocity agreement with Great Britain. Any observer of these parties in their
early days would have assumed without hesitation that these
policies naturally would have been those of the other party. By
the spring of 1923 it was clear that the republican IRA could
not hope to defeat the Free State forces. As President of Sinn
Féin, De Valera issued a proclamation announcing the cessation
of hostilities by April 30, and a similar proclamation was issued by
Frank Aiken as chief of staff of the IRA.

The general election of August, 1923, was a contest between
Cosgrave's party and the republican Sinn Féin led by De Valera.
The only issue was the treaty, its acceptance or rejection. Cos-

grave's party took the name of Cumann na nGaedheal. This name, meaning "League of Gaels," had first been adopted by a society founded in 1900 by Arthur Griffith. At first having only cultural aims, the society soon became a political body and a forerunner of the original Sinn Féin. De Valera's party retained the Sinn Féin designation.

The defeated republicans of Sinn Féin fought the campaign under considerable handicaps. According to the Fianna Fáil history, over 13,000 republicans were in jail or internment camps, others were in hiding, and despite the cessation of hostilities, Free State troops were still raiding the homes of known republican supporters. An election meeting held by De Valera at Ennis, Clare, in August, 1923, was disrupted by IFS troops who arrested De Valera. He was not released from detention until July, 1924.[3]

The election resulted in a sweep for the pro-treaty forces. Altogether they could count upon 102 votes out of 143.[4] The elected deputies of the republican Sinn Féin continued to refuse to sit in what they termed an illegal Dáil. The principal obstacle, from their viewpoint, was the parliamentary oath, stipulated in the treaty and included in the Free State Constitution.[5]

To continue the violent, revolutionary struggle was plainly absurd in view of the existing temper of the Irish people. Accordingly, Eamon De Valera's plan now was to induce his section of Sinn Féin to start a campaign to abolish the oath by amendment to the Constitution and then to enter the Dáil. He made a proposal to this effect at the Sinn Féin árd-fheis (national convention) in 1926 but failed to get clear majority support.[6] Thereupon he resigned as president of Sinn Féin and set about the organization of a new party which held its inaugural meeting on May 16, 1926. The new party, Fianna Fáil, was still avowedly republican and favored complete separation from Great Britain, but by constitutional instead of revolutionary means. Its domestic policies differed but little from those of Cumann na nGaedheal, now headed by William T. Cosgrave.

Articles 47 and 48 of the IFS Constitution provided for legislation by the Swiss device of initiative and referendum. De Valera planned to use this method to force a referendum on the oath. A petition was circulated and obtained the required 75,000 signatures but the Government refused to accept it on the ground that no procedure had yet been established by law for implementing the articles. The Government then moved quickly to abolish Articles 47 and 48 by legislative action.

In July, 1927, Kevin O'Higgins, the Minister of Justice, was assassinated, presumably by Republican gunmen. De Valera denied Sinn Féin's responsibility for the act and deplored it in rather mild language. The Government's reaction was to pass a drastic public safety measure and another act designed to deny Republicans access to the hustings. The new law required all prospective candidates for the post of deputy to swear *before nomination* that they would take the parliamentary oath if elected. Anyone who was elected and then refused the oath would have his £100 election deposit confiscated. De Valera then announced that the oath was merely "an empty formula" and that to subscribe to it "implies no contractual obligation, and . . . has no binding significance in conscience or in law. . . ." This remarkable example of casuistry represented an embarrassing reversal of De Valera's previous views, but it was the only way left to get into the Dáil, and this he had to do or resign himself to political impotence along with the die-hard Sinn Féin republicans.

The uncompromising republican Sinn Féin elected as leader Miss Mary MacSwiney. With small success they contested elections in a few constituencies until 1927. After that date they refrained from electoral politics until 1957 when two Sinn Féin candidates were successful but still refused to take their seats in the Dáil even though the oath had long been removed. Their reason for this refusal was their denial of legality to all Irish parliaments so long as the island remained divided and Great Britain still "occupied" the six Northeast counties. The proscribed IRA irregulars had never disbanded completely but retained a secret organization and committed acts of violence from time to time, specializing in attacks upon the Royal Ulster Constabulary and their barracks within the Six Counties until, allegedly, this policy of sporadic violence was abandoned in 1962.

Fianna Fáil, on the other hand, became the major party of

Ireland and soon developed the normal characteristics of major
parties: institutionalization, a party machine more concerned with
electoral victory and its spoils rather than with policies and principles, a program broad and vague enough to appeal to a wide
sector of the public, and, in order to attract voters of differing
views, a tendency to blur divisive issues. Together with its rival,
Fine Gael (successor to Griffith's Cumann na nGaedheal), it behaved in the manner we associate with major parties in a two-
party, parliamentary democracy.

The pro-treaty forces, Cumann na nGaedheal and their allies,
held power from the beginning of the Free State until 1932, but
despite its majority position Cumann na nGaedheal had a much
more confused history than did Fianna Fáil and many problems
concerning leadership. As the chart on p. 64 indicates, the original
Sinn Féin Party split on the treaty, with De Valera becoming the
unchallenged leader of the anti-treaty section. Most of the other
original party leaders were pro-treaty and in 1923 William T. Cosgrave, after Griffith died and Collins was killed in a civil war
skirmish, became the accepted leader of the new Cumann na
nGaedheal Party. This was a much more heterogeneous political
mixture than De Valera's Sinn Féin. Cosgrave's supporters included many of the more prosperous farmers, the urban middle
class, some former Unionists who thought Cosgrave more moderate
than the republican De Valera, and many of all classes who blamed
the republicans for the civil war. Because the Farmers' Party, as
well as a number of Independents, were also pro-treaty, Cosgrave
was able usually to count on their support when needed to keep
Fianna Fáil out of power. Cosgrave remained premier until 1932.
This decade following the treaty was one in which the Government had to tackle problems of discouraging difficulty. To begin
with, it was necessary to try to heal the wounds left by the civil
war and repair the extensive physical damage it had caused. Then
some sort of economic miracle was required, an "operation boot-
strap," to pull Ireland out of the economic doldrums. The Free
State was a poor, agricultural country now cut off from the industrial North and having virtually no industry of its own. Without substantial economic improvement one could only expect a

speed-up in the depressing spiral of emigration, additional unemployment, and then more emigration. Without any reliance upon economic theory or ideology, Mr. Cosgrave and his colleagues began a piece-meal program of tackling one deficiency after another and making what use they could of Ireland's slender resources. Sugar beet production was stimulated and a board appointed by the Government to manage sugar production. The Agricultural Credit Corporation was created to assist the farmers. The Shannon hydroelectric scheme was started under the government-created Electricity Supply Board.

Subsequent Fianna Fáil governments also invested heavily in public enterprises, such as Aer Lingus (Irish Air Lines), established in 1936. The Bord na Móna was established to undertake fuel production from the mechanized harvesting of turf (peat). It supplies all the fuel used by the Electricity Supply Board in its steam-powered plants, and can do so more cheaply than if oil were used. Gaeltarra Éireann, governed by an independent board, fosters industry in the Gaeltacht, operating tweed and toy factories and cottage industry as well as marketing the products. An Foras Tionscal was created to make direct grants for industrial development in the Gaeltacht. Córas Tráchtála Teoranta has the task of promoting exports by advising private producers in better methods of making exportable goods. The Industrial Credit Company can invest government funds in both public and privately owned concerns and guarantee loans to private companies. The Industrial Development Authority is another statutory body particularly concerned with industrial development and its desirable diversification. It advises the Government in these matters and conducts campaigns to attract foreign industry. It is empowered to lend money, within limits, to new industries for construction costs. It announced in 1967 that in the preceding two years some 212 important new industries with foreign participation had been started or substantially enlarged. Many of these were British but a number were American or German with a scattering from other countries. The Irish industrial expansion is helped by the existence of an ample labor supply, free access to the British market, tax exemption for ten years on profits made on the export of Irish-made

goods, and, for establishments located at the Shannon Free Air-
port, total tax exemption until 1983. These and other incentives
have been effective in attracting foreign capital investment. This
admixture of State and private enterprise had its beginnings under
the Cosgrave administration and its culmination, to date, in the
Programmes for Economic Expansion, discussed later.

When De Valera, with Labour support, was able to form his
first government in 1932, one of his first actions was to refuse to
continue the payment of land annuities as agreed to in the treaty.
The British Government responded by imposing duties on Irish
produce and this drastically cut the demand for farm produce.
The political response of the Irish farmers was the founding of the
National Farmers and Ratepayers' League under Frank Mac-
Dermot. When another well-known, independent deputy, James
M. Dillon, joined the party, its name was changed to National
Centre Party.

At the beginning, De Valera's attitude was tolerant toward
those in Sinn Féin who had refused to follow him into Fianna
Fáil. Immediately after the inauguration of Fianna Fáil, the IRA
leaders attempted to arrange a conference of themselves, Sinn
Féin, and the new party on the basis of a preagreement to re-
pudiate the treaty, restore the 1916 Republic, disarm and de-
mobilize the Free State forces, and entrust national defense to the
IRA. This repudiation of the basis for the existence of Fianna
Fáil and a total acceptance of the Sinn Féin–IRA viewpoint, despite its unpopularity with the majority of the Irish people,
naturally was rejected by unanimous vote of the Fianna Fáil national executive. However, when De Valera came to power in
1932 he ordered the release of the republicans who had been imprisoned by orders of the Cosgrave-created military tribunal. He
again allowed publication of the newspaper *An Phoblacht*, which
had been suppressed during the final months of the Cosgrave Government.

He also dismissed General O'Duffy from his post as chief of
the civic guard. This action, taken in February, 1933, had been
demanded by *An Phoblacht*. De Valera also ordered the cancella-
tion of all firearms permits and the police collected the arms of

all who had such permits. This affected the members of O'Duffy's new National Guard organization but not the IRA members because, although armed, they had never asked for permits.

Emboldened by this toleration, the IRA began to drill and march without weapons. Allegedly, a captain in the IRA, when charged with illegal possession of arms, refused to recognize the competence of the court and was sentenced for contempt but was released by orders of the Minister of Justice before completing his sentence.

The principal Irish enemy of the IRA and Sinn Féin was the Cosgrave party. Inflamatory attacks upon this party were printed in *An Phoblacht*. "Free speech and the freedom of the press must be denied to traitors and treason-mongers." [7] A Republican speaker, Frank Ryan of the IRA, was reported in the *Irish Press* (November 11, 1932) as having said: "while we have fists, hands and boots to use, and guns if necessary, we will not allow free speech to traitors."

The reaction of the Cosgrave supporters and the veterans of the IFS forces who had suppressed the rebellious IRA in the civil war was the expansion of the Army Comrades' association led by Dr. T. F. O'Higgins, brother of the murdered Kevin. The ACA, now open to all, whether IFS veterans or not, acted as guards at meetings of the Cosgrave party. For a time it seemed as if the civil war might break out again—with the death of Irish democracy as a probable final result.

De Valera's policy was one of pacification. The IRA men who had fought the Free State forces in the civil war were given military pensions on the same basis as the IFS veterans. To many Irish, the continued intransigence of the IRA seemed pointless. Ireland was a free, self-governing country except for the "occupied" Six Counties, and the end of partition could not be achieved by killing a few Royal Ulster constables. A minority of the IRA called for a turn to political action and a combination with the trades unions to work for a socialist republic. The majority, however, led by Maurice Twomey and Seán MacBride, who determined the policy of *An Phoblacht*, continued to press for physical action. There were still a few statues in public parks recalling the days of British domination or honoring British monarchs and soldiers. These could be blown up one after another. Moving picture houses that exhibited films considered objectionable by the IRA were damaged. None dared show the film made of the coronation of King George VI in 1937.

De Valera acted against both sides in the interest of public order. The Wearing of Uniform (Restriction) Bill was passed in March, 1933. This was directed against O'Duffy's Blue Shirt paramilitary organization. The IRA, not uniformed, was tolerated for some time thereafter. The military tribunal had acted to sentence some IRA men for acts of violence but few were convicted before the regular courts, in large measure because witnesses were unwilling or afraid to testify against IRA men. But certain outrages aroused strong public indignation. A retired Vice-Admiral named Somerville, who was highly popular in his community, was murdered in his own home, allegedly because he had advised local youths who had asked him about enlisting in the British navy. A· month later there was a similar murder, and in June, 1936, the Government declared the IRA to be an unlawful association and proscribed it under Article 2A of the Constitution. Subsequently a detention camp was established at the Curragh, County Kildare, for known members of the IRA and some Sinn Féin members who were merely suspected of IRA connections. Many of these were detained for periods of as long as one year. This camp was still in use in the late 1950's. In November, 1961, the Lemass Government reconstituted the special military court to deal with IRA offenses following a border foray in which a constable of the RUC was murdered. On February 26, 1962, the Dublin newspapers received messages from one James McGarrity who styled himself Secretary of the Irish Republican Publicity Bureau. The messages announced that the IRA had decided to stop its "campaign of resistance to British occupation." The reason given was public apathy toward the issue of partition. It was estimated that at its peak strength in the 1950's, the IRA never numbered more than some four hundred members and that by 1962 it had shrunk to about sixty.[8] Despite these small numbers the governments of the Republic and Northern Ireland had been compelled to spend many millions on extra police forces and the fortification of police stations.

Although Sinn Féin is not strictly a secret society, the close alliance between Sinn Féin and IRA and the proscription of the latter as an illegal organization by the Republican governments, has made the Sinn Féin leadership shy of public appearances or interviews. Contact with the public is maintained chiefly by statements sent to the general press and by the party's own monthly paper, *The United Irishman*, published in Dublin. The paper lists no editors' names on its masthead although many articles are signed, possibly by pseudonyms.

It was the original plan of the IRA, and probably Sinn Féin as well, that the violence against the RUC would inspire reprisal raids from Northern Ireland and that these, in turn, would outrage the Irish Government, which would be impelled to break relations and start a chain of events leading to actual warfare in which the Six Counties could be taken by force. From the start it was plain that the IRA could not ignite the fuse to a general explosion. Both governments suppressed the IRA and imprisoned those members it could catch. The Roman Catholic hierarchy condemned its activities in the strongest terms.

Why the IRA continued with its campaign of violence long after it was obvious that no practical political results could follow from it may be explained, in part at least, by the persistence of the traditions of rebellion against constituted authority and of the resort to physical action as an outlet for economic and social frustrations.

In 1933 De Valera found his party and his government compelled to deal with attacks from two directions. On the one hand the Sinn Féin republicans and the remaining armed members of the IRA were creating public disturbances and in their encounters with the National Guard threatening to renew the civil war. In the parliamentary battle, Cumann na nGaedheal was trying to secure a union of all other groups and parties against Fianna Fáil. Accordingly, the curious combination of O'Duffy's National Guard, the National Centre Party, and Cumann na nGaedheal joined forces as the United Ireland Party. Cosgrave remained parliamentary leader and he, along with MacDermot and Dillon, were vice-presidents of the party, while the party presidency was given to General O'Duffy.

The UIP manifesto was moderate and pragmatic. It called for the unification of Ireland as a dominion of the British Commonwealth, the ending of the Anglo-Irish economic war which had resulted from De Valera's withholding the land annuity payments, the creation of statutory corporations to undertake neglected agricultural and industrial enterprises, and the replacement of the proportional representation electoral system by single-member districts. All of the above came to pass except the reunification of Ireland and the electoral reform. The latter was adopted finally by Fianna Fáil, and opposed by the party which had originally proposed it, but twice rejected by the Irish voters.

De Valera's government had acted quickly to ban the National Guard, but the Guard was reconstituted as the Young Ireland Association, and when this was banned, it became the League of Youth. Before long it became clear that O'Duffy had borrowed ideas as well as paramilitary organization from European fascism. He favored a corporative state economy and seemed to look forward to a one-party policy, the first step being the abolition of proportional representation. He urged farmers to embark upon a tax strike and refuse both rates and annuity payments, which were still collected by the IFS Government. The alliance of the National Guard and Cumann na nGaedheal was never a comfortable one. It would seem that the views of the parliamentary members were centrist and by no means fascist, while O'Duffy was moving constantly toward the extreme right. In September, 1934, a prominent party member, Professor James Hogan of Cork, resigned and issued a statement in which he described O'Duffy as politically "utterly impossible." Other members shared Professor Hogan's views and in September, 1934, O'Duffy resigned as party chairman and was replaced as head of the League of Youth by Commandant Cronin. When he left, General O'Duffy was followed out of the party by some of the Blue Shirts, but O'Duffy and his followers ceased to be of any political importance. Some of them went to Spain under O'Duffy's command in 1936, where they fought with the Franco forces, constituting, in the words of an English war correspondent, Franco's only genuine "foreign volunteers."

Differences also developed between Commandant Cronin and the parliamentary members of the UIP and in October, 1936, Cronin was removed by the standing committee of the party. He left along with some of the League of Youth members, and to all intents, this episode concluded the attempt to unite the parliamentary party with an extraparliamentary, autonomous movement. There was no longer a need for guards at Fine Gael meetings, as the UIP had now generally come to be called. Fine Gael, "Tribe of Gaels," is almost identical in meaning to Cumann na nGaedheal, "League of Gaels," to which the UIP had essentially reverted. Without the semi-fascist O'Duffy element, Fine Gael was practically the Cosgrave party as it had been, with the addition of one or two outstanding members, notably James M. Dillon. MacDermot had resigned because of disagreement with the views of other leaders in October, 1935.

The two major parties have had few fundamental policy differences. Fianna Fáil has been more ardent than Fine Gael in devotion to the revival of the Irish language. Both parties have advocated and advanced government enterprise in various segments of the economy; both have embraced welfare-state policies. Although its republican bias might have led logically to the immediate declaration of an Irish Republic by Fianna Fáil as soon as it came to power, this action was deliberately postponed by De Valera who, in his 1937 Constitution, avoided use of the word "republic" [9] because of his persistent hope that Northern Ireland might finally be induced to join the Irish State if it still maintained a nominal British connection.

In Commonwealth and foreign affairs there was no real difference between the major parties. Neither wished to sever the Commonwealth relationship but both resented the compulsory nature of Ireland's membership. Irish statesmen were in the forefront of the moves, along with Canada and South Africa, to secure British agreement to the complete independence of the dominions in foreign as in domestic policies. The Free State representatives played an important part in the intra-Commonwealth diplomacy leading to the Balfour Report and its subsequent formalization in the Statute of Westminster (1931), which gave legal basis to the independence of the dominions. The IFS had joined the League of Nations in 1923 and succeeding Irish governments were eager to underline international recognition of Ireland's nationhood by maximum participation in international bodies.

Despite the economic depression of the 1930's, exacerbated by the Anglo-Irish tariff war, De Valera retained much of his popularity with the electorate. His parliamentary opposition was now provided by an amalgam of parties organized in 1936 under the name of Fine Gael. During this period, as noted previously, conflicts between O'Duffy's Blue Shirts and the IRA had compelled De Valera to outlaw both groups and in 1936 to reestablish military courts and detention camps.

His principal accomplishments in the 1930's were the several constitutional changes culminating in the new Constitution of 1937 and the trade agreement with the United Kingdom ending the economic war.[10] This trade agreement exempted Irish goods from British duties although a quota was placed upon agricultural produce. In return, Ireland removed duties upon certain categories of British goods. The annuity dispute was settled by a payment to the British Treasury of ten million pounds and the British Government gave back the treaty ports to the Irish authorities.

This last-named arrangement facilitated the declaration of neutrality by the Irish Government when World War II broke out in September, 1939. The neutrality policy had almost universal support in the State of Ireland. It was justified in the main on the ground that, so long as British "occupation" continued in the Six Counties of "Northern Ireland," no Irish government could become a military ally of Great Britain. The claim to "one Ireland" was emphasized by official objection to the presence of both British and Allied troops in Northern Ireland and by the dispatch of fire brigades from Dublin and Dún Laoghaire to the assistance of Belfast firemen after a German bombing of Belfast in April, 1941.

The neutrality policy had the complete support of both major parties (a rare example of unanimity) and of almost all other deputies. One of the very few dissenters was James Dillon, who spoke in favor of an Irish-American alliance in 1941 after the United States had become a belligerent. Because of this stand, he was expelled from Fine Gael. The other extreme was represented by the IRA, which threatened the British Government with war if British troops were not removed from the Six Counties. When its "ultimatum" was ignored, the IRA exploded bombs in London, Coventry, and in Ireland as well. De Valera could not permit this violation of his declaration of neutrality, so as many known or suspected IRA as could be found were rounded up and placed in a detention camp.

Neutrality was not merely a policy of convenience or one based upon a cool calculation of national interest, but a symbol of Ireland's independence and unmistakable proof that, Commonwealth member or not, Ireland was the complete master of its own foreign policy.[11]

The first postwar general election was held in 1948. After sixteen years in office, Fianna Fáil was replaced by an alliance of other parties under Fine Gael leadership. This interparty government, as it was called, included the left-wing Clann na Poblachta (Republican Party) led by Seann MacBride, the Labour Party, and the far from radical Clann na Talmhan (Farmers' Party), as well as a few independents. Such a grouping could not be expected to support a government offering a coherent policy program in contrast with that of Fianna Fáil. It represented simply a swing away from Fianna Fáil. The Minister of Finance in this first interparty government was Patrick McGilligan, who was responsible for an innovation—a state capital budget as suggested by the English economist, Lord Keynes. This was continued by succeeding governments and became of increasing importance. The taoiseach in this interparty government, Fine Gael leader John A. Costello, was responsible at this time for the decision to withdraw Ireland from the Commonwealth of Nations and assume the designation of "republic" for his country, which had been known since 1937 simply as Eire or the State of Ireland. Although this decision may have cost Fine Gael a few votes of former Unionists who had preferred it to Fianna Fáil because it seemed less anti-British, Fine Gael in fact increased its representation in the Dáil at the next general election in May, 1951, by nine seats. However, the coalition had broken apart for reasons detailed elsewhere.[12]

The next (Fianna Fáil) government lasted only three years. Although Fianna Fáil has remained the largest single party in the Dáil since 1932 and the only one able to maintain a one-party administration in power, it has rarely had a clear majority. If its strength drops below 70 seats in a chamber of 147, it may be replaced by a coalition of the other parties. This happened in the general election of May, 1954, when only 65 Fianna Fáil deputies were elected while Fine Gael had 50. This enabled Fine Gael to construct another interparty government. This second coalition lasted only three years because an economic crisis in 1956 induced voters to turn back to Fianna Fáil, which returned to power in March, 1957, with an absolute majority of 78 seats. It was at this high point in his long career that Eamon de Valera resigned office and was succeeded by his tanaiste, Seán Lemass. De Valera was then free to stand for the presidency of the Republic, which he won that same year.

It was during this administration that the Whitaker Report was published and the first Programme for Economic Expansion was inaugurated in 1958.[13] Fianna Fáil continued to dominate the Government. Although it lost eight seats at the general election of October, 1961, it picked up two at the next general election in April, 1965. In 1964 Mr. Lemass introduced the second Programme for Economic Expansion, a plan for the period 1964 through 1970. He also met with the Premier of Northern Ireland, Terence O'Neill, in an attempt to improve relations between their two parts of the island. In December, 1965, he signed a free-trade agreement with Prime Minister Harold Wilson which promised to be a boon for Irish agriculture and to open the way for Ireland to go along with Great Britain into international economic arrangements such as the European Economic Community.

In 1966 Mr. Lemass retired for reasons of health and was succeeded by John Mary ("Jack") Lynch, elected taoiseach by Dáil Éireann on November 10, 1966. His chief rival for the premiership was George Colley, who retained the important post of Minister of Industry and Commerce in the new cabinet.[14]

It may be of some significance that the 1965 election saw the return of twenty-one members of the Irish Labour Party, the largest number elected since 1927. At this same election only three independents won seats, the smallest number since the inauguration of the Free State until 1969 when only one independent was victorious.

In 1964 and 1965 Fine Gael appeared to shift to the left in its policy program. Declan Costello, a son of the former taioseach, induced the party to set up a policy committee with several subcommittees, each to concern itself with a specific social, cultural, or political problem. In Mr. Costello's phrase, the objective was to draft a plan for "the just society." In 1965 Fine Gael advocated extended social welfare benefits and substantially increased support of education.

Immediately after the general election of 1965, James M. Dillon resigned as parliamentary leader and president of the party at a meeting of Fine Gael deputies and senators. He gave as his reasons his age and the fatigue he had felt for some time. He believed that the party should be led at the next general election by a younger and more energetic man. The meeting then chose Liam Cosgrave, son of De Valera's old opponent, as leader of the Oireachtas party. At the next árd-fheis in October, Mr. Cosgrave was elected president of Fine Gael.

At the Fine Gael árd-fheis of May, 1968, an unusual number of important party posts were vacant and contenders for these offices had to pledge support for the "Just Society." The more radical members of the party, sometimes called "the young tigers," suggested that the party name be changed to Fine Gael–Social Democratic Party. The change was supported by nine branches but opposed by the older leadership of the party, including Cosgrave and Sweetman. It was defeated in the meeting but it was agreed to canvass party delegates throughout Ireland to settle the issue conclusively.

Declan Costello and his "young tigers" were unable to wrest the party leadership from the conservatives. Liam Cosgrave and Gerard Sweetman still seem to command the support of a majority of the party and Fine Gael remains substantially what it was—an old-fashioned, non-ideological kind of party; a band of deputies and senators backed at the polls by electors who have long held to a tradition of voting the Fine Gael label or who support a Fine Gael candidate because of personal rather than party loyalty. Historically, Fine Gael branches, like those of Fianna Fáil, have existed for campaign action and not to discuss or help develop party policies. In these respects, Fine Gael resembles the British Conservative Party rather than ideological parties like the British and Irish Labour Parties, whose adherents regard them essentially as extra-parliamentary associations which seek to elect members pledged to support legislation based upon the association's goals.

The attempt by Declan Costello to give Fine Gael an ideology resulted in a crisis of leadership. In January, 1969, James M. Dillon retired from politics entirely. Previously, Declan Costello had announced his retirement for reasons of health and in January, 1969, turned down an appeal to reenter the Dáil. It remains to be seen whether or not the older leadership is correct in its apparent assumption that Fine Gael can survive as a major party without developing a significant alternative to the policies of its larger rival and by continuing to rely upon personal ties and traditional party loyalties rooted in the treaty issue of almost a half-century ago.

In any case, the "Just Society" program was not without influence, as can be seen in Fine Gael's current policy statement issued in January, 1969. It advocated greatly increased social and welfare services, including health services, to be financed by a combination of insurance and state grants. It urged that public housing be removed from the control of the local authorities and be made the concern of the national Government only. It advocated free university education for all qualified applicants, an increase in noncontributory old-age pensions, and an increase in family allowances by two-thirds.[15]

Notes

1. This point should not be overstressed. On the whole, the Labour Party was pro-treaty.
2. *Supra*, Chapter I, footnote 29.
3. *The Story of Fianna Fáil, First Phase* (Dublin, 1960), pp. 5, 6.

4. William J. Flynn, *The Oireachtas Companion and Saorstat Guide for 1928* (Dublin [1928]).

IRISH FREE STATE GENERAL ELECTION, AUGUST, 1923:

Cumann na nGaedheal	63
Sinn Féin Republicans	43
Labour	14
Farmers	15
Independents	17

5. The oath read:

I, ... do solemnly swear true faith and allegiance to the Constitution of the Irish Free State as by law established and that I will be faithful to H. M. George V, his heirs and successors by law, in virtue of the common citizenship of Ireland with Great Britain and her adherence to and membership of the group of nations forming the British Commonwealth of Nations.

6. The árd-fheis was held on March 9 and 10, 1926. An amendment to veto De Valera's proposal failed by a vote of 177 to 179, but there were 85 abstentions and De Valera regarded the vote as a repudiation of his leadership. See *The Irish Independent*, March 11 and 12, 1926.

7. Quoted in O'Sullivan, *op. cit.*, pp. 296, 297.

8. See dispatch, *The New York Times*, February 27, 1962, p. 1.

The 1969 civil disorders and communal riots in Belfast, Londonderry and elsewhere in Northern Ireland, sparked by old racial-religious fears and prejudices undoubtedly led to a substantial increase in the number of IRA adherents in the Republic.

9. Article 5: "Ireland is a sovereign, independent, democratic State." In 1945 De Valera asserted that Ireland had been a republic ever since 1937. He said that the *word* "republic" had not been used in the Constitution because so long as part of Ireland was not governed under the Constitution, that "sacred" name, Phoblacht na hÉireann, should not be used. He "explained" the use of the royal signature validating the documents appointing Irish diplomats as signifying merely that the Irish Republic had chosen to associate itself with members of the British Commonwealth. See N. Mansergh, *Britain and Ireland* (London, rev. ed., 1946), p. 96.

10. For the constitutional changes, see *infra*, pp. 111–17.

11. Mansergh, *op. cit.*, p. 94.

12. *Infra*, p. 221.

13. *Infra*, p. 210.

14. Lynch received 52 votes to 19 for Colley in the party caucus.

15. See the *Irish Times*, January 17, 1969.

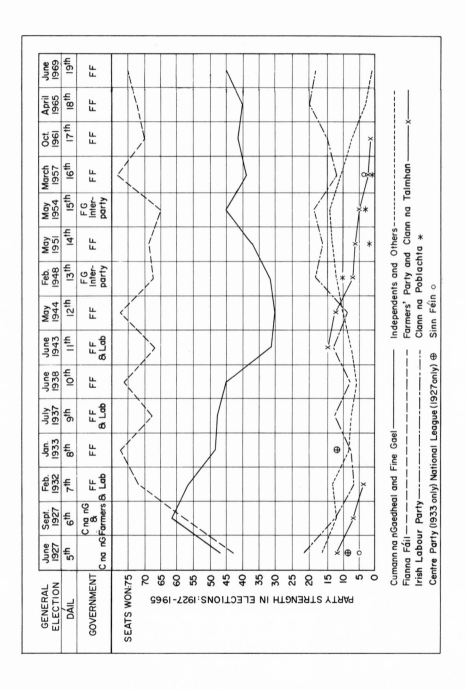

PARTY STRENGTH IN ELECTIONS: 1927-1965

III

THE IRISH SOCIETY

To understand the politics of any country it is necessary not only to know something of its political and social history, but also to know the nature of the society that has resulted from this history. It is important to be aware of the predominant beliefs and values that hold the society together, its class structure, and the location of centers of social power, informal as well as formal. With these facts in mind it is then possible to understand the political behavior of the society which is one result of the interplay of these forces in this environment.

To begin with, a prime fact is the self-conscious quality of Irish nationalism. The other Celtic groups also display this characteristic to a considerable extent. The Scots, Welsh, and Bretons, the last descended from Cymric tribes who left Britain at the time of the Roman conquest, are all somewhat self-consciously, and at times belligerently, nationalistic. No doubt this is the result of their feeling of belonging to a minority group in a larger and richer political entity.[1] Their language, customs, and history have given them a strong in-group feeling, reinforced by real as well as fancied discrimination against them, practiced by the majority groups. In the case of the Irish, this discrimination and injustice was real enough and sufficiently prolonged to explain the aggressive nationalism of some Irish. This strong national feeling is based upon a consciousness of race, of belonging to a peculiar people descended from the heroes of the Golden Age, the defenders of a great civilization who were the victims of ruthless, foreign invaders who were inferior in everything but force of numbers. The truth or falsity of this belief is unimportant. The fact that it is held gives it significance.

The emphasis given to nationalism in Irish politics is evidenced by the names chosen by several of the political parties. Sinn Féin is literally translated "Ourselves," with an exclusive connotation indicated by the frequently used translation, "Ourselves Alone." The two major parties formed out of the original Sinn Féin were Cumann na nGaedheal (League of the Gaels), which became Fine Gael (Gaelic Union), and Fianna Fáil (Soldiers of Destiny). The name Fianna Fáil is redolent of Irish history and legend. It was the romantic appellation of a body of warriors and huntsmen who constituted a guard and task force of the ancient Irish high kings. Fál is a poetic name for Ireland, alluding to the Lia Fáil or Stone of Destiny on the Hill of Tara which, in pre-Christian days, was supposed to utter a sound when mounted by the legitimate high king at his accession. Minor parties, on the other hand, have chosen names indicative of their special ideology or interest: Clann na Talmhan (Farmers' Party), Clann na Poblachta (Republican Party), Irish Labour Party, and National Progressive Democratic Party.

The myth of a peculiar and unique Irish race gives support to Irish nationalism. In truth, the Irish are a mixture of West European stocks, although there are several characteristically Irish physical types, recognizable as such, to strengthen the racial myth. A great many Irish do not conform to any of these types. The family names give some evidence of the more recent elements in the national mixture. The old Irish tribal patronymics are common, but these, sometimes now given Irish spelling, are found alongside English names, reminders of the Cromwellian and Williamite settlements and now widely borne by Roman Catholic Irish who, no doubt, are descended from seventeenth-century settlers absorbed by intermarriage. The common Irish name Walsh means

"Welsh." The names of the Hibernicized Norman barons, such as Fitzgerald and Burke, are common too, but in most cases probably indicate tribal connection rather than actual descent.

The racial myth has less significance today than it had in the nineteenth century when Irish nationalists depended heavily upon the financial support of the "Irish exiles," particularly in the United States. Irish parties today do not expect or need such support. There is less talk of the Irish race and most educated Irishmen, if they use the expression at all, do so with Shavian skepticism.[2]

Language is one of the factors that most emphasize distinct nationality. A strong sense of national identity can exist without a language peculiar to that nationality, but the existence of a separate national tongue is a constant reminder of the difference between the nation and foreigners.[3] Irish nationalism has long been hung on the two pegs of religion and language, both proscribed or suppressed over a considerable period by the English rulers. A result of the centuries of English domination was the near extinction of the Irish language except among poor peasants of the barren West and in Kerry and Cork. Three factors were involved: deliberate discouragement in the schools where a teacher had his salary reduced by the inspector if any of his pupils replied in Irish to the inspector's questions; the greater utility of English; and the general feeling that Irish was the language only of the poor and ignorant.

In 1853 the Ossianic Society was founded to encourage the study of old Irish and publish ancient texts. This was a matter of interest to scholars and had nothing to do with a popular revival of spoken Irish. But in 1876 the Society for the Preservation of the Irish Language was created to encourage the speaking of Irish. Disputes within this society led to the founding of a rival Gaelic Union in 1878, which was succeeded by the Gaelic League in 1893. Avowedly nonsectarian and nonpolitical, its moving spirit was Professor Douglas Hyde, an Anglo-Irish Protestant, destined to become the first president of Ireland under the Constitution of 1937. From the beginning Hyde argued that only a revival of the Irish language and culture could give content and meaning to

Irish National identity and justify Ireland's claim to be an independent nation-state. The league became very popular and its publications were widely read. Indeed, it became the greatest single influence in the revival of pride in Irish traditions and nationality and inspired the poets and playwrights of the Irish literary revival. It was responsible for the closing of public houses on Saint Patrick's Day and the latter's official establishment as a national holiday.[4]

De Valera, an old member of the Gaelic League, never abandoned the attempt to revive the Irish language despite the cost and difficulty involved. The policy of discouraging Irish speech, long enforced by the British-dominated Irish governments, was reversed and schools given a subvention for every pupil taking classes in modern Irish. Parents who do not want their children to spend time learning Irish must pay the school the equivalent of the lost subvention.

Only along the Connaught coast and in parts of Kerry and Cork had Irish remained the mother tongue of many and the only language of some. But these areas, the Gaeltacht, contained the poorest agricultural land in Ireland—some eighty percent was mountains or bogs—and yet almost the only employment was in farming. Naturally these areas had the highest emigration rate in the country. To try to reverse this trend, succeeding Irish governments set up a number of industrial establishments by means of government grants and managed by special agencies created to improve living conditions in the Gaeltacht.[5] Private firms also were given inducements in the form of loans and tax exemptions to encourage them to invest capital in enterprises located in Gaeltacht areas.

A possible factor in the failure of the Government's program to increase the use of Irish in the Gaeltacht or even to maintain it unchanged, is the fact that Irish farmers are not so much impressed with the beauties and national significance of Gaelic as were the scholars of the Gaelic League and their current followers. As practical people with a living to make, they are aware of the importance of a knowledge of English. It is said that many of them have abandoned the use of Irish in the home so that their children will get practice in English, which is no longer used or even taught in the Gaeltacht schools.[6]

Some Irish people seem to have an ambivalent attitude toward the language. Many city children resent having to study it and this resentment probably reflects a parental attitude. A frequent criticism is that modern Irish has no literature of merit and does not prepare one to read the Irish classics. This remark is made, as a rule, by those who cannot read Irish. Scholars familiar with the literature in both languages claim that there are writers of high literary merit, such as Mairtin Ó Cadhain, whose works are available only in Irish and whose merits are unknown to those who read no Irish. It is doubtful that many of the children who learn some Irish in school maintain their skill in its use after they leave, but many cherish at least a smattering of it and applaud government efforts to foster it as incontrovertible evidence of a distinct Irish nationality.

As of 1961, some 716,420 people could speak Irish, an increase of almost 127,000 since 1941. This brings the number of Irish-speakers close to the 800,000 speakers of Cymric (Welsh) in Wales and the similar number of Bretons who can speak Cymric in Brittany. The other two Celtic languages are extinct or nearly so. Cornish seems to have been lost nearly two centuries ago and Manx is virtually extinct.

Because the Irish revival policy was a reflection of Irish nationalism, few politicians dared to raise objections to it. In the general election campaign of 1961, Fine Gael took the plunge and advocated that Irish no longer be used as a medium of instruction in schools, except in the Gaeltacht, and that candidates for the civil service no longer be compelled to pass an examination in Irish. Fine Gael reaffirmed this stand in 1966. The Irish Labour Party, in its 1969 policy statement, declared in favor of "no compulsory examination subjects," that is, no compulsory Irish. This left Fianna Fáil as the only major party still favoring the requirement of Irish as a subject for the school leaving certificate.[7]

English remains the language of the great majority and, for most of these, the only language. An informal poll taken by a reporter for the fortnightly review *Hibernia* in Pearse Street,

Dublin, indicated that only 12 out of 122 persons questioned were able to translate a short warning announcement in Irish of the kind used on electric poles by the Electricity Supply Board.

Debates in the Oireachtas are conducted in English with an occasional interjection or introductory sentence in Irish. There is nothing like the genuine bilingualism of the Canadian Parliament. In divisions, "yea" and "nay" have been replaced by the Irish "ta" and "nil," but any attempt to conduct a debate in Irish arouses the resentment of the many T.D.'s who cannot understand it. Bills are printed in both languages but the Irish version is a translation. It became the custom for the governor general and his successor in this function, the ceann comhairle, to indicate completion of the legislative process by signing only the English version, which thus becomes the official one.[8] Official letters from government departments usually begin with a salutation in Irish and close with the Irish equivalent of "Yours truly," but the body of the letter is in English. Despite increased subventions, the number of "A" schools, where all subjects are taught in Irish, dropped from 106 in 1940–1941 to 84 in 1956–1957. This in spite of the fact that in 1940–1941, the grants to all-Irish and bilingual schools amounted to £14,487, and in 1956–1957 to £47,381. In most places parents are opposed to the all-Irish schools because the children, whose Irish is sometimes fragmentary, fail to learn enough of the non-language subjects.[9]

As an integral part of the Irish revival program, a speaking knowledge of Irish was made compulsory for all who wish to become teachers in the National Schools or civil servants. It is also a required subject for entry to the colleges of the National University. This does much to explain the emphasis given to the study of Irish in the schools.

In general, the opponents of the Government's efforts to revive the Irish language emphasize three points: the revival has been very costly, especially to a relatively poor country; it prevents the students from spending their time and effort upon more useful subjects; finally, it has been a conspicuous failure. Dr. J. J. McElligott, a member of the Commission on Higher Education from 1960 to 1967, wrote in his reservations to the majority report of the Commission: "I question if the revival of Irish as the generally spoken language of the people is an attainable objective." The emphasis given to Irish studies, he believes, has resulted in the neglect of "other and more worthwhile targets of educational policy . . . with consequent adverse effects in the field of higher education." [10] As evidence of the waste involved, Dr. McElligott notes that in 1964 and 1965 in the universities there were 62 teachers assigned to Irish, Welsh, and Celtic studies as compared with 43 to economics and 48 to both French and German. Despite this, of the 303 primary degrees with honors awarded in all the colleges, only one was in Irish and one in Celtic languages, and 22 in groups which included Irish as a subject. No doubt the overemphasis is most conspicuous in the primary (national) schools where the pupils spend almost half their time on languages, of which about two-thirds is devoted to Irish.[11]

Despite the views of Dr. McElligott and those who agree with him, the Irish revival effort continues and probably will continue for some time as a policy of Irish governments. It has now been institutionalized in a number of ways so that a great many civil servants, teachers, and others have a strong vested interest in its continuance.

Irish nationality is emphasized too by restoring the native form and spelling of Irish personal and place names instead of the English changes or corruptions. This is done even when speaking or writing in English. The harbor and village of Dún Laoghaire (pronounced "Dun Leary") had been called Kingstown ever since George IV landed there in 1821, but had its ancient name, meaning the castle or fort of Leary, revived when the Free State came into existence. In 1922 the well-known port of Cork, called Queenstown to commemorate the landing there of Queen Victoria in 1849, had its name changed back to Cóbh (pronounced approximately "Cove," meaning "harbor"). Dublin remains Dublin although its official Irish designation is Baile Átha Cliath.

As noted earlier, the talented Irish writers of the nineteenth century began to turn to native themes and legends for inspiration. They wrote in English but their stories, plays, and poems were calculated to remind their readers of the more romantic incidents of Irish history and legend and to inspire national pride. This was the case with many of the works of William Butler Yeats, James Stephens, and others, while the Abbey Theatre, founded by Lady Gregory, Yeats, and John Millington Synge, provided an opportunity to display the plays of the founders and later of other native writers of genius, such as Seán O'Casey. In general, they contributed a proud consciousness of Irish nationality, although Synge's *Playboy of the Western World* was regarded as an insult by many Irish when it was first presented.

A factor in producing the sometimes aggressive and defiant quality in Irish nationalism is the fact that it is in part the outcome of recent national independence. In everything but the formal, legal sense, Ireland is an ex-colony except for the Six Counties of Northern Ireland which are still, in the view of Irish republicans, subjected to British imperialism. Peoples that have emerged recently from colonial status to independence are likely to wear their nationality with ostentation and sometimes with an air of challenge or defiance, as if they expected outsiders to look down upon it. This has been true of many countries and not merely those where the race-color situation provided an additional complication. It has been true of Canada and Australia. No one could call Irish nationality either new or synthetic. Nevertheless, the Irish people long suffered from a malaise concerning their national identity. Their ancient nationality was denied by the English Government, which insisted that they were simply "West Britons." At the same time they were subjected to a sometimes crude and sometimes subtle denigration and insult by the Ascendancy, whose members seemed to regard them as often amusing and even likable folk—but of a clearly inferior strain. The result of this treatment was an acute case of what the writer has termed "the colonial complex." [12] The struggle to escape from colonialism to independence is certain to produce an upsurge of emotional patriotism which may sometimes find shrill expression. In a sense, therefore, Irish nationalism tends to have the self-conscious and exaggerated characteristics of the new nationalisms. A political result of these feelings may be the reaching of decisions under their influence to the disregard of "practical" considerations which lack such emotive appeal. An obvious Irish example of this is the expensive and, on the whole, ineffective attempt to restore the use of the Irish language.

  — All the Celtic peoples—the Welsh, Scots, and Bretons as well as the Irish—have retained strong national characteristics. English acculturation in Ireland was never complete among the peasants, where its principal result was the considerable replacement of the Irish tongue by English. Certain folk tunes and dances and superstitions were remembered as well as some of the old legends, although the medieval Irish of the bards became a closed language to the speakers of modern Irish. It required the efforts of the Gaelic League to bring the ancient literature to light again.

There was a tendency for English acculturation to spread into the realm of sport. Handball and hurling (a strenuous variety of field hockey) had long been played in Ireland, but cricket too was becoming popular in the Irish countryside during the union period and the middle class was even taking up the "effeminate" game of lawn tennis, much to the disgust of the superpatriots, until Archbishop Croke of Cashel and the Gaelic Athletic Association tried, with considerable success, to stamp out these English games. Today, little cricket is played in the Republic except at some of the Dublin schools. The Gaelic Athletic Association was founded in 1884 as a "non-political and non-sectarian Association," but neither modifier was strictly accurate. Its rules barred from membership all ranks of the British forces and police and provided for the suspension of any member who associated, socially or in sports, with the British soldiery. The GAA proved to be valuable to the original IRA in its recruiting drives and was suppressed by the Government during World War I. The GAA sponsored hurling and football clubs throughout Ireland.[18] The football, called Gaelic football, possibly is not an old Irish game but, according to some, is a blend of two English games, rugby and association football (soccer). Hurling, on the other hand, is doubtless an ancient Irish sport. Both hurling and Gaelic football are popular games wth the Irish people and the county matches draw huge crowds.

But in a colonial or ex-colonial territory a contrary reaction to local nationalism also occurs. As noted previously, the Protestant Ascendancy, to begin with, looked down upon the Irish, partly because many of the Irish gentry had been forced to emigrate and most of the remaining Irish were peasants and laborers. There is a parallel with the behavior of the Norman conquerors of England who expropriated the lands of nearly all of the Anglo-Saxon gentry and looked down upon the English people. On the whole, the heirs of the Ascendancy continued to identify themselves with England and to scorn everything Irish. Those who could afford it had their sons educated in English schools. In this they were joined by a certain number of middle-class, native Irish who became completely Anglicized, even in their religion. There were also Irish who remained Roman Catholic but in other respects identified themselves with the British connection. Hopeful of achieving social equality with the Ascendancy families, these people were known as "Castle Irish" or "Castle Catholics," the reference being to Dublin Castle, whence the Lord Lieutenant exercised English control.[14] Politically, the Castle Catholics simply voted with the Ascendancy and supported the Unionist cause.

In its negative aspect (hatred of England), Irish nationalism often has been a dominating factor in Irish politics. It is maintained by a memory of ancient wrongs. Nor are all the wrongs so far in the past. The reprisals of the constabulary and the "Black and Tans" of the period of the Troubles, after World War I are well within the memory of elderly people. Younger people have learned about them not only in school but from the lips of their elders. Naturally the counterviolence of the IRA was justified as patriotic and commendable. Until recent times a record of activity in the struggle for independence and especially of participation in the Easter Rising of 1916 was almost a necessary preliminary to a successful political career.

The continued separation from the Republic of the six northeastern counties (Northern Ireland) is still considered an outrage by most Irish nationalists. This reaction is now intellectual rather than emotional and most Irish citizens are neither deeply nor constantly concerned about partition. Feelings on this issue are much more intense in the North. When Mr. Lemass made overtures to Captain O'Neill, the Prime Minister of Northern Ireland, most citizens of the Republic approved, whereas O'Neill's leadership was instantly challenged by the right wing of his own party. Subsequently, Southern sympathy was general for the Northern Catholics civil rights drive and for their demand for universal suffrage in municipal elections. Despite the riotous behavior of Ian Paisley and his fanatical followers, however, the Irish people remained calm. O'Neill's Unionist Party was badly split and he was forced to resign because of his moderate position and advocacy of electoral reform.

A complete account of the partition issue would be outside the scope of this study. The subject has been written about extensively, usually in strongly partisan fashion. In brief, citizens of the Republic tend to regard the "Six Counties" of Northern Ireland as Irish soil forcibly occupied by a foreign power, and their people inherently a part of the Republic. The Ulster Protestants, who form a bare majority of the population of Northern Ireland, regard their exclusion from the Republic as protecting them from the poverty and galling restrictions of a Church-dominated South. In Northern Ireland, they point out, there is no clerical censorship; birth control is not illegal nor is divorce forbidden; trade with Great Britain is free; British social welfare benefits are enjoyed; there is a higher standard of living. Finally, the Protestant Ulsterman's fierce loyalty to the British connection prevents him from having a feeling of real community with the Irish of the South.

Nevertheless, despite the civil rights demonstrations and Orange riots of 1968 and 1969, there has been a slow but definite improvement in North-South relations. One of the earliest manifestations of this was an agreement to share in the development and distribution of hydroelectric power. In February, 1965, the Royal Ulster Constabulary and the Civic Guard of the Republic agreed that warrants issued in one jurisdiction would be enforced in the other as soon as enabling legislation could be enacted in Dublin and Westminster. In the summer of 1965, the tourist boards of the Republic and Northern Ireland agreed to pool their efforts in attracting tourists to the island. Border formalities have been minimized now that the IRA has allegedly given up its border raids. The Anglo-Irish trade reciprocity agreement, concluded in December, 1965, facilitated an increased flow of goods between North and South.

The Southern equivalent of the Orange extremists is the dwindling band of IRA irregulars, who in recent years have found an outlet for their emotions and energies chiefly in destroying monuments to English monarchs and administrators—monuments left over from the period of British rule. This seems to arouse little resentment among the Irish public, many of whom, no doubt, retain a certain admiration for the daring deeds by the IRA lads of the past who attacked the RUC on its home territory. In 1958 the large bronze statue of Lord Gough in Phoenix Park was destroyed. The statue of Lord Nelson, perched high upon its column like the one in Trafalgar Square, dominated both O'Connell Street (formerly Sackville Street) and the statue of O'Connell at its base until an explosion demolished it and the upper half of the column on March 8, 1966. This act may well have been intended as a dramatic commemoration of the approaching fiftieth anniversary of the Easter Rising.

Hatred is an intoxicating emotion—and easier to arouse than love of one's fellows. Irish nationalism on the positive side—the willingness to work for Ireland's progress in ways not involving the fight against England and to sacrifice personal profit to the public good—is no more common in Ireland than elsewhere.

The class structure of Irish society in certain respects reflects the colonial past. As in all ex-colonial societies, the former ruling class has lost its power and, in the case of Ireland, much of its wealth. Some of the titled families have left Ireland. Few can any longer be described as rich. The rents do not roll in as they once did and not many of the landed gentry or peerage, whose mansions survived the burnings of the Troubles, can afford to maintain these great houses in their old style. Although in the "social column" sense the titled families have the highest social prestige, they are an anachronism in the Irish Republic. They play little part in its public life and none at all in politics. Some have UK titles and seats in the House of Lords, but the lords no longer have a voice in Irish affairs. Scions of these families have no place in the Irish parties nor do they attempt to secure nomination for the elections to the Dáil. Their origins would make this difficult anywhere and impossible in many rural constituencies. Some, despite centuries of Irish land-holding, do not identify themselves with Ireland as much as with England, and certainly not with the Irish Republic. They have something in common with the French aristocracy following the establishment of the Third Republic, as regards their aloofness from political life.

Most of the nontitled members of the former Ascendancy are, like the titled families, little more than bystanders in politics. Of English descent and Protestant religion, they too often failed to become truly Irish in feeling and identification. If they can afford the expense, they send their children to England for their education. Some return for their university studies to Trinity College, Dublin. They tend to associate with their own kind, to regard Ireland as provincial, and to prefer the English way of life. Some of these families still farm the demesne land of their inheritance, the remainder of their former property, once worked by tenants, having been taken over by the Land Commission. In general, their farms are far above the average in efficiency and good management. Some Anglo-Irish farmers are active in farm organizations.[15] Few have any public role in political life. No doubt their British background and accent would be a handicap on the hustings even though some, such as Sir Anthony Esmonde, T.D., have overcome this disadvantage. It has been suggested that a prime reason for the failure to secure election of ex-British Brigadier O'Gowan in County Cavan was his British upper-class accent and manner, even though he is an ardent republican and an advocate of the reoccupation of the Six Counties by force of arms. Of course it may well be that O'Gowan's policy of violence had even less appeal than his accent to the farmers of Cavan, who would find themselves in the front lines of such an encounter.

Traces of the old, gay life remain. Racing and fox hunting are still the favorite pastimes of the gentry and the historic hunts still flourish with their pink-coated huntsmen and beautifully matched packs of hounds. The internationally renowned annual horse show of the Royal Dublin Society, with its accompanying festivities, and the Royal Irish Yacht Club, which still flies the blue ensign of the Royal Naval Reserve, are reminders of the vanished importance of the Ascendancy, although these institutions are no longer monopolized by the Ascendancy families.

Middle-class Protestant families are mainly urban and concerned with business and the professions. They have tended to be Unionist in politics but this class produced all the early leaders of Irish nationalism except O'Connell. There is no such separation from Irish politics as in the case of the rural gentry, but with the virtual disappearance of the Unionist Party in the Republic, former Unionists have had to vote for other parties or refrain altogether from political activity. There is no sharp separation on religious grounds among the urban middle class. There is a tendency for these Protestant families to be endogamous, but interfaith marriages do occur and in nearly all cases the children of such marriages are reared as Roman Catholics. It is possible that in time the Protestant urban middle class may be largely assimilated by the rest of the urban middle class and its origins forgotten. This is happening in smaller places and rural areas where Protestants are a tiny minority. In Dublin, however, with a rather large Protestant minority, assimilation is a much slower process.

In general, the middle class is nonrural and its members are mainly in the professions or in commerce. The small number of large-scale manufacturing enterprises and the predominantly agricultural and pastoral character of the national economy means that this middle class is relatively small. It is, as one would expect, the most active class in politics and its members are the energetic partisans, politicians, and candidates. With some exceptions, even most of the rural candidates for election to the Dáil are of the middle class.

Although the manual working class in the cities is thoroughly unionized, it has not been active politically as a class, and has produced few political leaders. This situation will be discussed in greater detail in connection with the history of the Labour Party.

The rural working class consists of small farmers and farm laborers. Most farms are operated by the farmer and his family. Some of these farmers may work elsewhere for wages, but the

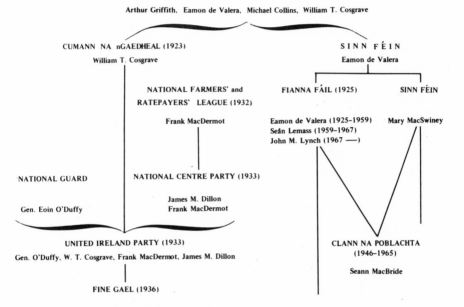

SINN FÉIN
and Its
Descendants

SINN FÉIN (1905)

Arthur Griffith, Eamon de Valera, Michael Collins, William T. Cosgrave

CUMANN NA nGAEDHEAL (1923)   SINN FÉIN
William T. Cosgrave   Eamon de Valera

NATIONAL FARMERS' and   FIANNA FÁIL (1925)   SINN FÉIN
RATEPAYERS' LEAGUE (1932)

Frank MacDermot   Eamon de Valera (1925–1959)   Mary MacSwiney
                            Seán Lemass (1959–1967)
                            John M. Lynch (1967 —)

NATIONAL GUARD   NATIONAL CENTRE PARTY (1933)

                          James M. Dillon
Gen. Eoin O'Duffy   Frank MacDermot

UNITED IRELAND PARTY (1933)   CLANN NA POBLACHTA
Gen. O'Duffy, W. T. Cosgrave, Frank MacDermot, James M. Dillon   (1946–1965)

                                                Seann MacBride
FINE GAEL (1936)

W. T. Cosgrave (Dáil leader and President, 1933–1944)
Gen. Richard J. Mulcahy (President, 1944–1959)
John A. Costello (Dáil leader, 1944–1958)
James M. Dillon (Dáil leader and President, 1959–1965)
Liam Cosgrave (Dáil leader and President, 1965 —)

class of those permanently employed as wage laborers is relatively small. Landless farm workers are economically and socially at the bottom of the scale. Rural Ireland has more farm labor than is needed and only the constant emigration of farmers' sons and daughters prevents a serious amount of unemployment.

Mention may be made of one other element in the Irish population: the few thousand tinkers who travel about the countryside in horse- or donkey-drawn caravans and live in these or in tiny tents by the roadside. They sometimes make a living by casual labor but are mainly concerned with horse-trading, fortune-telling, begging, and the usual pursuits of gypsies, although the tinkers are not of gypsy stock. In the winter they sometimes find shelter in the city slums. These people are hardly an integral part of Irish society, but form a subsociety of their own. They are widely believed to make a living chiefly by poaching and petty theft. It need hardly be said that this small but ubiquitous, picturesque, seminomadic and quasi-pariah group has no political role whatever. These tinkers are evidently the descendants of landless, homeless, and unemployed peasants compelled to wander about in search of a living. Without a fixed abode their children have no chance to acquire any education and their reputation for thievery makes them unwelcome in most localities. The reintegration of these unfortunates into the general Irish community is a still uncompleted task.

For more than a century the Irish economy was predominantly agricultural, pastoral, and poor by western European standards. Until very recently almost all Irish manufacture was concentrated in Northern Ireland. It was said, with small exaggeration, that the Guiness brewery was the only important export industry in the Republic. Guiness's stout, together with the produce of the whiskey distilleries, represented a substantial proportion of all manufactured exports. Altogether, manufactures supplied only about ten percent of visible exports contrasted with the eighty-five percent of farm produce, including meat and cattle.

The difficulty experienced by Ireland in expanding industrial production has been blamed on various factors. Often mentioned is the lack of coal, iron, and other basic raw materials. It may be noted that this lack also exists in Ulster, and in countries such as Switzerland and Japan which have built up extensive industries. Some Irish commentators have blamed Irish apathy and lack of ambition. A factor, perhaps, has been the tendency for the more enterprising youth of both sexes to leave the countryside and emigrate because Ireland has lacked attractive employment. Thus the meagre home market is further impoverished by emigration. Another problem has been the scarcity of investment capital. Foreign investors did not find Ireland attractive and local accumulations of capital were usually invested abroad, a condition typical of underdeveloped economies.

Already noted in Chapter II was the start made by Mr. Cosgrave in the early days of the IFS to overcome economic stagnation by government-created and financed enterprises and the continuation of this policy under Fianna Fáil administrations. Progress was slow and difficult at first. In recent years it has been accelerating and the population loss has been checked with a rejuvenating effect, both literally and figuratively, upon Irish society. The GNP for 1961 showed a real increase of four percent over 1960 and, for the first time, industrial production outvalued farm products. There were over 41,000 more industrial workers in 1964 than in 1958.[16]

The industrialization program has checked the population drain although it has not yet been eliminated. The birth rate provided a net increase in total population of 62,411 in 1966, representing a rise of 4.4 percent, coinciding with the lowest net emigration figure yet recorded: 83,855. Once before, in 1951, there had been a small net increase of 5,486, but the 1966 figure is far more encouraging as evidence of a possible reversal of Ireland's population loss. It should be noted that the growth occurred mainly in urban areas and that population continued to diminish in Connaught and the Ulster counties of Cavan, Donegal, and Monoghan.[17]

The drift to the cities will continue as industry expands. It is possible, as well, that there will continue to be some loss of population so long as Irish wages and living standards remain below those of Great Britain. As noted in the Whitaker Report, many emigrants are employed persons leaving for better jobs. When industrialization has raised Irish incomes to the British level, one may expect to see an expanding population which will stimulate the economy and reverse the cycle of a shrinking home market, a slowed industrial growth and, as a result, more emigration. Once a net increase in population has become established, it will have more than economic results. Irish faith in Ireland's future will be restored and Irish genius, skill, and enterprise will find satisfactory employment in Ireland rather than abroad. No longer will one hear the kind of cynical remark made to the author by a man once prominent in Irish politics: "How can one be a patriot in a dying country?"

Irish population density is still low by the standards of developed West European countries. This means higher unit costs for public services, especially in the rural districts where population continues to shrink. Another result of emigration is the disproportionate number of the very young and the elderly. In 1961, almost one-third of the population was under 15 years of age and over 11 percent was 65 or older. As a result, a large proportion of the population is economically unproductive. Another factor in Irish demography is the low marriage rate, 5.5 per 1,000. Age at marriage averages over 26 for women and over 30 for men. Many remain unmarried. Thirty-two percent of males aged 40 to 45 are bachelors and 22 percent of females in this age bracket are spinsters. The illegitimacy rate is low but the fertility rate is high. It is certain that a rise in industrialization and a drop in emigration will change this demographic pattern radically. Employment will make more and earlier marriages economically feasible, marriageable young men and women will remain in Ireland, and the estimate of a population in excess of three million by 1976 may prove to be far too modest. By that date Ireland may have to grapple with new problems of urban sprawl and population density.

Imports and exports have expanded rapidly since 1956. In 1965 imports had a total value of £371.7 million. This represented an excess of £151 million over the total value of exports. This unfavorable trade balance has been an Irish financial problem from the beginning, although the 1964 excess was the highest on record. The imports indicate a steady improvement in living standards as measured by number of motor vehicles, domestic electrical equipment, and the like.[18]

The GNP has risen steadily and by 1966 was more than 75 percent higher than in 1958. Savings and domestic fixed capital formation doubled and consumers spent £125 million more on goods and services than in 1958. Some of this additional consumer spending was due to the burgeoning tourist industry. In 1966 visitors spent an estimated £65.1 million, a substantial "invisible export" helping to correct the adverse balance of trade. According to an estimate in the *Irish Times* of January 1, 1969, tourism earned £92.5 million in 1968 and the government tourist board, Bord Failte Éireann, hoped that tourist spending would reach £100 million in 1969.

The Government continues to expand its enterprise. In 1965 it bought the British and Irish Steam Packet Company, which carries about half the general cargo traffic and more than half the livestock exports to Great Britain. The Pigs and Bacon Commission, which handles the export and sale abroad of pork products, proposed during 1965 to spend £100,000 on sales promotion in Britain. Even the export of Irish racing greyhounds is controlled by Bord na gCon, a statutory agency created in 1958.[19]

The taoiseach announced in January, 1969, as reported in the *Irish Times*, January 24, that a provisional estimate for 1968 indicated a record rise in national production of five percent over 1967. The economic statistics over the past several years give evidence of a successful effort on the part of the Irish Government to provide by public investment, in default of private, the needed capital to initiate productive enterprises and to provide for their management by statutory boards. Although these boards are dependent for their funds upon government and legislative action, they have remained relatively free of political interference in their policies and, in general, have earned the respect and cooperation of the Government and the Dáil. For example, in January, 1969, the Minister for Industry and Commerce, Mr. Colley, moved the Export Promotion (Amendment) Bill, 1969, to provide Córas

Tráchtála, the board responsible for promoting foreign trade, with £4.5 million for its work over the next two years. A prime objective of this board is to encourage the diversification of exports and to reduce Irish dependence upon the British market.

Despite recent industrialization, Ireland is still an agricultural, or rather, a pastoral country. There are about 12 million acres of farmland, of which almost 8½ million are used for pasture and over 2 million for hay. The remainder, about 1¼ million acres, are planted with other crops, including fruit. Obviously, Irish farms are mainly engaged in livestock raising, even though the average farm is too small for the most efficient production of cattle. The emphasis on cattle means a low average yield per acre over the entire farming area. The typical small farm supports a family, if not too numerous, but at a level not much above subsistence. At current production rates and farm income, Irish farms cannot support an increase in population. The number of males engaged in farm work dropped by almost 53,000 between 1960 and 1965. Even so, to secure a substantial improvement in living standards there should be fewer people living on farms than there are at present.

Irish farms are often inefficient by European standards. The fields are frequently irregular in shape, which makes efficient cultivation difficult, and separated by great untidy hedges which have been allowed to accumulate and expand over the years until they are ten to fifteen feet in depth. There is little standardization of quality in farm produce, even that intended for the city markets.

A factor in the drift away from the farm is the fact that, for years, the average income per person on the farm has remained below the national average.[20] Added to the low living standards is the absence of the excitement and entertainments of city life.

The long, low, whitewashed stone cottage with its overhanging, thatched roof is a picturesque kind of farmhouse but it provides substandard living conditions. Cooking is done in a fireplace over a turf fire, which is also the only source of heat for the dwelling. Few of these houses have running water, although a number have electric light—thanks to the rural electrification program. Often there are no sanitary facilities at all, not even a privy.

Sanitation standards are deplorable. The diet in many farm families is ill balanced; often its mainstay is bread and butter and tea without milk. Little milk, cheese, or beef is consumed. The meat is usually bacon.[21] Today almost everyone has had a primary education, so illiteracy is rare, but in many farm families nobody reads anything. The wives of many farmers go through lives of drudgery. Almost their only respite from toil is provided by the church visit on Sundays and a chat with other women after mass. They have no "days off" and no luxuries. Many of them have to carry home in buckets all the water used in the household.[22]

More than one-third of all Irish farms are from 30 to 100 acres in size. Seven percent are between 100 and 200 acres and only 2 percent are larger than 200 acres. Farms of 50 acres or less occupy 42 percent of all Irish farmland in the Republic. Most are worked entirely by the owner and his family. Only about one farm laborer in seven is a permanently landless hired hand.

A significant feature of the Irish economy is its close tie with that of Great Britain, which has always provided the nearest and by far the most important market for Irish exports, particularly cattle, meat, and dairy products. The total exports from Ireland in the year September, 1964 to September, 1965, were valued at something over £151 million. Of these, more than £92 million were accounted for by exports to Great Britain.[23] Great Britain, in turn, is the source of most of Ireland's imports. All this is a matter of economic geography and has persisted despite political differences. Great Britain also provides the closest and most important supply of employment for unemployed Irish of both sexes.

Potentially of great importance to the Irish economy is the free-trade agreement with Great Britain concluded in December, 1965, by the taioseach, Mr. Lemass. This should prove to be of enormous benefit to Irish farmers. Under the terms of the agreement all the cattle, sheep, and most other products Ireland can export have gone to England duty free from July 1, 1966. Ireland will cut duties on British imports by ten percent a year until such imports are free of all duties—by July 1, 1975. This provision is to permit the hitherto protected Irish industries time to adjust to free competition with British industries. The Government has also promised that State aid to Irish industry will be increased. The agreement provides that Ireland may lower duties or eliminate them on imports from Northern Ireland by negotiation between the two Irish governments. Northern Ireland has also welcomed the agreement as leading to more trade with the South. Another result of the agreement is that Ireland will be free to join EFTA and GATT.[24]

If the trade agreement succeeds in its objectives it may do much to transform Irish society. Hitherto, the pace of industrial development has been slow and insufficient to provide work for many willing and able Irish people. Capital investment has been tardy and many Irish enterprises inefficient because unable to find the capital necessary for plant modernization.

The low productivity and slow development of the Irish economy has sometimes been attributed to defects in the "Irish character." It has been alleged that few Irish workmen or craftsmen are interested in the quality of their product or even in good workmanship. This is said to be the case despite the existence of beautiful objects in glass, metal, and wood dating from the eighteenth century and testifying to the excellence of Irish crafts in that period. It is said that the Irish people lack ambition and enterprise. One Irish cynic suggested that the Republic adopt, as the most appropriate national motto, the expression: "Ach, sure it'll do." Insofar as such comments are justified, the lack of ambition, enterprise, and pride in one's work may well be due to the constant threat of unemployment and, for many, a fairly permanent condition of underemployment. This tends to result in poor work habits, "ca'canny," and the use of time-wasting methods to "make the job last," such as the astonishing number of "tea-breaks" that punctuate working hours in some trades.

Many Irish also believe that attitudes toward work and toward employers, formed during Ireland's colonial past, still affect the behavior of Irish farm laborers and city workmen. For generations, when any enterprise on the part of a tenant, or any improvement of his property, would lead at once to an increase in his rent, slovenly work habits were thoroughly established. Lingering effects of these attitudes and habits may be observed in the disposition to resist the introduction of new and better farming techniques and the tendency to procrastinate. One Irish commentator remarked that the typical Irish farmer spends much of his time opening and shutting gates and gazing at jobs he intends to get at next year. Another tendency is to trust to luck and take chances that everything will come out all right. "He's a chancy man," the Irish farmers say of one another. It must be kept in mind, as well, that the more ambitious and vigorous members of the poor farmer class have tended for more than a century to seek their fortunes overseas.

It is certainly the case that the educated and intellectual elite of Ireland are likely to regard Irish society, even in Dublin, as rather provincial, and to feel the strong attraction of the metropolitan society of London. Some writers have objected to literary censorship and have removed themselves to more tolerant countries. This may be a minor factor in the future, as censorship of both books and plays has recently been eased. In any case, censored books usually can be obtained without difficulty, although not displayed in the bookshops.[25] Of course, Irish writers leave Ireland for reasons other than censorship. They have larger audiences and wider opportunities elsewhere. It is a common complaint that Dublin is no longer a stimulating artistic, literary, and intellectual center. Those who subscribe to this opinion point to the mediocre folk comedies that are presented at the Abbey Theatre in place of the great plays of the past. But here too there may be changes. Conceivably a prosperous and economically resurgent Ireland may encourage an intellectual and cultural revival as well.

Another factor of interest in any political study is the educational system of the country under examination.[26] Before the establishment of the Free State, Irish popular education was controlled by the National Board of Education, which had been created in 1831. This was done in order to try to supervise the many parish schools called "hedge schools" that had been started locally, nearly all of which were in the charge of the parish priest. The board did not overturn this system but laid down rules regarding the curriculum, books to be used, and teaching methods. The principal instrument of control was the inspector and before 1900 the amount of the teacher's salary depended upon the annual oral examination conducted by the inspector. After 1900, regular salaries were paid without regard to the annual inspection. The curriculum was devised and the teaching of history designed to make the Irish children feel themselves part of the English nation. The Irish language was not taught before 1879; after that it was permitted as an "optional" or extra subject which could be taken if passing grades in other subjects were maintained. By 1921, something over one-third of the National Schools had some Irish instruction. The failure of the National Schools to substitute British for Irish nationalism was due, in all probability, to the attitude of the teachers who were able to supplement and contradict the material in some of the required reading.[27] The Irish language however, was not revived and the number of Irish speakers steadily diminished, due to the greater utility of English and to social and economic factors which led parents to demand English for their children.

After 1921 an abrupt change took place. At first it was laid down by the Minister of Education that the Irish language and history should be given top importance, that infant instruction should be entirely in Irish, and that Irish history and geography should be taught at all levels in the Irish language. This proved to be impractical because many teachers as well as pupils knew little Irish. Also, it was felt that some teachers were poorly prepared in general. Accordingly, five preparatory colleges for prospective teachers in religious orders were established under Catholic auspices and a sixth for Protestant students. They are boarding schools and students enter at the age of fourteen. The course lasts for six or seven years. This type of training has been criticized as too narrow, too rushed, and too cloistered. The students lack the intellectual stimulus of a university atmosphere. They do acquire fluency in Irish, which is the medium of instruction and the language in daily use. At the end of this course the students take the leaving certificate examination to qualify for entrance to one of the six National Teacher Training Colleges. Three are for Catholic men teachers and two of them train only Christian Brothers, De la

Salle Brothers, or other members of a male teaching order. Two train nuns or Catholic laywomen and the sixth trains both male and female Protestants. (This Church of Ireland Training College is associated with Trinity College, Dublin, which provides some of the instruction.) The course at these colleges lasts for two years—one year for university graduates. Entrance is limited by college accommodation and is competitive. Successful candidates usually have taken honors in six or more subjects in the leaving certificate examination. They must also pass additional tests in oral Irish and singing and be approved by an interview board.

Teachers of special subjects, such as art, music, and physical education are trained in other specialized schools or training centers. The colleges mentioned above cannot train a sufficient number of teachers to staff all schools and some laywomen teachers are admitted to the profession on the basis of honor standing at the leaving certificate examination after a course of study in an ordinary secondary school.

Attendance at a primary school is compulsory between the ages of six and fourteen. Almost all children attend one of the National Schools, which are entirely state-supported and tuition-free, although in most cases the pupils must supply their own textbooks. All of these schools are denominational in fact. The great majority are Roman Catholic (97 percent in 1948), a few are Protestant, and one is Jewish. In the case of the Catholic schools, the bishop or diocesan trustees appoint the school manager, who is almost always the parish priest. The school district is made to coincide with the parish. The manager oversees the upkeep of the buildings and other physical property and also approves the curriculum and appoints the teachers, subject to their qualifying under Department of Education rules. There is no lay supervision other than that of the department. Part of the cost of new school buildings is met otherwise, but most (86 percent in 1963) comes from a State subvention. About one-third of the schools belong to a religious congregation, usually a teaching order, or to the parish priest.

The subjects taught include religion, Irish, English, arithmetic, history, geography, music, and sewing. There are some additional

optional subjects such as physical training, drawing, manual training, and the like.

Altogether in 1966 there were 4,797 National Schools with an
enrollment of over 500,000 pupils mostly between the ages of 6
and 14, but some younger and some as old as 18. The teachers
numbered 14,614, of whom 1,858 were untrained. A few National Schools (81 in 1963–1964) gave some work in secondary
education, called a "Secondary Top." In 1963–1964 there were
6,700 pupils in these courses, the great majority of whom were
girls, as most are given in National Schools operated by convents.

In 1963–1964 about 21,000 children attended private, non-
State-aided primary schools, most of them in the Dublin area.

The National Schools have been sharply criticized by some
educators as spending far too much time on languages to admit of
a thorough primary training in other fields.[28]

The primary education given in the National Schools is the
terminal education for most Irish children. Those who continue,
attend one of the secondary schools which have been tuition-free
since 1967. There were 585 of these schools in 1966 with 98,667
pupils. They are nearly all Roman Catholic and are owned by
dioceses, teaching orders, and convents or monasteries. They receive State aid in the form of a capitation grant. The registered
teachers of the required subjects must have a university degree,
postgraduate training in teaching methods, and a year's teaching
experience. There were, as of 1966, 6,795 full-time secondary
teachers and 4,302 of these were registered teachers. Secondary
school students numbered 103,558. They are about evenly divided
between lay and religious, and the women slightly outnumber the
men.

The secondary school pupils enter at about 13 or 14 years of
age and complete the course at the age of 16 to 19. They study
Irish, English, history, geography, mathematics, one other language
and either science, commerce, or domestic science. There are two
sets of national examinations, the intermediate certificate, taken
after three or four years, and the leaving certificate examination
which, if passed successfully, serves to admit to the university. The
former is to provide a suitable terminal certificate for those who

leave school for work at about age sixteen. The additional two years of the senior course are college preparatory work. Irish remains a compulsory subject.

Criticisms of Irish secondary education, as with primary education, include the objection that the curriculum is too heavily loaded on the linguistic side, with almost one-half of the pupils' classroom time devoted to languages, leaving too little time for the other important subjects. Some university teachers complain that students are often poorly prepared for university work in the sciences. This may reflect the lack of equipment and of well-trained science teachers in many secondary schools and, more generally, insufficient time devoted to science classroom and laboratory work. The history textbooks used in most schools have been criticized as tending to inculcate a narrow nationalism, overemphasizing the violent episodes in Irish history and failing to give the pupils a fair perspective on domestic and international politics.

Another matter of concern to Irish educators is the large number of National School pupils (some 8,000 each year) who drop out without reaching even the primary certificate stage. Presumably, many of those who intend to get a job rather than continue into secondary school do not bother to take the examination. Of those who pass the primary certificate examination, a large percentage do not enter a secondary school, and of those who start postprimary schooling, many do not finish.[29] The physical distance from a secondary school, particularly in Connaught and Northwest Ulster, is sometimes a factor, as is the economic and social background of the pupil.

The high dropout figure has been taken to presage a future scarcity of persons capable of manning a fully developed economy. Some rural schools are deplorable as regards physical condition and equipment. Many of the National Schools were built before 1900 and almost four hundred are over a century old. A number of the one- and two-teacher schools have no provision for drinking water on the school premises and about the same number have no flush toilets. Almost two-thirds of these smallest schools have only an open fireplace for heat in the winter.[30] Of course, every year some new schools are built, and existing ones enlarged

or repaired. The amount spent by the Government on main-
tenance of school buildings rose from £226,062 in 1959–60 to
£404,415 in 1964–65.

Of course, all the faults to be found with the Irish educational
system have been discussed at length in the studies listed in footnote 26 of this chapter, and a number of changes and reforms suggested. It is beyond the scope of this study to discuss them.

As regards higher education in Ireland, for a long time the
only university in what is now the Republic was Trinity College,
Dublin University, founded under Queen Elizabeth I in 1591. St.
Patrick's College, Maynooth, was founded in 1795 as a seminary
for the Catholic priesthood, and the Catholic University of Ireland
was established in 1854. Its first Rector was the distinguished John
Henry (later Cardinal) Newman. This was the academic ancestor
of the present National University of Ireland, which came to consist of three constituent colleges—the University Colleges at Dublin, Cork and Galway, and St. Patrick's, Maynooth, recognized as
regards its courses in the arts, philosophy, sociology, Celtic
studies, and science. It is otherwise a pontifical university conferring theological degrees.

No religious test is required at any of the colleges. However,
the entrance requirement of a knowledge of Irish effectively keeps
most Anglo-Irish students out of the National University. Most of
these have had a secondary education in England or in a private
school in Ireland where Irish was not taught. Without Irish they
are acceptable at TCD. Until recently the general entrance requirements at TCD were higher than those of the NUI, but in 1966–
1967 they were equalized, requiring a secondary leaving certificate
with honors in at least two subjects or the passing of a matriculation
examination. The NUI grants a liberal arts or science degree after
three years but requires four years for an honors B.Sc. TCD requires
four years' work for a degree.

Although not kept out of TCD by entrance requirements,
many Irish youths are discouraged from attendance there by a
religious prohibition. The Catholic hierarchy has issued these regu-
lations:

We forbid under pain of mortal sin:

1. Catholic youths to frequent that College;
2. Catholic parents or guardians to send to that College Catholic youths committed to their care;
3. Clerics or religious to recommend in any manner parents or guardians to send Catholic youths to that College or to lend counsel or help to such youths to frequent that College.

Only the Archbishop of Dublin is Competent to decide, in accordance with the norms of the instructions of the Holy See, in what circumstances and with what guarantees against the dangers of perversion, attendance at that College may be tolerated.

The offer of TCD to establish a Roman Catholic chapel for the college and in other ways try to satisfy the hierarchy have not been successful. One of the members of the Commission on Higher Education, 1960–1967, the Most Rev. Dr. Philbin, defended this prohibition on two principal grounds: first, the need for a university education can be met entirely and satisfactorily by the clerically controlled NUI, whereas if NUI did not exist Catholics might well be allowed to attend TCD; second, TCD ". . . is seen as having a neutral and secularist character, its strong Protestant traditions having gradually given ground to an uncommitted attitude in which currents of opinion more radically opposed to Catholicism may exert considerable influence. . . ."[31]

Despite this attitude on the part of the hierarchy, the taoiseach, Mr. Lynch, subsequently proposed the merger of NUI and TCD and in March, 1968, informed officials of both universities that Fianna Fáil remains committed to this policy. The merger is advocated because it is the assumption that a division of academic labor between the two institutions should enable both to concentrate upon their specialties and improve standards while avoiding wasteful duplication of courses. This proposal was still in the discussion stage in the spring of 1969.

In 1965–1966 there were over 11,000 full-time students attending NUI and about 3,000 at TCD. Ninety percent or more of the NUI students were residents of the Republic, whereas only about 50 percent of the TCD students fell into this category. Students from Northern Ireland constituted about 2 percent of the NUI student body and about 20 percent of that of TCD.[32] Foreign students therefore comprised about 30 percent of the TCD enrollment, a fact of some concern to the 1960–1967 commission, which felt that Ireland should restrict foreign registrants in view of the cost to the Irish taxpayer. Both TCD and NUI receive subsidies which in 1966–1967 amounted altogether to £3.7 million. The Royal College of Surgeons, Ireland, educates more non-Irish physicians than Irish. In 1965–1966 there were 546 foreign and 164 Irish students enrolled at the RCSI.[33]

Proportionately more Irish young people than formerly obtain a secondary education, and about one-quarter of all who achieve the secondary leaving certificate apply for admission to a university. Fifty years ago there were a few more than 5,000 university students in Ireland. There were almost 14,000 in the school year 1964–1965 from a smaller population. Subtracting the non-Irish students from this number, there are now about 316 university students per 100,000 of the population, proportionately about 40 percent more than in Great Britain and comparing favorably with the most advanced European countries.[34] One result is that Ireland, at considerable public expense, is educating many of its sons for export. As indicated by Dr. McElligott, a survey of 492 physicians graduated from University College, Cork, in the years from 1945 to 1954, secured replies from 408, and of these, 45 percent were practicing medicine in Great Britain. The more recent graduates have shown an even greater tendency to emigrate.[35]

There is controversy over the extent of the "brain drain." Professor Richard Lynn presented a paper late in 1968 entitled "The Irish Brain Drain," in which he estimated the loss to Ireland by 1968 of about 60 percent of all university graduates. His estimate was challenged by Garret FitzGerald, who claimed that of the mechanical and electrical engineers who had received their diplomas in 1958, only 20 percent were working abroad in 1962. More available employment in Ireland has cut the emigration rate for most professionals since 1958 and increased industrialization may be expected to cut it further.[36]

~ It seems hardly necessary to state that the Irish people are predominately of the Roman Catholic faith. Ireland as at present constituted, excluding the Northeastern counties, is possibly the most completely Roman Catholic country in the world and is becoming more so. As of 1961 the total population was 2,818,341, of whom 2,673,473 were Roman Catholics. Protestants and Jews, and those without religious affiliation, numbered 144,868. The majority of these, 104,016, declared themselves Protestant Episcopalians (the old Church of Ireland). While the total population decreased by .4 percent between 1936 and 1946, at the same time the number of Roman Catholics increased 6.3 percent in the towns. Most of the emigration has been from the rural districts where the number of Roman Catholics decreased by 2.8 percent, while non-Catholics fell in numbers by 13.1 percent in both urban and rural areas. Dublin County had the second highest proportion of non-Roman Catholics, 13.3 percent, in 1946. In 1891, Protestants had constituted almost one-third of the population. Wicklow County, near Dublin, has the highest remaining proportion of non-Catholics.[37] It was 20.1 percent in 1881 and 14.2 percent in 1946. In the West Protestants have always been few in number. In Clare and Galway less than one percent of the population is Protestant.

The reasons for this drift would seem to be these: both groups are subject to the emigration drive; the Protestant group is more prosperous, on the whole, and tends to have a lower birth rate; marriages between Protestants and Catholics are not uncommon and the children of such marriages are almost always reared in the Roman Catholic faith.

A political result of this situation is that no party or movement of an antireligious or anticlerical stripe can develop. Beyond this, no person who expects to become a public figure in any capacity can be openly nonreligious. To be sure, this is not peculiar to Ireland, although the piety of the Irish people reinforces the ban upon avowed atheists. Protestants, however, are not excluded from public life and there have always been a few Protestants in both Dáil and Seanàd.[38] This willingness to vote for Protestants seems to derive from a Southern Irish tradition of religious tolerance which developed during the struggle for Roman Catholic emancipation in which the Church became identified with tolerance and nondiscrimination on sectarian grounds. To some extent, also, it may derive from the fact that Roman Catholic politicians never attack Protestant adversaries on the issue of religion, in line with the policy of all Irish governments since 1921 to try to prove groundless the fear of Roman Catholic rule harped upon by Northern Unionists. In any case the Protestants are far too few to develop political communalism and so to inspire a countercommunalism by Roman Catholics.

To say that Protestants do not suffer from political discrimination does not mean that they play an important part in politics or that the Church of Ireland (the disestablished Protestant Episcopal Church) exerts much, if any, influence as a body upon political affairs. It is simply the church of the remaining minority of the Ascendancy families and of those Irish whose ancestors became Protestant converts during the long history of English rule. There are a few Presbyterian as well, mainly located in and around Dublin, and these include some of the more important merchant families. Other sects exist only as tiny and unimportant groups. It is safe to say that in the Republic of Ireland we have a community which is totally Roman Catholic insofar as religious influence upon public policy is concerned. Clerical influence in politics will be discussed later.[39]

˜ The Irish Republic is the political expression of a society still predominantly pastoral and agricultural, relatively poor and underdeveloped by western European standards, although improving rapidly in this respect. Its population is unusually homogeneous. There are no sizable minorities, as the Anglo-Irish Protestant minority has been assimilated in all essentials. The Roman Catholic faith is all but universal and this faith and Irish nationalism are reinforced by a clerically controlled educational system.

Notes

1. As Conor Cruise O'Brien has remarked:
    Nationality becomes, I think, self-conscious in the degree to which it is negated. Powerful nationalities express nationality overtly in times of war or when they feel threatened. . . . Smaller nationalities have lived most of their historical lives in analogous conditions (letter to the author).

2. Shaw derided the notion of an Irish race: ". . . don't talk to me about that hackneyed myth, the Irish race. There is no Irish race. We are a parcel of mongrels: Spanish, Scottish, Welsh, English, and even a Jew or two . . ." (G. B. Shaw in *New York Journal-American*, March 17, 1946, reprinted in Shaw, *The Matter with Ireland*, Dan H. Lawrence and David H. Greene [eds.] [New York, 1962], p. 294).

   An exception to the current independence of American funds on the part of Irish parties must be noted in the case of the Ulster Republicans as represented by Bernadette Devlin, M.P., and her U.S.A. fundraising tour in the summer of 1969.

3. In conversation with the writer at King John's Castle, Limerick, an Irish youth remarked rather belligerently (in English), "You have no language of your own in your country. I wouldn't belong to a country that didn't have its own language."

4. See "Myles na Gopaleen" (Brian Ó Nualláin), "The Gaelic Past" (column), *Irish Times*, August 13, 1959.

5. These measures have not proved sufficient to save the Gaeltacht. In 1946, 48.3% of the Gaeltacht population spoke Irish. By 1961 this had dropped to 47.5%. In the rest of the country during this same period the percentage of Irish speakers had risen from 16.7 to 24.1% (*Statistical Abstract of Ireland 1966* [Dublin: Stationery Office, 1966], p. 55, table 46).

   During this period the total population in the Gaeltacht dropped from 400,489 to 345,604.

6. See the *Irish Times*, February 17, 1965, p. 11, for a comment to this effect by Cara, a society for promoting the use of Irish.

7. In January, 1965, the (Fianna Fáil) Government issued a White Paper on the Irish language outlining a ten-year plan to make Irish "the general medium of communication." A feature of this plan was an increase in the annual bounty for Gaeltacht pupils from £5 to £10. Some advocates of Irish revival thought this plan was half-hearted, offering far too little to save the Gaeltacht from eventual extinction.

8. Nevertheless, Irish national feeling, or possibly a sense of humor, induced one T.D. (T.D. means Teachta Dala, deputy of the Dáil) to insist that British libraries, entitled to free copies of Irish publications under a reciprocal arrangement, write their applications for these in Irish. See question by McAuliffe, T.D., Dáil Debates, 176, 11, July 21, 1959, 1491. Presumably in order to encourage the use of Irish in the Dáil, deputies have been provided with a booklet giving Irish equivalents of 150 phrases. The translated phrases include: "talk sense," "that is not the answer to my question," and "what about the election speeches?" See J. L. McCracken, *Representative Government in Ireland, A Study of the Dáil Éireann, 1919–1948* (London, 1958), p. 134, n. 1.

9. See T. J. McElligott, "The Language," *National Observer*, II, No. 1, July, 1959, 3–4. According to a strong advocate of the revival of Irish, the interest in the language is confined to the middle class and is of little concern to the great majority, who have no schooling beyond age fourteen. Father Ó Catháin asserts that the quality of Irish speech

and comprehension in "A" schools is very good, although the general
teaching standards of these schools have been questioned.

The marks assigned to Irish in the examinations are higher than
those given in any other subjects except the combined three mathe-
matical examinations. Bonus marks are also given to students for
writing certain papers in Irish instead of English. The "A" schools
get a 25% increase in their capitation grant from the Government.
But the number of secondary schools classed as "Irish and bilingual"
has dropped from 235 in 1960–1961 to 209 in 1965–1966. *Statistical Abstract of Ireland 1966*, p. 247.

10. Commission on Higher Education, 1960–1967, *Presentation and Summary of Report* I (Dublin: Stationery Office, 1967), 110 ff. Nevertheless, the commission advocates the revival of Irish and the establishment of postgraduate scholarships for Irish studies. Of the 26 members
of the commission, only 3 raised objections to the Irish revival program.

11. See p. 100 n. 28.

12. This has two chief manifestations. Some colonials tend to give unduly
high value to everything native to the colony and assume that their
arts, customs, and products are the best there is. Others turn their
backs upon the colony and identify themselves with the imperial power,
looking down upon local manners, customs, and products. See M.
Ayearst, "The Colonial Complex," *The Canadian Forum*, Vol. XIV,
No. 157 (October, 1933).

13. Archbishop Croke's letter of December 18, 1884, long appeared in the
GAA manual. In the words of Sir James O'Connor, it displayed "a
curious mixture of class jealousy, anti-British feeling, and the most
extravagant nonsense." The letter called for the abandonment of English
games and manners and a return to the rude, manly sports of Ireland.
Much of it is printed in O'Connor, *History of Ireland, 1798–1924*, II
(London, 1925), 240, 241.

Conor Cruise O'Brien believes that the GAA was highly significant
in stimulating Irish nationalism because of its popularity in rural
Ireland, its exclusion of British police and soldiers, and its refusal to
sponsor "foreign" games. See Conor Cruise O'Brien (ed.), *The Shaping
of Modern Ireland* (Toronto, 1960), p. 16. See also David Greene,
"Michael Cusack and the Rise of the GAA," *ibid.*, pp. 74–84.

14. This traditional attitude persists in some cases. It was Castle Catholics,
not members of the former Protestant Ascendancy, who objected in
1959 to the extension of the hospitality of a Dublin club to Lord
Altrincham, the journalist who had been guilty of criticizing Queen
Elizabeth's style of public speaking. It is of such that an Irish wit remarked: "He'd give everything save his immortal soul to be Protestant."
Quoted by O'Connor, *op. cit.*, II, p. 225.

15. An outstanding example is Dr. Juan N. Greene, founder and past
President of the National Farmers' Association. He is of Anglo-Irish
Protestant background and comes of an old land-holding family.
Through the association he has had influence upon agricultural policies
but has kept aloof from party politics. The NFA is an educational or-

ganization as well as a communication medium between its members and the minister of agriculture. Partisan activity would diminish its influence both with its members and the Government.

16. *Statistical Abstract of Ireland, 1961*, and dispatch by Hugh G. Smith, *The New York Times*, January 9, 1962.

17. *Statistical Abstract of Ireland, 1966*, pp. 12, 20, 21, 22, 23, 26. The 1966 census recorded a population of 2,880,752. It had been 4,402,752 a century earlier. In the last 65 years Dublin and suburbs almost doubled in population and Cork more than doubled. Small places lost inhabitants or remained stationary. See also James McGilvray, *Irish Economic Statistics* (Dublin: Institute of Public Administration, 1968).

18. *Ibid.*, Section V, External Trade, pp. 135–40.

19. *Weekly Bulletin of the Department of External Affairs*, No. 690 (February 8, 1965), pp. 5–8.

20. See address by Dr. J. N. Greene, "A Survey of Irish Agriculture," *The Advancement of Science*, No. 56 (March, 1958); *Documents on Ireland*, No. 16 (May, 1964); and *Statistical Abstract of Ireland, 1966*, III, 68–111.

21. It may be noted, however, that the Irish people are amply fed. According to UN statistics, daily calorie consumption averages 3,440 per person, which exceeds that of both Great Britain and the United States. It is possible that this figure may be exaggerated by failing to take into account the food consumed by tourists who visit Ireland in the number of about one million a year, and who are not included in the population base.

22. See the *Irish Times*, April 17, 1968, p. 7, for report of a talk by Mrs. Ethna Viney at the Christus Rex Congress, Rosslare.

23. *Trade Statistics of Ireland* (Dublin: Central Statistical Office, September, 1965).

24. See the *Irish Times*, December 15, 1965. A summary of the agreement is on p. 6. Of course, the trade agreement cuts both ways. In a speech at the National Management Conference held at Killarney and reported in the *Irish Times*, April 29, 1968, the taoiseach observed that an immediate result of free trade would be the loss to imports of about one-third of Ireland's domestic market. This could be counterbalanced only by increased exports. Early in 1969 Mr. Lynch observed that although production in 1968 reached record levels, the 1968 balance-of-payments deficit was still large (see the *Irish Times*, January 24, 1969).

25. See Michael Adams, *Censorship: the Irish Experience* (Dublin, 1968). This gives the history of Irish censorship from the passage of the first censorship bill in 1926, but is concerned only with the censorship of printed works.

26. For facts and opinions about the Irish educational system see: Seán Ó Catháin, S.J., *Secondary Education in Ireland* (Dublin, n.d.) [1958].
Documents on Ireland, Survey of Higher Education, No. 15 (July, 1964).
Investment in Education (Dublin: Stationery Office, n.d.) [1965].

(Report of the Survey Team appointed by the Minister For Education in October, 1962).

I *Presentation and Summary of Report,* Commission on Higher Education, 1960–1967 (Dublin: Stationery Office, 1967).

II *Report,* Vol. I, Chaps. 1–19, Commission on Higher Education, 1960–1967 (Dublin: Stationery Office, 1967).

It may be noted that a second volume of this report will be issued as well as a volume of appendices and volumes containing the written and oral evidence considered by the commission.

Statistical Abstract of Ireland, 1966, Section VIII, Education, pp. 245–53.

Statistical Abstract of Ireland, 1967, pp. 244 ff.

All of the above documents as well as interviews with Irish teachers have been used in the following paragraphs on education.

27. Ó Catháin, *op. cit.,* p. 3. For a bitter attack upon the educational system during the period of British domination, see Patrick Pearse, *The Murder Machine* (Dublin, 1912).

28. The time distribution in National Schools is approximately as follows, the figures indicating hours per week: religious instruction, 2½; Irish, 6⅔; English, 3⅓; arithmetic, 5; history, 1; geography, 1; other subjects, 3. Total: 22½. History and geography are taught in upper standards (grades) only.

29. *Investment in Education,* pp. 138 ff.

30. *Ibid.,* pp. 247–49.

31. I *Presentation and Summary of Report,* p. 50.

32. *Ibid.,* p. 20.

33. *Ibid.,* pp. 88, 108.

34. II *Report Volume* I, p. 76.

35. I *Presentation and Summary of Report,* p. 108.

36. See *Hibernia,* XXXIII, No. 1 (January 3–16, 1969) 15, and **XXXIII,** No. 4 (February 14–27, 1969) 7.

37. Figures are derived from *Census of the Population of Ireland, 1946* (Dublin: Stationery Office, 1952), III, 13, 15, 16; *Census of the Population of Ireland, General Report,* (Dublin: Stationery Office, 1958), p. 165, and *Statistical Abstract of Ireland,* 1966, p. 53. The net emigration between 1956 and 1961 was 215,641 (*Statistical Abstract of Ireland* [Dublin, 1961]).

38. In 1959 there were four Protestant T.D.'s. McCracken notes that the largest number was fourteen in the Dáil of 1923 and the first Dáil of 1927. The smallest number was three in that of 1948. On the average, Protestants have composed six percent of the membership, a proportion corresponding closely to their proportion of the total population. See J. L. McCracken, *Representative Government in Ireland* (London, 1958), table 10, p. 92. However, McCracken's calculations are based upon all Dáils, whereas recent elections have seen the return of only 3 or 4 Protestants. There should be 7 or 8 if they were elected in proportion to their incidence in the population.

39. *Infra,* pp. 210–225.

IV

THE CONSTITUTION

The background of the Constitution of the Irish Free State was outlined in Chapters I and II where the 1921 Anglo-Irish treaty was discussed. Obviously, with such a background this constitution could not be the free choice of the Irish people or their representatives. Nevertheless, a committee of the Provisional Government was appointed to draft a constitutional document for presentation to the British Government. As already noted, the original draft, prepared by Michael Collins, Darrell Figgis, and others, was in fact a bargaining gambit which the Irish leaders had no hope of getting accepted because it ignored several of the treaty requirements. They hoped, however, to pry more concessions from the British Government by presenting these proposals than they would get by adhering strictly to the treaty provisions. British parliamentary draftsmen then altered the Irish document to emphasize Commonwealth status, include the parliamentary oath, and provide for the withholding of the royal assent to bills, legal appeals to the Judicial Committee of the Privy Council and proper references to the Crown and the Crown's representative, the Governor General. Some alterations were made, as well, in the structure and powers of the Senate in order to provide for representation there of the former Unionists, unlikely otherwise to secure any representation at all. The cabinet system of parliamentary government embodied in the Constitution turned out to be entirely suitable to Irish political conditions, although it was accepted reluctantly by the Free State leaders.

In October, the Dáil adopted the Irish Free State (Saorstat Éireann) Bill, 1922. It was then passed by the British Parliament and made effective by a royal proclamation on December 6, 1922.

The Irish Free State so created certainly was much less than sovereign. Its Constitution had to be construed in accord with the terms of the treaty, and any constitutional clause or law adopted by the Dáil found contrary to the treaty would be null and void. Under the treaty the British Government controlled certain Irish ports and the Irish military establishment was restricted in size. The fundamental Irish objective of a republic was forbidden by the treaty. The required retention of the British monarch as nominal chief of state was, to Irish republicans, the most offensive feature of the treaty and the IFS Constitution, a feature underlined and emphasized by the parliamentary oath.

From the viewpoint of a constitutional lawyer, the validity of this constitution might be derived from the British Act of Parliament confirming it or, on the other hand, from the will of the Irish people as expressed through their deputies in the Dáil. The former view was taken by the Judicial Committee of the Privy Council in *Moore v. Attorney-General for the Irish Free State* [1935] A.C. 485, 497, whereas the IFS Supreme Court held that the Constitution derived its authority by reason of its adoption by the third Dáil, sitting as a constituent assembly *The State* [*Ryan and Others*] *v. Lennon* [1935] I.R. 170, 203. Note that the Irish case refers to the "*third* Dáil," containing the implication that this institution had a legal existence antedating both Constitution and treaty. An ironic result of this decision was that, by declaring the IFS act of 1922 to be the sole source of constitutional authority, the Statute of Westminster, 1931, which purported to give the dominion parliaments the right to repeal any British act applying to them, and hence the IFS Parliament the right to release itself from the limitations of the treaty, was held not to apply to the IFS. This may have been one reason for De Valera's decision to have his

1937 Constitution ratified by plebiscite, even though, because of the extension of the power to amend by the legislature, it would seem to have been within the competence of the Oireachtas to adopt whatever constitution it liked.[1]

In spite of the treaty restrictions, it was possble for the Irish leaders to insert some of their own ideas into the IFS Constitution. The assertion, "all lawful authority comes from God to the people," seemed to imply the existence of a law superior to the treaty. This "natural law" concept was accepted by Chief Justice Kennedy in the case mentioned above as invalidating Article 2A of the Constitution (Amendment No. 17) Act, 1931. This article empowered the Government to arrest persons and intern them without trial for an indefinite period. The Chief Justice's view did not prevail as the other two justices did not agree with it. This case also upheld the validity of the 1929 amendment passed by the legislature extending its own power to amend the Constitution by an additional eight years.

Another Irish contribution was the deliberate subordination of the executive branch to the legislature. The latter would be chosen directly by the people; the British cabinet system had not been accepted with enthusiasm by the Irish negotiators. Furthermore, the executive power in Ireland had been the instrument of British rule. Accordingly, the Constitution was emphatic about the predominance of legislative authority and did not display the distrust of legislatures exhibited in several of the European post-World War I constitutions.[2] The clearest expression of this legislative supremacy was Article 50, empowering the Oireachtas to amend the Constitution by ordinary act for a period of eight years. In effect, this made the treaty the only actual limitation upon the IFS Government and reduced the Constitution to nothing more than a nominal restriction. The Public Safety Act, 1927, provided that if any part of it were repugnant to the Constitution that part should be deemed to be a constitutional amendment. This provision was held by the courts to be valid.[3] Legislative supremacy applied to the Dáil but not to the Senate. The second chamber, discussed later in this chapter, was given strictly limited powers designed to prevent it from thwarting the will of the Dáil for longer than a specified period. The executive council and its president (cabinet and prime minister), were appointed by and responsible to the Dáil alone.

The cabinet system and some other features were in the British tradition, familiar to Irish parliamentarians and lawyers. In certain respects, however, the IFS Constitution reflected the post-war trends in constitution-making. For example, a bill of rights was included. Much of this was traditional—freedom of speech and assembly, for example—but the newer idea of social rights found expression in the requirement that free, elementary education for all was to be obligatory. The legislature was also subordinated to the direct legislative action of the voters through the Swiss devices of initiative and referendum which had been embodied in a number of the new European constitutions and reflected the extreme, academic democracy of the period after 1918.[4]

Two other features of the IFS Constitution deserve particular mention. A certain distrust of parties and party leadership and a fear that corruption would be the end result of party government led to the adoption of large electoral districts, in which several deputies would be chosen by means of the single-transferable-vote system of proportional representation.[5] It was expected that this would inhibit the development of two strong, major parties and that the Dáil would consist of a number of groups and Independents who would debate each issue on its merits and support a government of national union.[6] In harmony with the nonparty government idea was the plan of a real executive power, the executive council, which should consist of twelve ministers, at least four to be members of the Dáil. The other eight would be extern-ministers, not members of the Dáil and required to resign their seats if they were deputies when appointed to office. Under certain circumstances, not more than three of the extern-ministers might be allowed to become members of the Dáil or Senators. The four Dáil members in the ministry would be a cabinet of the familiar British type in all essentials. The president of the council, significantly not given the title of prime minister, would be chosen by the Dáil and he in turn would choose the other three, who would then require confirmation by the Dáil. This cabinet would be collectively responsible and would have to resign if they lost the confidence of a majority of the Dáil. The extern-ministers would not be chosen by the president of the council, but be nominated by a committee of the Dáil, representative of all groups. They would be chosen as experts in the work of a particular ministry rather than as politicians, and each nominee would be voted upon separately by the Dáil. Once confirmed, extern-ministers would have the right to attend sessions and debate and would have the obligation to answer questions, but no right to vote. They would hold office for the life of the Dáil, even if the Government were defeated, and could be removed only by a kind of impeachment procedure. This plan, obviously based upon the Swiss federal executive, was actively debated in the Dáil and finally accepted with several modifications. Extern-ministers were to be chosen by a committee of the Dáil and were to hold office for the life of that Dáil, but their number was not fixed. The president of the council might have as few of them as he liked. They might be members of the Dáil but might not be members of the executive council, and so would have to secure the approval of their departmental activities and policies by that body because it prepared the estimates.

Had the multiparty situation with a large bloc of independents prevailed in the Dáil, it is conceivable that the extern-minister scheme might have operated somewhat as planned. But the governments were party governments from the beginning, and although three extern-ministers were appointed in the first Dáil to be elected under the Free State Constitution, and four in the following Dáil, all were Dáil members, party men picked by the party leaders and confirmed by a party vote. They were not obviously chosen for any special knowledge of the work of their departments.[7] Generally they behaved as members of a collectively responsible executive body. However, from 1924 to 1927 two of them were very much at odds over tariff policy. One, the Minister for Agriculture, was a free trader, while the Minister for Posts and Telegraphs was a high protectionist. Both disagreed with the Government's intermediate policy of selective tariffs based upon the advice of a tariff commission. The disagreement was aired in public to the embarrassment of the Government. The Government's inability to impose cabinet discipline upon extern-ministers may well have been a major reason for the Constitution (Amendment No. 5) Act of 1927, which allowed the president of the council to take all twelve ministers into the executive council if he wished. This was done thereafter and no more extern-ministers were appointed.

The changes in the executive branch, made by the De Valera Constitution of 1937, increased the authority of the prime minister.[8] In line with De Valera's desire to emphasize the native Irish character of the State, the president of the executive council (prime minister) was given the title *taoiseach* (pronounced approximately "teeshock"), a Gaelic word meaning "chief." The deputy premier was now to be called *tanaiste*, a Gaelic word meaning "heir designate to the chiefship." The taioseach has more control over his ministers. He may dismiss them at will, whereas the president of the council could not do so without himself resigning and reforming a ministry for the approval of the Dáil. Except for the president's right to refuse a dissolution to a defeated taoiseach and his right to refer certain bills to the Supreme Court for a decision on their constitutionality, the executive-legislative balance of power was little changed by the 1937 Constitution. The president, unlike the British monarch in picking a prime minister, has no choice under any circumstances in the appointment of a taoiseach. The latter must be nominated and approved by the Dáil, which also approves all ministerial appointments. The taoiseach now advises the summoning and dissolution of the Dáil, whereas previously the Dáil itself set the dates of its sessions. The taoiseach was also empowered to include two senators in the Government. Previously no more than one might be a minister.

The 1937 Constitution is not as flexible as that of the IFS. Article 51, a transitory provision, gave the legislature three years after the Constitution came into effect in which it could pass amendments by ordinary law. This was used only twice as compared with the frequent passage of amendments before 1937. During this three-year period the courts no longer regarded implicit amendments as valid. One of the two amendments mentioned above, as passed by the legislature, was designed to facilitate the declaration of neutrality in World War II. The other amendment placed a serious limitation upon civil liberties. In effect it denied to the courts the right to inquire into the constitutionality of any law declaring itself to be "for the purpose of securing the public safety and the preservation of the State in times of war or armed rebellion." It gave to the Oireachtas alone the authority to decide whether or not such a condition exists. This means that the Government, with legislative approval, may set up internment camps for the detention of suspects without trial, and for an indefinite period, whenever it likes. In fact, such camps were established and used from 1939 to 1945 and again in 1955 for the detention of suspected IRA activists.

The failure of the extern-minister plan and the evolution of the Irish Government into a cabinet with practically complete control over the legislative program is the result of the development in Ireland of what is virtually a two-party system instead of a system of many small parties and numerous independent deputies envisaged by the IFS constitution-makers. That cabinet control of the time and business of the Dáil is as complete as that of the British cabinet over the House of Commons is evidenced by the fact that the time set aside for private members' motions and bills (three and a half hours per week, divided between Wednesdays and Fridays) is normally preempted by the Government for the discussion of financial business.[9] Private members' bills have scarcely any more chance of success in Dublin than they have at Westminster. As in Great Britain, the Government has a monopoly of money bills, and a private member's bill which may involve incidental expense must receive government approval of its money aspect before it reaches the committee stage. Nearly all bills are discussed in committee of the whole, which ensures the final decision being left to the government majority. As in Great Britain, the legislature has given in to the Government's requests to delegate considerable legislative authority to ministers why may be empowered even to amend an act of the Dáil by a ministerial order.[10]

A natural outcome of this development is a shift of actual power from the Dáil to the permanent Civil Service. Without any adherence to theoretical socialism by government or public, a large section of the Irish economy operates on a state socialist basis. Several statutory bodies are concerned with such matters as the underdeveloped areas, the turf (peat) industry, electricity, sugar, and so forth. These boards plan and carry out their plans with very little interference from the Dáil. Nor are they closely controlled by the ministers.[11] Their financial statements are tabled in the Dáil, but the deputies have neither the time nor the information and expert knowledge to delve into them. Questions asked about them are usually few and superficial. The lack of a permanent, continuing, subject matter committee system in the Dáil prevents it from performing intelligently one of the prime functions of a legislature: acting as the public's representative in overseeing the work of the permanent administration. In the long run, of course, the Dáil holds the purse strings, but its use of this power is of necessity guided by the government of the day. Accordingly, the taoiseach and his inner group of cabinet colleagues are the only elected officials who have genuine control over the work of these nondepartmental authorities and in practice the cabinet, as a rule, must defer to the opinions of the experts permanently in charge of them.

Apart from the statutory bodies, the Civil Service in Ireland, as in other countries, is not as firmly under ministerial control in fact as it is in theory. Ministers are politicians, temporarily in charge of departments about which, to begin with, they may know practically nothing. They have little choice but to accept the advice of their departmental subordinates. Some higher civil servants in Ireland claim that the relatively poor intellectual and educational qualifications of some ministers often compel the Civil Service to take the initiative in policy-making; they also complain that, despite briefings, such ministers fail to defend these policies properly and strongly in cabinet meetings and in the Dáil. Such allegations are by no means peculiar to Ireland but are made in all countries with a cabinet system involving temporary political department heads. Fortunately for Ireland, there is general agreement that the Irish Civil Service, although it has some of the tendencies characteristic of bureaucracies, has so far escaped any serious corruption. Possibly because of the relatively small number of opportunities in business and the professions, the Civil Service has attracted a fair number of the more capable graduates of the schools and universities. Because all civil servants must pass an examination in Irish, it is said that candidates who are fluent in Irish sometimes succeed when those who lack this skill, but are otherwise superior, are rejected.

The original IFS Senate (Seanád Éireann) was created without enthusiasm by the makers of the Constitution because they wished to avoid national disunity so far as possible and to compromise with the expressed ideas of the Unionists sufficiently to induce their acceptance of the Free State. From the start, it was certain to be unpopular with labor and the republican left because in their eyes it provided a last-stand rallying point for the defeated and hated Ascendancy. Unlike the Dáil, it had no revolutionary history or tradition—quite the contrary. It did not come into existence until four years after the Dáil had been functioning without it. Like many of the second chambers in colonial legislatures, it consisted in part of nominated members, and some of these were chosen to represent the class now unlikely to secure any spokesmen in the Dáil. The first Senate included, as nominated members, 12 of the hereditary aristocracy (8 peers and 4 baronets). Twenty-four of the 60 senators were Protestants.

The unpopularity of the Senate was due to its composition rather than to any fear of serious conflict with the Dáil. Its constitutional powers, to request a joint session with the Dáil to discuss money bills and to compel a popular referendum on other bills by a three-fifths' majority vote, were abolished in 1928 before they had ever been used. From the start, the Government, with the evident approval of the Dáil, tended to ignore the Senate and behave almost as if the Oireachtas were a unicameral legislature and the Senate's approval of bills a mere formality.

The original Senate was unlikely to precipitate serious quarrels with the Dáil at the start of its existence. Half the senators were the nominees of the president of the council and the rest had been chosen by the Dáil by single transferable vote. Despite the presence of a number of senators who were members of the former Ascendancy, all owed their seats to the government and had been chosen with care. The arrangements for subsequent replacement of senators, however, left room for possible trouble in the future. The Senate was supposed to be a continuing body. Every 4 years one fourth of the senators were to be replaced, or possibly reelected, by all Irish voters aged 30 or more who would pick the 15 winners by single transferable vote from a panel of 45, 30 nominated by the Dáil and 15 by the Senate. To these might be added the names of any retiring senators who wished to stand again. This elaborate method was discarded in 1925, allegedly because it was unwieldy and because poor candidates were chosen. If the latter were true, the deputies and senators, who picked the nominees, were themselves to blame.[12]

Before the next election it was proposed by the Cosgrave Government to reform the method of electing the Senate. The real reason for the change may have been the fact that a few organized interest groups, not connected with the political parties, succeeded in getting their candidates elected. After 1928 the Senate still had sixty members. One third of these would retire every three years and be reelected or replaced. The Senate and Dáil each nominated 20 candidates by single transferable vote and the 20 new senators would be elected from the slate of 40 by the two chambers acting as an electoral college and using the single-transferable-vote method.

The important result of these reforms was to begin the process of turning the Senate into a partisan body. This created another problem. Given time, a government might hope to place a safe majority of its partisans in the Senate, but governments may be forced out of office at any time. Because of the long tenure and gradual turnover in Senate membership it was likely that a new government might encounter obstructive action by a senate dominated by the opposition.

When De Valera became President of the Council in 1933

there was evidence of antagonism between the chambers even though, in general, the Senate was not obstructive. The antagonism became open and obvious over the question of dealing with General O'Duffy's Blue Shirts. This organization was a uniformed body of young men formed to protect the speakers of Cosgrave's United Irish Party from heckling and the disorderly tactics of Republican youth. In time, the Blue Shirts, who are discussed elsewhere,[13] began more and more to resemble a paramilitary, fascist type of organization. Fianna Fáil's reply was the recruiting of an auxiliary force with uniforms like those of Casement's Irish Brigade, allegedly officered mainly by former IRA men. To some Cosgrave supporters this force seemed to offer more threat to peace and security than did the Blue Shirts, who were unarmed. Before this issue had come to a head, the Senate had refused to pass De Valera's bill to abolish the parliamentary oath, on the ground that the bill was unconstitutional. The Senate had also turned down two bills enlarging the franchise in local government elections, on the ground that the changes would bring the national party struggle into local government—to the detriment of the latter. When De Valera sent to the Senate the Wearing of Uniform (Restriction) Bill, clearly aimed at the Blue Shirts, it was attacked as grossly partisan legislation. The Senate rejected the bill by a vote that was almost entirely partisan.[14] De Valera's immediate move, on March 22, 1934, was the introduction of a bill to abolish the Senate. He argued that second chambers in general are unnecessary, and that this senate was positively a menace to orderly government by its obstructive actions and its revival of revolutionary sentiment.[15]

The Senate tried to get the Dáil to agree not to abolish the Senate until another second chamber was devised. The Dáil, however, did nothing of the sort and when the Senate's suspensory veto period had elapsed, a simple resolution of the Dáil was all that was needed to abolish the Senate. This was not done at the earliest possible moment and the Senate continued a day-to-day existence, under sentence of death, for some time. It seems likely that De Valera considered the second chamber to be no particular menace so long as it could be abolished at a moment's notice and that he

waited to abolish it until he was ready to introduce his new constitution, which could be discussed and adopted without the critical comment and possible attempt at obstruction by any second
chamber.[16] The Constitution (Amendment No. 24) Bill, 1934, was
adopted by resolution of the Dáil for the final time in May, 1936,
and went into effect when signed by the Governor General on
May 29.

Neither De Valera nor his tanaiste, Sean T. O'Kelly, were
strongly opposed to having some kind of second chamber so long
as it did not represent the former Unionist Ascendancy and so long
as its powers were circumscribed enough so that it could not interfere seriously with the Government's program. An *ad hoc* committee was appointed to prepare a scheme for a second chamber
and the draft of the new (De Valera) Constitution, published
April 30, 1937, provided for one. This new senate was ingeniously
designed to do two things: to provide a "sober, second thought"
but without power to nullify the Government's legislative program; to provide a forum in which nonpoliticians of distinction in
various fields might give the country the benefit of their advice.
The first objective was to be accomplished by allowing a suspensory veto amounting to 180 days and also permitting the Senate to
combine with at least one-third of the Dáil to request the president
to call for a national referendum on a bill of importance. The possibility of a prolonged holdover in the Senate of a defeated party
was prevented by requiring senatorial elections not more than
ninety days after dissolution of the Dáil.

The new Senate was composed as follows: the taoiseach
named eleven senators (over one-sixth of the total membership);
the remander were elected, 3 by Trinity College, Dublin, 3 by
the National University, and 43 by an electoral college consisting
of the members of the Dáil plus 7 members of each county and
borough council chosen by these bodies by single transferable
vote. This electoral college would then choose senators from a
panel composed of candidates chosen to represent various national
interests. The taoiseach and the leader of the Opposition would
each name 2 to represent public administration and the Dáil would
pick the rest—5 to represent culture and education, 11 for agri-

culture, 11 for labor, 9 for business, and 7 for public administration. Established vocational groups might add as many as 75 additional candidates. These groups included chambers of commerce, trades unions, and teachers' associations.

This scheme accomplished one of its two objectives. No longer was there any possibility of serious and prolonged conflict between Dáil and Senate. The second objective was not achieved. Important nonpolitical groups failed to secure representation. Under the terms of the Seanád Electoral (Panel Members) Act, 1937, the returning officer published the names of bodies having the right to nominate vocational candidates. In the case of "labour, whether organised or unorganised," he admitted for the first election, the claims of the Ballingarry Cottage Tenants' and Rural Workers' Association.[17] This was an obscure and allegedly moribund body in a County Limerick village of about five hundred souls. Nevertheless, under the law when certified by the returning officer, it had as much right to present a nominee as had the Irish Trade Union Congress. In disgust, the latter body refused to make any nominations at all. In only a few cases (when a vocational group picked a candidate with political connections) did it succeed in getting a senator to represent it. Nineteen of the forty-three new senators were either ex-deputies or ex-senators. Many highly distinguished, nonpolitician candidates failed to poll a single first-preference vote. There were six candidates on the cultural panel identified with the revival of the Irish language, including the President of the Gaelic League, the Director of the Irish Folk-Lore Commission, and respected academicians, but the successful candidate was a high school principal from the Gaeltacht. Among De Valera's eleven senators were two politicians who were by no means supporters of his, Sir John Keane and Frank Mac-Dermot, and the Gaelic scholar Dr. Douglas Hyde. His remaining eight choices, however, seemed to be based on partisan criteria rather than any other.

The electoral college operated on a strictly partisan basis and often chose candidates whose connection with the panel they were supposed to adorn was tangential, to say the least. It was also claimed that bribery sometimes influenced votes. So that the likelihood of bribery might be reduced by making it too expensive, the electoral college was enlarged in 1947 to include senators as well as deputies and the entire membership of county and borough councils; its membership was thus increased to about nine hundred. So elected, the Senate has remained the second chamber of the Oireachtas without further change.

As regards the Dáil, the principal change made by the 1937 Constitution was the reduction in the number of deputies from 153 to 138 and an increase in the number of constituencies from 30 to 34. These changes had the effect reducing the number of 4- and 5-member districts and increasing the number of 3-member constituencies. This had the intended result of increasing the difficulty of election for independents. In fact, only 8 Independents were elected at the first election under the new Constitution whereas there had been 12 in the previous Dáil. The only Independent to win a seat in a 3-member constituency was Alfred Byrne, the very popular Lord Mayor of Dublin.

In 1947 the number of constituencies was increased to 40, and as there had been a net decrease in population since 1937, the number of 3-member districts was again increased at the expense of those electing 4 or 5 deputies. There were now 9 constituencies with 5 deputies, 9 with 4, and 22 with 3. It is obvious that major party government would like to come as close to the single-member district system as is possible under the Constitution.[18] Nevertheless, a slight shift in the contrary direction took place at the next revision. In 1961, 143 deputies were elected from 38 constituencies. Nine of these still returned 5 deputies, but the number of 4-member districts was increased to 11, and the number of 3-member districts reduced to 18. Apart from the Labour Party, which won 15 seats, 11 Independents or nominees of very minor parties secured election. Four of these were chosen in 5-member districts, 4 in 4-member districts and 3 in 3-member districts. Four of these were the last deputies to win in their districts and would not have been elected in one returning fewer members, but one headed the poll and one came second in 4-member constituencies. One was the second man to be elected and 3 came fourth in 5-member constituencies.[19]

Of all the features of the IFS Constitution that were objectionable to most Irish Republicans, the most unacceptable, after the oath of allegiance, was the institution of a governor general as nominal executive, personal representative and nominee of the Crown. This office, based on that of Canada, was considered an offensive reminder of the British monarchy by Griffith and the other pro-treaty leaders of Sinn Féin, but was accepted by them as necessary for the time being. The drafters were able to word the Constitution so as to leave the governor general no discretionary power as to the naming or acceptance of the president of the council (prime minister) chosen by the Dáil and no authority to refuse a dissolution request by the president of the council. As of 1922, this went beyond Canadian practice. In addition, the IFS leaders insisted that the choice of a governor general should be theirs, although they had to secure British approval of their selection. This again was in advance of current custom in the dominions. The practice of having each dominion choose its own governor general was not a formal part of British Commonwealth public law until a resolution to this effect was adopted by the Imperial Conference of 1930.

With the above understanding, only Irishmen were appointed to this office, the first being T. M. Healey, K.C., a barrister, former Member of Parliament, and a Roman Catholic. From the beginning, the office was deliberately minimized and the governor general was not permitted to play any role in political life or even take much part in social and ceremonial activities. When the Dáil passed a law delegating certain legislative authority to the executive, it was made clear in the wording that any powers given to the governor general were to be exercised only on the advice of the executive council (cabinet) and the draftsmen avoided the use of the traditional phrase, "Governor General in Council."

When the Free State was established, the Governor General opened Parliament by addressing a joint session of Dáil and Senate on December 12, 1922. There was a modest amount of ceremonial display, including a military guard of honor. The Governor General read a message from the King and then gave the "speech from the throne" outlining the Government's proposed program. This procedure was repeated in October, 1923, after the next general election, but never thereafter. From the beginning, the Labour Party delegation boycotted these appearances of the Governor General, and a majority of Fianna Fáil as well as many of Cosgrave's party did not relish this public display of the British connection. Accordingly, after 1923, new sessions began with almost no formalities, not even a "speech from the throne" outlining projected government policies. Except for campaign speeches by party leaders and the party's election manifesto, the deputies had to wait for the actual introduction of government bills to know the details of the legislative program.

When Fianna Fáil first came to power, the governor general was James McNeill, who had had a distinguished career in the Indian Civil Service and who had served as the first Irish high commissioner in London. He had succeeded T. M. Healey as Governor General in 1928. De Valera's intention to minimize this symbol of the British Crown became apparent when two of his ministers, Messrs. O'Kelly and Aiken, hastily departed from a reception at the French legation as soon as the Governor General arrived. Correspondence between De Valera and McNeill brought out the fact that it was now government policy for ministers to boycott all functions at which the Governor General appeared. McNeill regarded this as an insult and also protested his omission from the guest list at a state reception for the Eucharistic Congress which had been held in Dublin. The Governor General published this correspondence, contrary to explicit instructions from De Valera, and was abruptly dismissed from office some five months before the expiration of his term.

De Valera then advised the appointment of the last Irish Governor General, Domhnall Ua Buachalla (Daniel Buckley), a man so obscure that many people had never heard of him before his appointment. He was a retired general merchant from Maynooth who had served in the Dáil but had been defeated in several attempts to secure reelection. He did not live in the old viceregal mansion in Phoenix Park which had been the residence of his predecessors and is now the official residence of the President of the Republic. Buckley was almost never seen in public. He seems to have done no more than the minimum required by law, mainly the affixing of his signature to bills passed by the Oireachtas. Legally he still had the formal powers, never used, to reserve bills to ascertain "the pleasure of the Crown" and to recommend appropriations. These remnants of Crown Colony status were abolished by the Dáil in 1933. The oath of allegiance was also abolished in that year. The Constitution (Removal of Oath) Bill became law, over the Senate's veto, on May 3, 1933. The removal of the nominal powers of the governor general by the Constitution (Amendment No. 20) and the Constitution (Amendment No. 21) Bills became effective on November 2, 1933. The Constitution (Amendment No. 22) Bill abolished the right of appeal from the Irish courts to the Judicial Committee of the Privy Council. This became law on November 16, 1933.

The abdication of King Edward VIII in 1936 provided De Valera with the opportunity of abolishing the office of governor general. The day after the abdication, December 11, he summoned the Dáil into special session and introduced two bills under a guillotine closure allowing about twelve hours of debate on each measure. The Constitution (Amendment No. 27) Bill, 1936, removed from the Irish Constitution both the king and his representative, the governor general, as far as domestic matters were concerned. Henceforward, the Dáil would be summoned and dissolved by the chairman of the Dáil on advice of the executive council. Bills would become law when signed by the chairman of the Dáil. The other bill introduced at the same time was the Executive Authority (External Relations) Bill. So long as Ireland remained in the British Commonwealth of Nations as then constituted, it was necessary legally to recognize the formal functions of the monarch in the field of foreign affairs. The reference to this was worded clumsily so as to avoid the use of the word "Crown." [20] The bill provided that Irish consuls and diplomats be appointed by the executive council and that King George VI be the "person" entitled to act for the Free State in external relations, on advice of the executive council. To clear up all remaining loose ends the Executive Powers (Consequential Provisions) Bill repealed the act of 1923 which had provided a salary for the governor general, distributed his remaining functions, and appropriated a gratuity and pension for Buckley, whose five-year term had not quite expired.

Amendment No. 27 left Ireland in the unusual situation, for a parliamentary government, of having no permanent, formal chief executive to ratify the appointment of a new ministry. De Valera took care of this in his 1937 Constitution with the provision of a nationally elected president who, however, was not declared chief of state. It has been suggested that De Valera was anxious to suppress the republican aspect of his constitution until such time as the six counties of Northern Ireland might be induced to join an all-Ireland union.[21] It was not until Costello decided to break with the Commonwealth and formally declare Ireland a republic in his Executive Authority (External Relations) Act, 1948, that the president was admitted to be the chief of state of a sovereign republic.

Mr. Costello's sudden decision to take this step is still surrounded by some mystery. It was directly opposite to the policy of full Commonwealth membership which had been advocated four years previously by the Fine Gael President General Mulcahy, and never repudiated by any party spokesman or conference. It would appear that the new policy was announced by the taoiseach without cabinet consultation. Indeed, it was not announced in Ireland but in Ottawa, in September, 1948, while Mr. Costello was attending a Commonwealth conference. It was rumored that he was infuriated by real or fancied insults offered him or Mrs. Costello, and, by implication, his country, at the conference. He may well have been influenced by the possible political advantage to be gained by satisfying the republican sentiments of the Clann na Poblachta supporters of his coalition and perhaps winning away some votes from Fianna Fáil.[22]

The office of president of the Republic was designed with care by the author of the Constitution, De Valera, for although most of the president's functions are formal in nature and have to do with his position as chief of state, he may, under certain circumstances, exert a potentially powerful influence politically. It was said that De Valera expected that he himself, upon retirement from party leadership, might occupy the presidency, where he would be in a position to warn and advise his successors, if necessary.

The president is elected directly by popular vote for a seven-year term and is once reeligible. He has a council of state consisting of the taoiseach, the tanaiste, the chief justice, the president of the high court, the chairmen of the two legislative chambers, the attorney general, former presidents, prime ministers, and chief justices, and seven others named by the president. His formal functions include conferring the seals of office upon ministers approved by the Dáil, signing passed bills, and so forth. Unlike the governor general, he may, on his own authority, refuse a dissolution to a prime minister whom he believes to have lost the confidence of the Dáil. After consulting his council of state, but not bound by their advice, he may send a message to the Oireachtas and convene either or both chambers. If the Senate appeals, against a decision of the ceann cómhairle (chairman of the Dáil), that a bill is a money bill, the president may appoint a committee to decide this appeal. If petitioned by a majority of the Senate plus one-third or more of the Dáil deputies, he may refuse to approve a bill (unless it be a money bill or a constitutional amendment) and submit it to a popular referendum or the result of a general election. With the same exception as regards money bills and constitutional amendments, he may also submit bills to the Supreme Court, before approving them, for an advisory opinion on their constitutionality.

The above extraordinary powers are rather like the "reserved" powers of a colonial governor, an "umbrella in the closet" to be used in emergencies only. In fact, there have been no attempts so far, on the part of the presidents of the Republic, to take the leadership of the Government away from the taoiseach. No president has used his message power to try to force his policies upon the Government. The first president was a nonpartisan personage, Dr. Douglas Hyde, a Gaelic scholar and a Protestant but a strongly nationalist Irishman who may have been chosen partly to prove lack of religious prejudice. His tenure of office was uneventful except that on two occasions he deferred approval of a bill until he had secured an advisory opinion from the Supreme Court that the bill did not contravene the Constitution.[23] De Valera was annoyed by this use, unnecessary in his view, of one of the president's special powers, and Dr. Hyde was not renominated for a second term. Instead, De Valera backed the nomination of Sean T. O'Kelly, who had been De Valera's tanaiste. The choice of a strictly party candidate was defended on the ground that this kind of president would know how to get along with the Oireachtas and would not needlessly delay approving legislation. Although O'Kelly's entire political career had been that of a Fianna Fáil partisan, he had satisfactory relations with the Fine Gael coalition that succeeded De Valera and he was elected without opposition to a second term in 1952. In 1959, De Valera, whose age and failing eyesight made it difficult for him to continue as taoiseach, was nominated by his party for the presidency, which he won over the Fine Gael candidate, General Sean MacEoin, in a vote cast, it would seem, along party lines.[24] There were no public evidences of any conflict between him and the taoiseach, Seán Lemass, who had been his tanaiste and who succeeded him as leader of the Fianna Fáil Party.

The changes in the Constitution of the IFS and its successors have been in response to the existence of two major party groups in the Dáil: Fianna Fáil, and Fine Gael plus most of the rest. One or the other has had control of both executive and legislative power from the start. The single transferable vote has not prevented the development of what is essentially a two-party system, although it has militated against the sweeping party victories that occur in countries with single-member constituencies. It was perhaps his fear that in the future, lesser leaders, not having his prestige, might be unable to keep the party firmly united, that induced De Valera to urge the Irish voters to drop proportional representation in favor of single-member districts. Certainly this would have strengthened major parties at the expense of minor parties and Independents. Such a change, indeed, would have been in harmony with other constitutional amendments since 1922, some of which have tended to strengthen party control of executive, Dáil, and Senate, and none of which have weakened such control.

Although De Valera won the presidency, the electorate defeated his proposed amendment and voted to retain the right to number their choices and help to elect one of several candidates, rather than being compelled to pick the single winner or waste a ballot. The fact that Irish governments have been reasonably stable made the argument that proportional representation leads to weak and unstable executives seem academic and unreal in the Irish situation. This seems to be the widely held public opinion, even though the election of a number of independent deputies, facilitated by the Irish electoral system, together with the narrow majorities usually held by Irish governments, have tended to bring about elections before the end of the full, legal term which is now five years. In the 34 years between 1923 and 1957, there have been 13 general elections, giving the governments an average life of about 2½ years. In fact, the duration has varied from 2 months (June 23 to August 25, 1927), to 5 years (June 30, 1938, to May 31, 1943). The government elected in 1943 lasted only 11 months but subsequent administrations have remained in office about 3 years.

Another attempt by Fianna Fáil to get Irish voters to approve the substitution of the single-member-district system for the single transferable vote was made at a referendum held in October, 1968. Again the Irish electorate came out emphatically in favor of the existing system.

De Valera was elected President of the Republic for a second term on June 1, 1966, when he was eighty-three years of age. He will be ninety at the conclusion of this term. The election was again partisan. The aged President did no campaigning but his opponent, Thomas F. O'Higgins, sponsored by Fine Gael, campaigned as if contending for the office of taoiseach. De Valera's margin of victory was only one-twelfth that of 1959. He defeated O'Higgins by a mere 10,648 votes. Traditional loyalty to "Dev" in the rural districts barely overcame the large majorities won by O'Higgins in Dublin and Cork. Despite the fact that government policies are not determined by the president but by the Dáil and its leadership, O'Higgins in his speeches emphasized the need for increased social welfare benefits, improved educational facilities, the advantages of the Common Market, and other features of Liam Cosgrave's "just society" program.

The creation of the Free State and its successors did not disturb the Irish legal system based upon English Common Law. It remained in force and judges continued to be appointed from the ranks of practicing barristers (solicitors being eligible for appointment to the district courts). The appointments, of course, were now made on the advice of the Irish Government. In the British tradition, judicial appointments are for life and a judge may be removed from office only by a resolution passed by both chambers of the Oireachtas.

The lowest (district) courts handle only misdemeanors and small civil cases. The eight circuit courts deal mainly with contract and tort disputes. Above is the High Court with a presiding judge and six others. This court has full jurisdiction in both civil and criminal cases and exclusive original jurisdiction in all cases raising constitutional questions. At the pinnacle of the judicial hierarchy is the Supreme Court with the Chief Justice and four other justices on the bench. It hears appeals from the High Court and also, as noted earlier, may examine a bill passed by both chambers of the Oireachtas before its promulgation, if asked to do so by the president of the Republic, and give an opinion as to the bill's constitutionality.[25] This may be compared with the Canadian provision whereby the Supreme Court of Canada, at the request of the Minister of Justice, delivers advisory opinions on the constitutionality of provincial laws.

This power of judicial review, however, has not conferred upon the Irish Supreme Court that extensive veto power over legislation which the United States Supreme Court has exercised at times. There are two reasons for this. The written constitution of Ireland is that of a unitary, not a federal, state and so the problems of a constitutionally fixed distribution of powers among government units cannot arise. Furthermore, the Irish courts have held that there are no "natural law" or "higher law" limitations upon

the legislative power (the Common Law rule) and that only explicit constitutional provisions can limit it. This contrasts with the
virtual identification by the United States Supreme Court, at one
time, of the due process clauses in the United States Constitution
with natural justice, and consequently the assumption by the court
of the power to disallow any act of Congress or of a state legislature that it found to be "unjust." In fact, the Irish courts have used
the power of judicial review sparingly. One occasion of its use was
the refusal of the courts in 1939 to apply a part of the Offenses
against the State Act because they found it to be repugnant to
Article 40 of the Constitution guaranteeing the right to habeus
corpus procedure. As noted earlier, however, this right vanishes
when ignored by a law defining itself as a public safety measure.
The courts have held that the phrase used in Article 40, "save in
accordance with law," nullifies any constitutional attack upon an
act permitting indefinite detention without trial.[26]

Late in 1967 a committee of the Oireachtas chaired by
George Colley, T.D., Minister for Industry and Commerce and a
former Minister of Education, issued a report on constitutional
revision.[27] This committee was an interparty body of 11 members
—8 deputies and 3 senators. The report was a careful study of the
entire Constitution, article by article, followed by a collection of
annexes comparing Irish constitutional provisions with those of
other countries. The suggestions of the report were far from
startling. Indeed, it suffered some criticism in the press for its lack
of imagination. It began with the assertion that there was no intention of questioning the fundamental features of the Constitution.
Many of the changes suggested were very minor. For example, it
was proposed to remove reference to "Éire" in the English version
and say simply: "The name of the State is Ireland."

A daring suggestion, unlikely to appeal to constitutional
lawyers, was the proposal of some committee members that the
office of President of the Republic be abolished and the presidential functions transferred to the taoiseach. The committee rejected this suggestion but recommended that Subsection 4 of
Article 12.4 be removed. This is the provision whereby a retiring
or former president may renominate himself.

Article 13.1 provides that the president appoint the taoiseach
on the nomination of the Dáil. The committee observed that a
multipartisan Dáil might be unable to agree upon a nominee and
suggested giving the president the power to designate as taoiseach
the man most likely, in his opinion, to secure the confidence of
the Dáil, this appointment to remain in force unless rescinded by
a vote of no confidence. Indeed, this would be in accord with
customary parliamentary practice.

Another committee suggestion was that a specified number of
members of the Oireachtas be given the right to compel the president to convene one or both chambers in special session. Under existing law, the president alone makes this decision (Article 13.2.3).

The committee agreed that the size of constituencies might
well be lowered by reducing the population requirements, which
now vary from 30,000 to 20,000, to between 22,500 and 17,500.
They suggested further that the desirable average size should be
about 20,000, that rural constituencies be of lower population
within the legal limits, and that this population differential be mentioned in the Constitution itself.

The arguments for and against proportional representation
were given in the report but no recommendation was made on this
subject, a matter of current partisan dispute.

No significant change in the composition or election of the
Senate was advocated. In particular, the use of vocational nominating bodies as envisaged by Article 19 was rejected on the
ground that this procedure would bring "politics" into the affairs
of these bodies, to their detriment. In consideration of the possible university merger, the committee suggested that the wording
of Article 18.4 be altered to say that the six university senators
would be allocated by ordinary law.

Article 28.3.3 allows the Senate and Dáil by joint resolution
to suspend certain constitutional provisions in time of national
emergency. In fact the language is so broad as to place no limit
upon the emergency powers of the Government approved by such
a joint resolution. Once passed, the resolution remains in effect
until removed by the action of each chamber. Emergency powers
voted during and after World War II still exist. The committee

recommended, therefore, that emergency powers should lapse after a term of three years unless extended by another joint resolution of the two chambers. A recommendation intended also to give additional protection to civil liberties was made concerning Article 38.3, permitting special courts. The committee suggested that abuse of this provision might be prevented by adding the requirement that such courts could be established only in case of war or armed insurrection, by an Oireachtas declaration of a state of national emergency, or by joint resolution of the two chambers creating such courts for a limited period.

A peculiar feature of the 1937 Constitution is the list of family and religious rights it includes in Articles 41, 42, and 44. Possibly because of their own religious background, Irish judges have been scrupulous in enforcing these to the letter. They have gone so far as to invalidate an English judgment granting costs in a divorce case simply because the costs were part of an action for divorce. Article 42, giving parents the right to control the education of their children, was held by the courts to invalidate a power conferred by statute upon the Minister for Education to control the choice of school by children between the ages of six and fourteen.[28] In some Irish cases the judges would seem to insist upon parental authority in disregard of any consideration of the welfare of the child.

These rules reflect Roman Catholic doctrine.[29] Together with the mention in Article 44 of the "special position of the Holy Catholic and Apostolic and Roman Church as the guardian of the Faith professed by the great majority of its citizens . . . ," they are not calculated to allay the fear of "Rome Rule" among Ulster Protestants, even though the Constitution also guarantees freedom of conscience and religion.

The Colley Committee did not suggest any change in the parental authority provision but proposed some relaxation of the absolute prohibition of divorce. It was argued that to permit persons married according to the rites of any religion to have their marriage dissolved only on grounds allowed by that religion, would be acceptable to persons of all faiths; at the same time, it would not open the way to easy divorce by renouncing the former religion. It would also permit Roman Catholics to secure annulments from the Church authorities, a step illegal under the existing Constitution. The committee also suggested that the legal complications created by Article 41.3.3 concerning foreign divorces, which are all invalid in Ireland, be eliminated by repealing the paragraph altogether and allowing legal problems in which divorce and marital status play a part to be settled under the accepted rules of international law.

As regards the recognition of religions in Article 44.1, the suggestion was made that the legally meaningless mention of the "special position" of the Roman Catholic Church be deleted as offensive to some non-Catholics and as giving a semblance of basis to the Orange opposition to the reunification of Ireland. Another suggestion was that the list of "recognized" religions also be deleted because it seemed to discriminate against sects not listed.

Notes

1. John Maurice Kelly, *Fundamental Rights in the Irish Law and Constitution* (Dublin, 1961), p. 4.
2. See Agnes Headlam-Morley, *The New Democratic Constitutions of Europe* (London, 1929), pp. 29 ff.
3. Kelly, *loc. cit.*
4. *Constitution of the IFS*, Articles 6–10, 47, 48, 50.
5. This distrust seems to have stemmed from some knowledge of the American spoils system and from difficulties some of the drafters of the Constitution had had with the leaders of the old Nationalist Party and the United Irish League. See Andrew E. Malone, "Party Government in the Irish Free State," *Political Science Quarterly*, XLIV (1929), 363–78.
   In urging the adoption of the single-member district in place of PR, however, Fianna Fáil speakers claimed that PR had been foisted upon the IFS by the British to try to ensure the election of Ascendancy representatives.
6. See speeches by Dr. Eoin MacNeill and President Cosgrave, *Freeman's Journal*, April 28, 1923.
7. The departments concerned were agriculture, post office, fisheries, and local government.
8. The new Constitution was approved by plebiscite held simultaneously with the general election of July, 1937. It was approved by a narrow majority, 685,105 to 526,945 (*Official Gazette*, July 16, 1937). This would have amounted to a rejection had the provisions of the former

Constitution applied. Article 50 required an absolute majority of the electorate or a two-thirds' majority of those voting.

The text of the 1937 Constitution in both Irish and English is contained in a publication of the Stationery Office, *Bunreacht na hÉireann* (*Constitution of Ireland*), obtainable from the Government Publications Sale Office, G.P.O. Arcade, Dublin 1. The English text is available also in *International Conciliation*, Pamphlet No. 343 (October, 1938) 352–95. This pamphlet also has the transitory provisions (Articles 51–63) not printed in the current official text.

9. McCracken, *op. cit.*, p. 167.

10. *Ibid.* Pages 167 and 168 cite the Emergency Imposition of Duties Act, 1942, which allows the Government to impose new duties by executive order, and the Supply and Services (Temporary Provisions) Act, by which it may suspend customs duties.

   In 1935, for example, while 47 acts were passed, no fewer than 684 statutory rules and orders were issued. See Donal O'Sullivan, *The Irish Free State and its Senate* (London, 1940), p. 526, for a table showing the steady increase in the number of such orders.

11. The Ceann Cómhairle (speaker) refused to permit a question addressed to the Minister of Industry and Commerce about the work of An Foras Tionscail (the body concerned with stimulating industry in underdeveloped areas) on the ground that the Minister had no official responsibility for the work of this authority. See *National Observer* I (January, 1959), p. 7.

12. As noted by Warner Moss, *Political Parties in the Irish Free State* (New York, 1933), 49 n.

13. *Supra*, p. 54.

14. It was defeated 34 to 18. The majority included 25 UIP (Cosgrave Party) senators, 5 members of the Independent Group, and 4 Independents; the minority consisted of 12 Fianna Fail, 4 Labour, and 2 Independents.

15. O'Sullivan, *op. cit.*, 369–79, gives an extensive summary of De Valera's arguments.

16. The evidence for this statement is found in these words by De Valera: "I wanted to get rid of a Second House, and particularly I wanted to get rid of the previous Second House whilst a certain piece of constitutional work was being done . . ." (Dáil Debates, lxix, 1608).

   De Valera's lack of enthusiasm for second chambers in general was expressed in these words:

   > My attitude is that, even though some of us be largely indifferent to the question of whether or not there is a Seanád, if a large section of the people of the country think, that there is something important in having a Seanád, then, even if we ourselves are indifferent to it, we should give way to the people who are anxious for it (Dáil Debates, May 11, 1937, p. 56).

17. O'Sullivan, *op. cit.*, p. 571.

18. See Basil Chubb, "Ireland 1957," D. E. Butler (ed.), Chapter 3, *Elections Abroad* (London, 1959), pp. 184–ff.
19. *Election Results and Transfer of Votes in General Election (October, 1961) for Seventeenth Dáil and Bye-Elections to Sixteenth Dáil (1957–1961)* (Dublin: Stationery Office, 1962).
20. Article 51 of the bill reads in part:

> Provided that it shall be lawful for the Executive Council . . . for the purposes of the appointment of diplomatic and consular agents and the conclusion of international agreements of any organ used as a constitutional organ for the like purpose by any of the nations referred to in Article I of this constitution.

21. McCracken, *op. cit.*, p. 159.
22. Shaw offered this explanation:

> To me it seemed that Mr. Costello and his Coalition were anxious to show that they were even more Irish, more Nationalist, more anti-Partition than Mr. de Valera, and could thing of nothing else that would do the trick then knocking off the Crown (G. B. Shaw, *The Matter with Ireland*, Dan H. Lawrence and David H. Greene [eds.] [New York, 1962],

According to T. P. Coogan, Mr. Costello's action may have been motivated by a desire to "take the gun out of Irish politics by giving the republicans their Republic." (*Ireland Since the Rising* [New York, 1966], p. 97).

23. This referral power has been used three times: in 1940 for the Offenses Against the State (Amendment) Bill, in 1942 for the School Attendance Bill (some provisions of which were found to be unconstitutional), and in 1961 for the Electoral (Amendment) Bill.
24. De Valera won by 120,476 votes. He had a majority in all constituencies except Dublin city, where MacEoin's majority was 2,000, and in Cork West, Longford, and Westmeath, MacEoin's home territory.
25. See n. 23.
26. Kelly, *op. cit.*, p. 20.
27. *Report of the Committee on the Constitution, December, 1967* (Dublin: Stationery Office).
28. *In re Article 26 and the School Attendance Bill, 1942,* 1943 I.R. 334. See Kelly, *op. cit.*, pp. 33–35.
29. Richard O'Sullivan, K.C., "The Background of the New Irish Constitution," *Politica*, III, No. 2 (March, 1938), 49, n. 2. This commentator writes that the article concerning education is "an incomplete and to that extent imperfect, statement of the teaching of Pope Pius XI in his Encyclical Letter on the Christian Education of Youth (*Divini illius magistri*)." It is possible also that the idea of vocational representation in the Senate may have been inspired by *Quadragesimo Anno* (1931) as well as by the corporative arrangements of Fascist Italy and Salazar's Portugal. See Basil Chubb, "Vocational Representation in the Irish Senate," *Political Studies*, II (1954) 97–111.

V

DÁIL ÉIREANN

The two chambers of the Oireachtas, the Irish Parliament, hold their sessions in the former town house of the Dukes of Leinster, the premier dukes of Ireland and chiefs of the Fitzgerald clan. The Sinn Féin Dáil of 1919 had met in the Mansion House but this is the seat of Dublin's city government and other quarters had to be found. The old preunion parliament building on College Green, across from Trinity College, had been taken over by the Bank of Ireland. This magnificent Georgian edifice was considered, along with Dublin Castle, as a possible accommodation. However, the Royal Dublin Society, the sponsor of the famous annual horse show, offered Leinster House, which the society then occupied, to provide temporary accommodation. The offer, made in September, 1922, was accepted; subsequently Leinster House was purchased from the Royal Dublin Society, which moved to new buildings in the outskirts of Dublin. A number of structural alterations were made in Leinster House to transform it into a suitable parliament building.

The original republican Dáil had no time or inclination to think of decorations or grandeur and the tradition of republican simplicity has been retained. As noted previously, the Governor General soon ceased to visit the Oireachtas and open sessions with a speech from the throne. There is no mace and no sergeant-at-arms, nor any display of the national arms or symbols, not even a flag.

A new Dáil, assembling after a general election, listens to the clerk as he reads the proclamation of summons and reports on the election returns. The newly elected deputies then sign the roll and take their places. They take no oath of office as none was substituted for the abolished parliamentary oath.

The first business of a new Dáil is the election of the chairman (ceann cómhairle) whose duties correspond, in general, to those of a parliamentary speaker. Under Standing Order 14 no minister or parliamentary secretary may be chairman, indicating the intention to have the chairman conduct business in a non-partisan manner. To begin with, the government party nominated one of its members to be chairman but, in contrast with British practice, the chairman was not reelected automatically when his party lost control of the Dáil. An exception to this occurred in the case of Frank Fahy of Fianna Fáil, who continued as chairman during Fine Gael administrations from 1948 until he retired in 1951. An element of British tradition may have influenced the statements of deputies who objected to Mr. Fahy's original election to the chairmanship in 1932 by a straight party vote over his distinguished predecessor Professor Michael Hayes, who had been ceann cómhairle since 1922. It is possible that Mr. Fahy's reelection was due not only to his merits as an impartial chairman but also to the narrow government majority which the taoiseach did not wish to reduce by the election of one of his own supporters. The Fine Gael Party, following Mr. Fahy's retirement, chose a Labour Party deputy, Patrick Hogan, who was supported also by Clann na Talmhan and Fianna Fáil. Mr. Hogan remained in office under Fianna Fáil administrations until 1968, when he resigned and was succeeded in the chair by a Fianna Fáil T.D., Breslin of Donegal. Retiring speakers at Westminster customarily accept a peerage and do not engage in party politics. In Ireland, retiring speakers have continued as deputies in the Dáil. Just as the Speaker of the House of Commons enjoys reelection without opposition, so in Ireland, since 1927, the ceann cómhairle is automatically reelected from his old constituency without thereby reducing the number of deputies elected by that constituency.

Patrick Hogan represented County Clare and in the 1961 general election was deemed to be elected under Section 3 of the Electoral (Chairman of Dáil Éireann) Act, 1937. Clare is a three-member constituency and three deputies were elected from it in addition to Mr. Hogan.

Like the British Speaker, the chairman takes no part in debate and has a vote only to break a tie. In this case he behaves like his British counterpart, not to bring victory to his own party if it has taken a stand on the issue, but to provide an opportunity for further consideration by the Dáil or to avoid decisive action. On the rare occasions when a chairman's vote has been required, these principles have been followed. In 1923 the Chairman voted against a bill requiring outlay of funds on the ground that only a majority of the Dáil, exclusive of the chair, should exercise the spending power. In August, 1927, the Chairman voted against a motion of no confidence, again on the ground that only a clear majority of the Dáil should have the power to upset a government. In 1934 the vice-chairman, presiding, voted for an amendment to keep the matter before the chamber.[1]

Originally the chairman of the Dáil wore no robe of office, but since 1946 he has presided in a simple black robe of academic type with green facings, worn over an ordinary business suit. He wears no wig and his robe is virtually the only concession to parliamentary pomp. It is Mr. De Valera's contention that the absence of ceremony and display in the Dáil was not due to a deliberate avoidance of British practice but rather to lack of concern about such matters and the press of important business.[2]

Sessions commence after the ceann cómhairle has taken his place on the dais, risen, and read a prayer, first in Irish and then in English. This has been done since 1932 as required by Standing Order 23. The deputies rise for the prayer, bless themselves before and after the prayer, and resume their seats.

In harmony with the original antiparty bias and the expectation that no single party could expect to dominate the Dáil, the seating does not follow the antiphonal pattern of Westminster.

The floor is level and benches are arranged on three sides of the chamber facing the center. Also in contrast with British custom, the taoiseach sits on the left-hand side of the ceann cómhairle, on the front bench, while the principal opposition spokesmen usually sit opposite, on the bench at the right hand of the chairman.

Except in the rare event of their exclusion by a two-thirds' vote of the Dáil, visitors are admitted to a gallery overlooking the chamber. They must observe proceedings through a heavy wire screen, possibly installed to prevent anything being hurled at the deputies by the wilder spirits of the IRA.

Besides his duty as impartial chairman, applying the standing orders, maintaining order, recognizing speakers, and the like, the chairman directs the preparation of the order paper which is printed for every sitting. The taoiseach determines the order of government business as it appears on this paper. The chairman also certifies money bills. He has the right to refuse to put a closure motion to the house if he considers the matter under discussion to require further debate. He presides over the committee of the whole house, contrary to British and American practice. He is always chairman of the committee on procedure and privileges.

A vice-chairman, called leas-cheann cómhairle, is elected for each dáil to preside in the absence of the chairman, but otherwise to act as an ordinary deputy although, in line with the recommendations of the committee on procedure and privileges, he refrains from vigorous participation in controversial debate and does not initiate such debates.[3] It is customary for the Dáil to elect as vice-chairman a deputy from the ranks of the opposition parties.

The ceann cómhairle also nominates, together with the finance minister, the clerk of the Dáil and the assistant clerk, whose appointments are confirmed by the taoiseach. The clerks keep the official minutes and advise the ceann cómhairle on procedural rules. As noted previously, the Dáil has no sergeant-at-arms but the Oireachtas has a captain of the guard who is in charge of the guards (police); they maintain order within the building and grounds and screen visitors. This officer, together with the superintendent of the building and grounds and the librarian of the Oireachtas, are appointed by the taoiseach on the recommendation of the minister of finance and the chairmen of Dáil and Senate.

Unless urgent business demands additional time, sittings of the Dáil are held on Tuesday, Wednesday, and Thursday afternoons and evenings from 3 P.M. until no later than 11 P.M., and on Fridays from 10:30 A.M. until no later than 2:30 P.M. The rules require a quorum of at least twenty deputies and, if a count is demanded and absence of a quorum established, bells are rung and three minutes allowed for members to assemble. If a quorum is still not present, the sitting must be suspended until a later hour or until the next regular day of meeting.

Business normally begins with questions addressed to the ministers, followed by private business, public business, and private members' business. The ministers read replies to questions previously submitted concerning their departments or subordinates. Very often the minister's answer will be followed by a further oral exchange between the questioner and the minister, although there is no formal debate. The questioner, however, may raise the matter again when speaking to the motion for adjournment.[4]

Private business refers to the field of legislation covered by private bills at Westminster: bills advocated by bodies outside of the Oireachtas in the interest of private individuals or specific local authorities. Such bills, under standing orders, originate in the Senate where they pass the first two readings and then are sent to a joint committee of Dáil and Senate, if the Dáil agrees. The joint committee considers evidence, listens to counsel for advocates and opponents of the measure, and discusses amendments. The Senate then has two more readings; when passed, the bill goes to the Dáil for a final reading there. If passed in the Dáil it becomes law.

Theoretically, private members are assigned one and a half hours on Wednesdays and two hours on Fridays, during which they may make motions or introduce bills, but Standing Order 80 permits the Government to take over these periods for financial business and this is done much of the time. In the fifteen-year period 1923 to 1937, only twelve private member's bills were passed into law.[5]

Public business consists of legislation and motions introduced by the Government. A minister moves for permission to introduce a bill. There is no debate on this motion but objections may be raised by a member. When the motion is passed a date is set for the next consideration when debate is joined on general principles. If accepted, the bill is debated in committee of the whole House. Virtually all public bills are so handled. As is usual, the rules of debate in committee of the whole permit deputies to speak more than once. Occasionally a bill is sent to a special committee after the committee of the whole has debated it but usually it is simply reported back to the Dáil after enough time has passed to permit the minister in charge of it to refine the measure in line with the decisions of the committee of the whole. When he reports to the Dáil, the amendments he has made are discussed. This is the fourth stage. In the fifth stage, only amendments concerned with wording are in order. After passage at the fifth stage, the bill is sent to the Senate, where the procedure is similar except that no leave to introduce is required. If the Senate amends the bill further, these amendments are considered by the Dáil in committee of the whole where they may be accepted or rejected. When passed by both houses in identical form the bill goes to the president for his signature. If the Dáil rejects the Senate's amendments, the bill becomes law without the Senate's consent. The suspensory veto of the Senate is effective for 90 days, but the bill does not become operative following its acceptance by resolution of the Dáil until after 180 days, when the president's signature completes its enactment. Money bills must originate in the Dáil and cannot be delayed by the senate for more than 21 days.[6]

Closure is not often used. Ordinary closure can be effected by a motion "that the question be now put." The chairman has the option of accepting or rejecting this motion. If accepted, it is voted upon without debate and may be carried by simple majority. The guillotine closure is also used at times, under which a specified amount of time is allowed for debate on each stage of a bill.

Select and special committees are chosen by a committee of selection which is elected by the Dáil at the start of a session. This committee is broadly representative of all parties and groups in the chamber including the Independents. The only permanent committee is the Public Accounts Committee which has a larger task than its name implies. It has general oversight of legislation. It is seriously handicapped in this work by its lack of research facilities and even adequate secretarial assistance. Coogan cites three bills which were amended regarding certain questionable or ambiguous provisions only after these were commented upon by "alert newspapers." [7]

The deputies are casual and informal in their behavior. Question time provides opportunities for lively exchanges between ministers and opposition spokesmen. The minister's prepared answer to a previously submitted question may be followed by a sharp response from the questioner. The chairman is tolerant of the backchat and informal interjections and comments with which some opposition deputies punctuate the speeches of government supporters. The rules permit the censure or suspension of deputies by resolution of the Dáil. Under Article 15, paragraphs 12, 13, of the Constitution, they enjoy the usual parliamentary immunities.

Attendance at sessions is not compulsory and the Dáil debates contain a number of complaints of absenteeism. On an ordinary day there may be hardly more than a quorum present. It would seem that many private members speak rarely or never. The actual motions and debates are left to the ministers and a few leading members of the Government and Opposition. [8]

The relative inactivity in the Dáil of the back-bench deputies may be due in part to their acceptance of the fact that, as individuals, whether pledged to the support the Government or not, ordinarily they cannot hope to affect policy decisions made in the cabinet or the fate of legislation based upon these decisions. It may also be due in part to their recognition of the fact that activity in the chamber is a minor consideration with their electorate and will have little or no effect upon the probability of their reelection.

It was the intention of the framers of the original Free State Constitution that the Dáil should be the real seat of power, the body that would freely debate and determine policies and the master rather than the servant of the ministers. Deputies, it was believed, would belong to a number of parties and in many cases would be Independents, accepting no party discipline.[9]

All commentators on Irish politics have observed that this ideal was never realized. The emergence of a party system contemporaneous with the establishment of the Free State and the domination of the major parties by leaders able, as a rule, to secure reliable support from their partisans among the deputies meant that, from the beginning, actual policy determination rested with the taoiseach and his ministers and Dáil debates were merely a prelude to the enactment of government bills. Even as regards the choice of the taoiseach, legally a matter for the decision of the Dáil, the identity of the taoiseach, as in the case of prime ministers in other parliamentary, two-party systems, was predetermined in most cases by the election results. Even though the Irish multi-member constituencies enabled the election of more minor party deputies and Independents than does the single-member-district system of Great Britain and the United States, and as a consequence major party victories tended to be less overwhelming, the leader of the majority party winning a substantial plurality became, in effect, the only possible candidate for the office of taoiseach.

This situation, in which the elections determined the choice of taoiseach, and in which there were actually only two serious contenders for this position, became well established during the long contest between De Valera and Cosgrave. In 1944, however, the parliamentary picture became more complicated with Cosgrave's resignation for reasons of health. Cosgrave's successor as leader of the old pro-treaty forces was General Mulcahy, whose vigorous military action in suppressing the anti-treaty Sinn Féin IRA during the civil war had made him many enemies. Accordingly, when the results of the 1948 elections made it possible for a coalition of the deputies outside of Fianna Fáil to command a majority, it was possible also for these deputies to decide upon their own choice for taoiseach, a choice not predetermined by the election. General Mulcahy, official leader of Fine Gael, the largest party in the coalition, was passed over in favor of his colleague John A. Costello, who had not been involved in the civil war fighting. It is evident that the absence of a party with a clear majority after any general election can throw the choice of prime minister to the Dáil or, more precisely, to the deputies of the parties and independents forming the coalition.

A prime minister chosen in this manner is necessarily much more confined in his choice of ministers than the leader of a single, united party. He is also confined in relation to policies because he must try to avoid alienating any one of his supporting parties or groups. Certainly this was Mr. Costello's situation in 1948. The various parties negotiated for ministerial posts before the alliance was agreed upon. When a controversy arose over the maternity and child welfare bill introduced by the Minister of Health, Dr. Browne, his resignation was demanded, not by the taoiseach, but by the Minister of External Affairs, Seann MacBride, in his capacity as leader of Clann na Poblachta, Dr. Browne's party.[10] Judging by his statements in the Dáil, Mr. Costello evidently accepted this procedure as constitutionally correct.[11] Altogether the interparty coalition of 1948 to 1951 was loose, uncoordinated, and undisciplined. Differences in policy objectives among the ministers were aired in public. There seems to have been a lack of communication and consultation at cabinet level. There was occasional use of the "free vote" when it was obvious that the various parties in the coalition were divided on the issue.

The weakness of the taoiseach in relation to his cabinet colleagues may have been due in part to Mr. Costello's methods and personality.[12] However, it was also in accord with the ideal, held by the framers of the IFS Constitution, of an independent Dáil and a subservient executive branch. In 1937 Mr. Cosgrave, speaking in the Dáil, said that when he was in power "in practice . . . it was not open for the Prime Minister to ask for and compel the resignation of a Minister. . . . Ministers, in my view, ought to possess security and a measure of independence." [13]

This was not Mr. de Valera's view. As the leader of a united party which usually, when in power, had a clear majority in the Dáil and which had to depend on Labour Party votes only on three occasions (the 7th, 9th, and 11th dáils), De Valera was inclined strongly toward the British type of parliamentary executive: a strong prime minister, a cabinet accepting collective responsibility, and a disciplined party support in the Dáil. In general, he was able to secure the acceptance of his concept of the position of taoiseach, which title, as Professor Chubb notes, with its significance of "chief," conveys more of the idea of superiority and leadership than the IFS designation of president of the council.[14] The 1937 Constitution explicitly gives him powers far greater than those of the former president of the council. He has the right to dismiss ministers, and it is implied that the President of the Republic usually will accept his advice as to dissolution, even if he has lost majority support in the Dáil, although the president is not legally required to do so.[15] It is fair to say that the Irish cabinet system as developed under successive Fianna Fáil governments closely resembles the British system, even though the institutional elaboration of cabinet committees and secretariat has not been duplicated in Ireland.

A factor in the strong leadership of the executive branch is the use of the committee of the whole Dáil to consider most legislation. Here the control of debate and voting by the taoiseach and his colleagues is unquestionable, whereas in special committees, as the standing committees are called, the domination by the ministry is not always so complete. Special committees are appointed annually and sometimes used instead of the committee of the whole to discuss and amend legislation at the third reading. An unusual procedure, permitted under the rules, is to have specified sections of a bill handled by a special committee and other sections in committee of the whole. However, there is little in the committee system to provide the rank-and-file T.D.'s an opportunity to challenge the leadership of the taoiseach and his ministers. The absence of permanent committee membership and chairmen in the American style means that the Government has little to fear from independent committee action.

Party discipline is strict. Party caucuses are held and the whips keep track of the voting patterns of their deputies. In a number of cases deputies have been expelled from a party for departing from the party's position on legislation. An exception to this was the permission given by Mr. Costello to a Fine Gael deputy of Presbyterian, Unionist background to speak and vote against the repeal of the Executive Authority (External Relations) Act and the Republic of Ireland Bill in 1948. This deputy, H. P. Dockrell, was not disciplined and continued to represent Dún Laoghaire and Rathdown as a Fine Gael deputy in subsequent elections.

The trend toward executive control of legislation can be observed in Ireland, as in other parliamentary systems, in the constant increase in the number of executive orders, authorized by statute. A façade of legislative control is provided by the requirement that in most cases these orders must be laid on the table and can be revoked by resolution of one or both chambers. In fact, the greater number of them go into effect without scrutiny by the deputies. Many of these orders have little political significance and most deputies have neither the expert knowledge nor the specific information needed to examine them intelligently. The Dáil is most vigorous in acting as a "watch-dog of the public purse." Debates on the estimates are often lively and sometimes influence appropriations. A committee of public accounts, with members chosen from all parties and groups and with the Leader of the Opposition as chairman, has the task of examining the reports and accounts of the comptroller and auditor-general. This committee can act to prevent misappropriation of funds but cannot affect policy decisions. Debates on money bills can produce minor changes and provide ammunition for the Opposition in subsequent appeals to the electorate.

The control of the Dáil by the executive branch is complicated by the electoral system, described later, which prevents the disproportionate overrepresentation of the winning party produced by single-member-district, plurality victory systems. Under Ireland's PR system, minor parties and Independents are certain to hold some seats and if the larger of the major parties lacks an overall majority the balance of power may be held by splinter groups or Independents. In 1948 there were twelve independent deputies and Mr. Costello found it necessary to include one of them in his ministry. In 1951 Costello was forced to resign by threatened withdrawal of the Independents' support.

It is possible, as noted by Professor Chubb, that a coalition of all other parties and Independents might again at some time force Fianna Fáil into opposition and that a series of weak coalitions might become the rule rather than the exception. The incoherence, instability, and relative inability of such governments to tackle urgent controversial issues, as was the case in the French III and IV republics, might eventually bring about popular demand for constitutional change.

This has not been the case so far. The leadership of Fianna Fáil was transferred from its founder, Eamon de Valera, to Seán Lemass and then to John M. Lynch without affecting party discipline.

British governments, with the growth of executive domination, have shown a tendency to enlarge the numbers of ministers and refine the specialization of their responsibilities. While Irish ministries remain small in comparison, they too have displayed a tendency to increase. In 1966 Mr. Lemass had thirteen ministers in addition to himself and six parliamentary secretaries who serve as assistant ministers. This represented an increase in the number of parliamentary secretaries over the previous year. The parliamentary secretary to the taoiseach functions as chief whip and as liaison officer between the taoiseach and the other ministers.

Altogether, the Irish Government, at least in the case of Fianna Fáil ministries, appears to be executive-dominated as completely as that of the United Kingdom and possibly more so. There is no Irish equivalent of the Conservative back-benchers' "1922 Committee" nor are Irish prime ministers under as many party directives and policy limitations as are British prime ministers of the Labour Party.

Notes

1. See McCracken, *op. cit.*, pp. 121, 122.
2. Conversation with the author, September 10, 1959, in the presidential mansion, Phoenix Park, Dublin.
3. *Second Report of the Committee on Procedure and Privileges. Office of Leas-Cheann Cómhairle*, April 20, 1928.
4. McCracken, *op. cit.*, table, p. 124, lists the total number of questions asked from 1923 to 1948. In 1948 the number was 2,653.

5. McCracken, *op. cit.*, p. 167.
6. *Constitution of Ireland*, Articles 20, 21, 22, 23, 24, 27.
7. Coogan, *op. cit.*, p. 141.
8. McCracken, *op. cit.*, table, p. 135, gives an analysis of entries in the general index of Dáil debates which bears out this statement.
9. This suggests that the Irish ideal was similar to that of English politicians between the first and second Reform Acts when party ties were loose and members of Parliament asserted their independence even when behaving in a partisan manner. See Richard Pares, *King George III and the Politicians* (Oxford, 1933), p. 192, and Norman Gash, *Politics in the Age of Peel: A Study in the Technique of Parliamentary Representation* (London, 1953), p. 109.
10. *Infra*, p. 221.
11. Dáil Debates, 12.4.1951, cols. 777–78.
12. Oddly enough, the one policy of prime constitutional significance introduced by Mr. Costello was his institution of a republican form of government together with resignation from the British Commonwealth of Nations, which was announced, apparently, without previous cabinet consultation and which reversed former Fine Gael policy (see *supra*, p. 118. It is almost unthinkable that a British prime minister would dare to commit himself to such an important change without securing the approval of his colleagues.
13. Dáil Debates, 14.6.1937, col. 348, quoted in Basil Chubb, "Cabinet Government in Ireland," *Political Studies*, III (October 3, 1955), 265.
14. *Ibid.*, p. 268.
15. Constitution of Ireland, Article 13, 2, 2.

VI

THE SENATE

The early history of Seanád Éireann and the amendments in its composition and powers have been discussed in Chapter IV. As noted there, the Senate is now composed of 60 senators: 11 named by the taoiseach, 6 by the 2 universities (3 by Trinity College, Dublin, and 3 by the National University) and 43 elected from 5 panels of nominees representing: (1) national language and culture, (2) agriculture, fisheries, and allied industries, (3) labor, organized or unorganized, (4) industry and commerce, including banking, finance, accounting, engineering, and architecture, (5) public administration and social services, including voluntary social services. Not less than 5 nor more than 11 may be elected from each panel.[1] The Constitution also provides that associations or vocational groups may by law elect senators directly in substitution for an equal number on the appropriate panel.[2] This latter provision has not been implemented by any enabling law. Fine Gael accepted as official party policy the recommendations of a commission which advocated that a trial be made of direct election of some senators by vocational bodies, but Fianna Fáil governments have ignored these recommendations.

The original Senate had fairly good relations with the Cosgrave administration. There were five Labour senators but they did not always vote as a bloc, nor did the fifteen senators who called themselves the Progressive Party and who were combined informally in general support of the Cosgrave Government. They were not under strict party discipline. The same was true of the Independent Group, consisting mainly of ex-Unionists who used to hold caucus meetings before sessions but took no pledge of unanimity. There was little disposition to obstruct for the sake of obstruction and, while the Senate used its suspensory veto on three Cosgrave bills, none was a vital measure. Some revisionary work was done in the Senate and most of the Senate's amendments were accepted by the Dáil. The chief complaint of the senators, then as now, was that virtually no use was made of their services for the unhurried consideration and refinement of noncontentious legislation. The Senate would be left for long periods with practically no business while the Dáil was overworked. Finally, usually near a recess period, the Government would send up a sheaf of bills with a request for immediate action.

The Senate's own bills were few in number. During the life of the original Senate, before 1928, 14 bills originating in the Senate were sent to the Dáil. Seven of these were accepted, 3 rejected, and 4 did not receive consideration.

Despite the facts outlined in the preceding paragraphs, it is fair to say that even during the Cosgrave administration, the Dáil's attitude toward the Senate was "one of detachment, dislike, and distrust. . . ." [3] It was this attitude, probably based on class antagonism more than anything else, which limited the usefulness of the first Senate. Nevertheless, its membership was generally of high caliber and its record contradicts the statement, "the first Irish upper house proved so inept as to be abolished." [4] When the Senate itself proposed that a joint committee of the two chambers be appointed to consider the Constitution, powers, and election of the Senate, the resolution was opposed by De Valera, not yet in power. Seán Lemass forthrightly expressed the Fianna Fáil view of the second chamber when he said:

> It is a body created, as we all know, not to improve the machinery of administration in this country, but to give political

power to a certain class that could not get that power if they had to go before the people at a free election. . . . The Senate was set up to put a certain section of the community into a position where they could influence the course of legislation—a section of the community that was always hostile to the interests of Irish nationalism, and that was always hostile to the Irish nation. And we think that this bulwark of imperialism should be abolished. . . .[5]

The Cosgrave majority in the Dáil accepted the Senate's proposal and the result was a reconstituted Senate elected by the two chambers as a united electorate from among candidates nominated by the two chambers separately, each picking a list by single transferable vote. In November, 1928, there were 19 vacancies to be filled, but some names appeared on both Dáil and Senate lists, so there were only 27 candidates. Fianna Fáil won 6 places, 3 of these going to ex-deputies. The Cosgrave party won 4 seats, 3 of these going to ex-deputies and the other to a senator whose term had expired. Party lines became much more sharply drawn and the senators of both major parties organized themselves under chairmen. Some of the new senators were distinguished more for their party loyalty than for outstanding ability.

As time went on the Senate became more and more a partisan body reflecting the party composition of the Dáil. As the electorate consists entirely of party politicians—except for a few Independents—and as half the nominees are also selected by the Oireachtas, this result was inevitable. Nonparty nominating bodies representing cultural or professional associations can hope to have their nominees elected only if they are chosen from among men of definite party affiliation.[6] In 1954 the Irish Agricultural Organization was able to secure the election of two nominees, one from each major party. Distinguished nonparty nominees get few first-choice ballots and are almost never elected. After this voting pattern became evident, eminent men who were not politicians tended to refuse nomination. Except for the six university senators and an occasional choice by the taoiseach, the typical senator is a party politician and often one who has failed of election or reelection to the Dáil.

Professor McCracken checked the number of former deputies elected to the Senate beteen 1938 and 1951. He discovered that the percentage varied between 29 and 39.[7] He noted also that the actual number of party politicians is greater than these figures indicate because they do not include the senators appointed by the taoiseach nor the party candidates who had failed to secure election to the Dáil. Some of the nominees of professional associations behave in the Senate like partisans, voting or abstaining in the party pattern. It was noted in *Fine Gael Digest* that Mr. Lemass had nominated the Fianna Fáil party secretary to the Senate where he became leader of the House. The official in charge of Fianna Fáil head-quarters publicity was also placed in the Senate by election, as was a party organizer from Munster.[8] The Fine Gael jibe regarding these senatorships was that Fianna Fáil was using them as remuneration for party workers. But Fine Gael practice is not conspicuously different. In 1948, when J. A. Costello was taoiseach, six of his eleven nominated members of the Senate were party candidates who had been defeated for election to one chamber or the other of the Oireachtas.

The Senate thus reflects the partisan composition of the Dáil and, although it contains some able and distinguished men, is far from being representative of Ireland's most outstanding talents in the fields named in the panels. It could hardly be otherwise when half the nominating and all the electing to membership in the second chamber of their legislative body is done by party politicians. Certainly, conflict between the chambers is highly improbable under this system. The taoiseach's party can be sure of electing a majority of the elected members and the taoiseach himself names eleven. Even in the unlikely contingency that all six of the university senators were constantly to oppose government bills, a government majority is still assured.

Secure in the Government's pocket, the Senate is more or less ignored. Senators still complain that the Senate could make a much greater contribution to the legislative process if it were allowed to give first consideration to noncontroversial bills in addition to the relatively few private bills. The Senate would have more time for this than the busier Dáil has. However, this is not done and the Senate is still left almost idle for long periods and then given a number of bills with a request for fast action. Senatorial amendments, however, are often accepted. Between 1938 and 1949, the Senate amended 77 bills and 70 were approved by the Dáil as amended. The other 7 were also passed with additional changes by the Dáil. In the same period, the Senate made recommendations for three money bills. One of these was accepted by the Dáil, one was further amended, and only one was simply rejected.[9] Between 1960 and 1966 the Senate suggested thirty-eight amendments and all but two were accepted by the Dáil.

The Senate no longer represents the Irish aristocracy or the former Unionists. Although it reflects the partisan composition of the Dáil and can offer no real opposition to the government of the day, its atmosphere is quieter and more dignified. Expressions of partisan sentiment are less pronounced. There are few interruptions and interjections during debates. The university senators contribute an element of academic detachment to the discussions. The Senate does amend legislation and its amendments are often accepted by the Dáil. It may be said therefore to perform, at least to some degree, the function of reviewing and revising which is the chief reason for the existence of a second chamber.[10] One senator expressed to the writer the belief that the Senate's opposition to De Valera's proposal in 1959 to replace the multimember constituencies by single-member districts was an important factor in the defeat of this proposal by plebiscite, even though it had the powerful support of De Valera and the dominant Fianna Fáil Party. However, few voters pay much attention to senate debates or proceedings and other factors were probably more influential.[11] Of minor importance in the Irish political system, the Senate has its uses and advantages to the major parties and would seem to have become a permanent feature of the Irish legislative institution.

A subsidiary senatorial function is to provide the taoiseach with the means of giving public recognition to men of distinction who are not politicians. This is done occasionally. Examples in the first Senate would be such literary figures as W. B. Yeats and Oliver Gogarty.[12]

Notes

1. Constitution of Ireland, Article 18.
2. *Ibid.*, Article 19.
3. O'Sullivan, *op. cit.*, p. 250.
4. A. W. and M. C. Bromage, "The Vocational Senate in Ireland," *American Political Science Review*, XXXIV, No. 3 (June, 1940), p. 519. It may be that the Bromages, in so writing, were thinking mainly of the later stages of the partisan Senate after 1928.
5. Dáil Debates, XXII, 140.
6. In the 1965 general election, 27 nominees of the Oireachtas were elected while only 16 of the outside nominees were successful.
7. McCracken, *op. cit.*, p. 151. In 1957 it was 35 percent, and in 1965, 25 percent.
8. *Fine Gael Digest* árd-fheis issue, 1962, p. 10.
9. McCracken, *op. cit.*, tables, p. 125.
10. Since 1948 the Senate has had a permanent Committee on Statutory Instruments which is supposed to investigate all legislation. However, like its counterpart in the Dáil, it has no research assistants or secretarial staff.
11. The President of the Irish Trade Union Congress claimed that the trade union campaign "tipped the balance in the referendum." See *Irish Independent*, July 23, 1959, p. 12, and *Labour*, July–August, 1959. *The Irish Review and Annual 1959* (supplement to the *Irish Times*, January 1, 1960), p. 7, also expressed the opinion that the trades union vote was decisive in retaining PR. The overall national majority for PR was 33,600, while the majority in Dublin city and county was 45,762, indicating that outside of this area De Valera's leadership and arguments had prevailed.
12. A contemporary Irish writer comments somewhat cynically: "In effect, the Seanad's main function is to fill the absence in the Irish Republic of an honours list." (Coogan, *op. cit.*, p. 140).

VII

MINOR POLITICAL PARTIES AND PARTY ORGANIZATION

The Irish Labour Party

In Ireland the Labour Party has only momentarily been able to achieve more than third-party status. Undoubtedly one reason for this failure has been the overwhelming importance of nationalism in the thinking of Irishmen of all classes and the emergence of the major parties out of the struggle for independence. Even though organized labor had a significant role in this struggle, the principal leaders, Griffith, De Valera, Collins, and the rest, were not connected with the unions and these leaders became the founders of the new parties which replaced the old Unionist and Nationalist parties.

It may be observed that this situation contrasts sharply with that in some other ex-colonial societies. In the West Indies, for example, most existing major parties began as labor parties and as the political manifestation of union solidarity. The union officials became the labor party candidates and some became the ministers in the semi-independent and, finally, the independent governments that emerged after World War II. With the political eclipse of the old ruling plantocracy, the transfer of policy decisions from the overseas service officials to the elected ministers and the fading out of the middle-class West Indian politicians (comparable to the Irish Nationalist leaders), the new leadership was supplied by vigorous and demagogic union officials who represented the newly enfranchised working class. These new leaders succeeded in combining an appeal to the economic interests of the Negro workers, the vast majority of the population, with the rising demand for political independence.[1]

In Ireland the nationalist movement in its beginnings was led by middle-class men, mainly Protestant and socially conservative in their views.[2] These leaders were succeeded by others who were Catholic but, in general, also middle class and far from radical in social and economic matters. The first important labor movement, on the other hand, was inaugurated as a truly radical organization by James Connolly in 1896. In that year he returned to Ireland from Scotland to found the Irish Socialist Republican Party, which stood for the total socialization of land and industry. Despite his fervid editorials and other writings in the columns of his party newspaper, *The Irish Worker*, the Irish working class remained indifferent. Some union leaders believed that Irish labor should continue to support the Irish Parliamentary Party as offering the best hope for eventual Irish independence. In fact, Connolly's views were far too radical to appeal to many Irish of any class. Eventually Connolly emigrated to the United States where he joined forces for a time with Daniel De Leon. Without Connolly's leadership, his small socialist party in Ireland almost disappeared.

Of much greater significance in Labour Party history was the founding of the Irish Transport Worker's Union by James Larkin in January, 1909. Larkin was born on a small farm near Newry but, like so many Irish lads in his situation, he went to England in search of work. In Liverpool he learned the techniques of trades union organization and tactics as an officer of the Transport Worker's Union. He returned to Dublin in 1907 to find Irish labor in a pitiful condition. Unemployment or underemployment was the lot of most workmen who were compelled to work, when they could, for miserable wages. The Dublin slums, where many of them had to live, were among the worst to be found in any

European city. The city government was in the hands of public-house keepers and slum landlords. Under these circumstances, Irish workmen were more than ready to accept Larkin's leadership and join his union.

From the beginning Larkin's aims went far beyond immediate economic gains for the working class. Like Connolly, he hoped to see a Marxist republic in Ireland and his union provided a disciplined and organized support far more effective than Connolly's socialist party. By making the union the basic organization and proving its value to its members, Larkin was able to show the Irish workman that united action could give him formidable bargaining power. The next step was to educate the union members in political philosophy and induce them to turn their combined efforts toward political goals.

Larkin's first step was to throw his union open to all workmen. Its name was changed to Irish Transport and General Workers' Union. At this point Connolly returned to Ireland to become the Ulster organizer and secretary of the IT & GWU. In 1912 Larkin and Connolly persuaded the Irish Trades Union Council to endorse the idea of having an Irish labor party. This action was facilitated by the electoral success of the British Labour Party in 1906. In 1914 the Irish TUC took the step of identifying itself as the political arm of labor. Its name was changed to Trades Union Congress and Labour Party. This did not meet with universal approval among trades unionists. Some labor leaders could see no rosy future for a labor party in Ireland and urged that labor's best weapon was political voluntarism, as in the United States. At all events the merger of TUC and Labour Party lasted only for some years. The TUC and ILP became separate organizations again in 1930.

The first real test of union strength came in 1913. Alarmed at the growth of the IT & GWU, the Dublin employers determined to crush "Larkinism" and tried to compel all employees to sign a "yellow dog" contract, a pledge to join no union. The IT & GWU responded by calling a general strike. The employers countered this by a general lockout. The union was in no position financially to withstand a long lockout and by January, 1914, it was forced to capitulate. Many believed that this would destroy Larkin's influence with Irish labor. In fact, however, Larkin had made use of the free time of the locked out workmen, mostly members of the IT & GWU, to recruit them into a paramilitary force he named the Irish Citizen Army, with its headquarters in the union's Liberty Hall. The army's pledged objectives were the emancipation of Irish labor and the establishment of an Irish republic.

During World War I Connolly and Larkin urged a boycott of the British war effort. Liberty Hall bore a banner reading, "We Serve Neither King nor Kaiser," and in 1916 the union decided to go so far as to display, illegally, the green flag symbolic of their hoped-for republic.

The Irish Citizen Army soon had a competing body in the National Volunteers who were recruited on a purely nationalist basis to serve as a counterforce to intransigent Ulster Volunteers in the North. A number of ICA members were attracted into the National Volunteers, which had middle-class leaders. Larkin thereupon reorganized his ICA into a purely working-class force, called by Clarkson the "first 'Red Army' in modern Europe." [4] As already noted, it was this army—together with the Sinn Féin republicans of the Irish Volunteers led by Padraic Pearse and the old Fenian, Thomas Clarke—that made possible the Easter Rising of 1916.

Larkin had left Ireland for the United States in 1914 and the leadership of militant labor had been left in the hands of Connolly. The latter's execution, after the crushing of the Easter Rising, removed Ireland's most colorful labor leader.[5] His ideas were consistent, his leadership vigorous, his aims truly revolutionary.[6] It is tempting to speculate upon the different course that Irish labor might have followed had Connolly remained to dominate its councils.

In April, 1918, Irish labor joined forces with virtually all other organizations in Southern Ireland to protest the British proposal to apply military conscription to Ireland. Except in Belfast, most Irish workmen joined the twenty-four-hour work stoppage.

The British Government then gave up the plan to conscript Irishmen, but Irish labor cannot claim the sole credit for the victory. Sinn Féin Nationalists, and the Church were united with labor on this issue.

The question which Irish labor leaders and Irish workmen had constantly to ask themselves was: "Am I an Irishman first and a laborite second, or vice versa?" As a rule, nationalist sentiment overcame the labor orientation. Throughout the whole history of the struggle for Irish independence the leaders of Irish labor were constrained to subordinate labor politics to the leadership of Sinn Féin. An outstanding example of this was the decision of the special meeting of the TUC in November, 1918, by a vote of 96 to 23, not to enter candidates in the elections of 1918 in order to avoid competition with Sinn Féin candidates.

The result of this decision was to remove Irish labor and its leadership from any part in the parliamentary and diplomatic aspects of the independence struggle. Although Labour candidates contested local government offices, none were nominated to parliamentary seats. Sinn Féin alone represented Ireland vis-à-vis Lloyd George. It is probable that the leaders of Irish labor believed that the independence battle was the first order of business in the view of all Irishmen and that an attempt by them to complicate the issue by nominating a list of Labour candidates might weaken the Irish side—and doubtless their men would be unable to beat Sinn Féin nominees. The result of this stepping aside by the Labour Party was to deny it any publicity or fame in the ensuing struggle and to reinforce the loyalty of the working class to Sinn Féin.

Nor was the Labour Party able to present a united front on the treaty issue. Some of its leaders were pro-treaty and it would appear that the urban working class generally favored the treaty, although the IT & GWU newspaper, now called *The Voice of Labour*, attacked both Griffith and De Valera editorially.

When the civil war broke out Irish labor took no part in any organized fashion. This neutrality may have been a factor in the success of the seventeen ILP candidates who won parliamentary seats in the elections of June, 1922.[7] This was a remarkable victory in view of the fact that the ILP had presented only 18 candidates. At first glance it might seem that the party had not suffered from its relative detachment from the burning issues of the time. Whatever the reasons for this relative success, the ILP delegation of 17 formed the largest bloc in Parliament after the pro-treaty group of 58 deputies because the antitreaty deputies, numbering 36, refused to take their seats in an "illegal" parliament.

Possibly rendered overconfident by their 1922 victories, the ILP presented 43 candidates in the "green election" of August, 1923. Only 14 of these won seats. One reason for the setback was a bitter internecine quarrel in the IT & GWU between the union's executive committee led by William O'Brien, the general secretary, and the Larkinites. This quarrel broke out after Larkin's return from the United States in April, 1923. The Larkinites took almost no part in the electoral battle and failed to support Labour candidates. The internecine fight resulted in the expulsion of Larkin from the union in March, 1924. After this had happened, Larkin went to the USSR where he was named British representative in the Communist trade union international. With his support, a rival to the IT & GWU was founded in Ireland. This was called the Workers' Union of Ireland and it secured as members a number of Larkinites who had belonged to the IT & GWU. Naturally these developments affected both the economic and political strength of Irish labor at a time when the depression of 1921 had increased unemployment and sharply decreased the number of dues-paying trade unionists.

The 14 ILP deputies in the 1923 Dàil represented proportionately a much smaller delegation than the 17 of 1922, because the Dáil had been enlarged to 153 members. The government party was Cumann na nGaedheal, with 63 seats. The Farmers' Party had 15 and there were 17 independents. Although it had one more deputy than the Labour Party, the Farmers' Party rejected the responsibility of serving as the official opposition and the Labour Party performed this function under the leadership of Thomas Johnson. Despite the debating preference this gave the ILP, its leadership was not outstanding and it was unable to exert any important influence upon legislation.

In subsequent Dáils ILP strength was varied but it has never been anything but a minor party, fighting an uphill battle against general indifference. In May, 1954, it secured its largest delegation before 1965, seating 19 T.D.'s. Its strength dropped to 12 in the elections of March, 1957, and one of these was the chairman of the Dáil, elected without contest. In the general elections of 1961, 16 ILP deputies were elected from among 33 nominees, including the automatically elected chairman of the Dáil. Of the 15 who had to contest the election, 6 led the poll, a probable indication of personal popularity as in every case they were the single candidate of the ILP in the constituency. In general, the ILP chose to nominate only a single candidate or, at most, two candidates in a multimember constituency. The party was heartened by the victory of 22 of its candidates in 1965 but only 18 Labour T.D.'s were returned in the general election of June, 1969.

The failure of the ILP to show political vigor or to grow in strength over the years may seem curious in view of the existence of well-established, strong, and disciplined trades unions in Ireland. Union members have proved to be loyal to union leadership in industrial disputes. In Dublin, where the ILP has been weak, picket lines during a strike are respected almost absolutely. In the United States the reasons often given for the failure of a strong labor party to develop are the tradition of political "voluntarism" and the upward social and economic mobility of the working class which militates against political class consciousness among union members. It would seem that these reasons would hardly apply to Ireland where the escape from working-class income and status traditionally has been more difficult than in the United States. It is true, however, that few Irish workmen are self-consciously proletarian.

Insofar as one may judge, the reasons for ILP weakness include the following: [8]

1. The Irish electorate, including the working class whether unionized or not, became strongly attached emotionally and by tradition to one or other of the two main contenders in the treaty dispute. These contenders evolved into the two major parties, Fianna Fáil and Fine Gael, and their working class supporters re-

mained loyal to them. More often than not, voters of this class were republican as well as strongly nationalist, and supported Sinn Féin before the treaty split and Fianna Fáil as soon as it was formed. At no period could the ILP count upon solid trades union support. Until 1965 it had been particularly weak in Dublin where organized labor has its greatest strength. It is strongest in the South —in Cork, Wexford, and Waterford—due it would seem, to the persistence of the Land and Labour League tradition in these counties.[9]

2. Because of the strong, traditional loyalty of their members to Fianna Fáil or some other party, union leaders are cautious in supporting the ILP. They are careful to avoid the appearance of trying to coerce their members. When they make public appearances to speak in favor of ILP candidates they make it clear that they do so as private citizens and not as union officials.

3. Although the Labour Party was founded by socialists and as late as 1927 named its principal goal to be the achievement of a socialist republic, thereafter its socialist aims were mentioned in a fainter voice. It still pays verbal tribute to its revolutionary founder and states, "it seeks to establish in all Ireland a democratic Republic based upon the social teaching of its founder—James Connolly."[10] However, the Constitution does not use the word "socialism" and merely lists as one of its objectives "to bring under public ownership such industries and services, including banking, as will promote the common good by the provision of better services for the community."[11] It has been ready at times to cooperate with the nonsocialist Fianna Fáil and its program differs little from that of the major parties. It has lacked, therefore, a rousing and militant appeal which might attract working-class voters away from their traditional allegiance to one of the other parties which have, in fact, supported state enterprise in many fields, as well as public housing, aid to the distressed agricultural economy of the West, and other welfare measures.[12] Its parliamentary leader in 1957, William Norton, issued a pamphlet advocating a mixed rather than a socialist economy, "a combination of public enterprise, co-operative endeavour and private initia-

tive . . ." to be rationalized by a national planning board.[13] His views seemed to be practically identical with those of Fine Gael on the partition and the Irish language questions.

4. The ILP has been plagued by serious disputes among labor leaders almost from its inception. When Larkin returned to Ireland in April, 1923, the only persons who greeted him on his arrival were members of his family and a representative of the British Communist Party. Not a single member of the ILP delegation in the Dáil was present even though Larkin was still officially the general secretary of the IT & GWU. Larkin fought back and at "illegal" meetings he secured the suspension of members of the union's executive committee who opposed him. This quarrel had serious repercussions in the "Green Election" of August, 1923, when, as noted previously, only fourteen of forty-three ILP nominees were elected. Larkin and his supporters virtually boycotted the election. In March, 1924, Larkin was expelled from the union by unanimous vote of the executive committee. In 1944 the IT & GWU, which had provided much of the ILP's financial support, formally disaffiliated itself from the party.[14] These splits in the labor movement were fatal to labor's chances of achieving political power.

5. From the standpoint of pure trades unionism there are excellent reasons for keeping the (all-Ireland) Irish Congress of Trades Unions nonpolitical. This body includes unions from Northern Ireland, many of whose rank-and-file are Orangemen, monarchists, political Unionists (Conservatives), and strongly attached to the United Kingdom. Some of the unions are organized as branches of British unions and rely upon their British brethren for help in time of need. To be a powerful body, the Irish Congress of Trades Unions must secure the cooperation of Protestants and Roman Catholics, Unionists and Republicans. The Irish Congress of Trades Unions was created by the amalgamation of the Congress of Irish Unions and the Irish Trade Union Congress. Negotiations to this end began in 1956 and the amalgamation took place in 1959. The first congress of the ICTU was held in September, 1959. It represented a total union membership in both the Irish Republic and Northern Ireland of about 450,000. The first

president to be elected was James Larkin, Jr. of the Workers' Union of Ireland.

6. In the loss of James Connolly, Irish labor lost its most militant and dynamic leader. James Larkin, Sr. might have replaced Connolly but the victory of O'Brien and the executive committee led to his departure. In any case, Larkin and Connolly were too radical, too far to the left to be acceptable to the majority of Irish workmen who were not prepared to accept the doctrines of Soviet Communism against which their church spoke out so vigorously. Had he been so inclined, James Larkin, Jr., not so prominently identified with Communism as was his father, might have become an effective ILP leader. However, except for several sessions as a deputy between 1954 and 1957, when he retired from party politics, he had generally kept aloof from political activity. Even when he was a candidate he did not campaign. From 1957 until his death in 1969 he devoted his energies entirely to union affairs.

In recent years, top leadership in the ILP has not been outstanding. In 1932 the party chairman, T. J. O'Connell, failed to win a seat in the Dáil and was succeeded by William Norton, considered at the time to be somewhat more radical than the conservative O'Connell. Although he remained party chairman and parliamentary leader until 1960, Norton displayed little vigor or aggressiveness as party leader. An intelligent and able man and an effective public speaker, he seemed to have become disenchanted with the party and discouraged about its future. In his personal manifestoes and election propaganda he played down his ILP connection. In 1957 he made no mention at all of the Labour Party in his campaign documents.[15] Although he began his career as a trades union official, his acceptance of a directorship in an Irish subsidiary of the General Electric Company tended, in the eyes of many, to identify him with big business rather than labor.

In 1960 Norton was succeeded as leader of the ILP by Brendan Corish. Mr. Corish is young and inexperienced and the effectiveness of his leadership is still to be established. The unusual success of the ILP in the 1965 general election would seem to speak well for it.

7. The British Labour Party has long attracted many intellectuals who dominate some of the constituency parties and are found as well in the high councils of the party at the national level. They have included such figures as G. B. Shaw, the Webbs, G. D. H. Cole, Harold Laski, and Sir Stafford Cripps. They helped to make the Labour Party intellectually respectable and more acceptable to the middle-class voter, and were generally more bold and adventuresome in their policy suggestions than the often stodgy leaders of the Trades Union Congress.

The Irish Labour Party in recent years lacked this intellectual leaven. Nor, on the other hand, was it a vigorous proletarian revolutionary movement such as Connolly had hoped to create. As a result, it often had trouble in finding suitable candidates. Many of its nominees were unimpressive, lacking the education and experience that could convince voters of their fitness for the post of deputy.

There is evidence that this situation is changing. Recently the ILP has recruited some professional men and even outstanding intellectuals. The cogent and lively debater and celebrated independent deputy, John McQuillan, who had at various times belonged to Clann na Poblachta and the National Progressive Democratic Party, joined the ILP in 1964. Among the Labour candidates who won Dublin seats were a doctor with a Dublin practice and a graduate of the National University.

A noteworthy instance of the new trend was the announcement by Conor Cruise O'Brien that he was joining the Labour Party. Professor O'Brien made this announcement in an address given at an ILP meeting on December 19, 1968.[16] In making the announcement, he took the occasion to analyze Irish political shifts since 1880. He identified three momentous moves, all to the left. The first was Parnell's and Davitt's "New Departure" from Butt's old Home Rule Party, a move which led to the destruction of landlordism. The second came at the close of World War II when the Irish Parliamentary Party had come to the end of its usefulness and the Sinn Féin movement dominated Irish politics. The third shift came with the triumph of Fianna Fáil in 1932 over the Cumann na nGaedheal, by now a conservative party. Professor O'Brien prognosticated a fourth shift, to come about because Fianna Fáil has repeated the history of successful major parties. It has become fat, complacent, and conservative, in his opinion, and dominated by satisfied men who do not want to disturb the status quo. The important question, in Professor O'Brien's view, is whether or not the ILP is prepared to take advantage of the time for another swing to the left. This will require it to abandon its old view of itself as a consciously minority party, hoping at best to be included in a Fine Gael coalition.

O'Brien believes the Irish people to be ready now for a move to the left. The evidence for this is a noticeable disregard of old taboos such as those that prevented public discussion of sex and Church discipline. Censorship appears to be "moribund." There is hope that the pervasive and almost totally conservative influence of the Catholic Church may also be changing. Pope John made it difficult to denounce socialism as anti-Christian and ecumenism as a device of the devil. Irish social attitudes are changing. Young people are interested in a moving, growing society and no longer in the civil war or ancient history. Party names such as "Soldiers of Destiny" and "Kith and Kin of the Gael. . . . strike them as rather ridiculous."

A recent announcement by the Labour Party provides some evidence that it may indeed be attempting a move to the left. Its latest statement concerning "worker democracy" sounds much like guild socialism. The statement included this definition: "the aim of worker democracy is to make the decision-takers in the place of work and in control of the enterprise responsible to those who work in it." [17] This is calculated to appeal to the expanding industrial labor force. As Ireland becomes more industrial and urban the rural segment of society will have proportionately smaller political influence. Trades union membership will grow and the new labor force is less likely to be attached emotionally, as were their fathers, to one of the two major parties. Under these favorable circumstances and with energetic and imaginative leadership, which the party lacked for so long, and with the help of its new intellectual adherents, the ILP may hope to have a more significant role to play in the Irish political drama.

Minor Parties

A number of other parties have been organized from time to time, many of them by politicians who have seceded from one of the major parties. The remnant of the old Nationalist Party was reorganized in 1926 under the leadership of Captain William Redmond, John Redmond's son. Calling itself the National League but generally known as "Captain Redmond's Party," it won eight seats in the first general election of 1927 but only two in September, 1927. It passed from the political scene thereafter and Captain Redmond joined Cumann na nGaedheal in 1932.

Disgust with the boundary settlement of 1925 induced Professor William Magennis, a National University deputy, to break with Cumann na nGaedheal and form a party called Clann Éireann. Clann Éireann agreed with Fianna Fáil as to the abolition of the oath. It also demanded immediate revision of the boundary settlement and the imposition of a tariff wall against foreign goods. Seven candidates of this party contested seats in the 1927 election but all were defeated.

Some minor parties have been created as splinter groups of major parties only to recombine later with other groups and finally with a major party. Frank MacDermot, elected as an Independent from Roscommon in 1932, became the president of a farmers' association and turned this into a political party called the National Farmers' and Ratepayers' League. The basis for the party was the disgust of many with the seemingly interminable disorder and violence over the treaty question and the repercussions on Irish agriculture of the economic war with Great Britain. Its program called for strengthening the influence of the farm interest upon government policies and an end to the cold war with Northern Ireland and England. The party was enlarged by the entry of James M. Dillon. The rump of the old Parliamentary Party, which had been led by his father, followed Dillon into the NF & RL, which then changed its name to the National Centre Party. As noted previously, the next alliance came in September, 1933, when the Centre Party joined forces with O'Duffy's National Guard and Cosgrave's Cumann na nGaedheal to become the United Ireland Party, and subsequently, Fine Gael.

The Farmers' Party had a history similar to that of other small parties. Although ostensibly a special interest party formed to represent the Irish Farmers' Union, its leaders tended to side with Cumann na nGaedheal and urged amalgamation with that party. This was rejected by the union but after the entry of Fianna Fáil into the Dáil it was evident that small parties could exert no influence at all unless allied with one or other of the two major parties. Accordingly the Farmers' Party T.D.'s voted for Cosgrave as president of the executive council after the September, 1927, election and the party soon was virtually absorbed by Cumann na nGaedheal. Most of the T.D.'s of the Farmers' Party who stood again in the 1932 election did so as candidates of Cumann na nGaedheal.

A reconstituted farm party under the name of Clann na Talmhan was formed in 1938 at a meeting in Athenry, Galway, by farmer delegates from several western counties. Its program was devoted entirely to the interests of the small farmer including government support of land reclamation and lowering taxes on farm lands. Possibly because Irish agriculture was feeling the effects of the worldwide economic depression at this time, as well as the effects of De Valera's economic war with Great Britain, the new party had considerable success in the next election. Fifteen candidates were elected in June, 1943, but Clann na Talmhan had to remain in opposition as the Government was formed by Fianna Fáil with Labour support. Subsequently the new farm party had diminishing success. Indeed it can hardly be called a party today because it has virtually no organization. It is rather a label shared by a few small farmer candidates from the west of Ireland. Five candidates of this designation were elected in 1954, three in 1957, and two in 1961. The traditional loyalty of the rural voter to the major parties, especially Fianna Fáil and the particular attention given by Fianna Fáil to the rural West, the creation of the Turf Board (Bord na Móna) in 1934, the various schemes for the improvement of the farm economy in the Gaeltacht—all have stolen the thunder of Clann na Talmhan and prevented it from becoming a party of even regional importance.

There have been other minor parties which have persisted despite a conspicuous lack of electoral success. One of these is Clann na Poblachta (Republican Party) headed by Séan Mac-Bride, son of the famous beauty and Irish patriot, Maude Gonne MacBride, immortalized by the poet Yeats. He was described as "half in and half out of the IRA." He thought De Valera too ready to compromise with England but he condemned the use of violence by the IRA during World War II. He attacked De Valera's economic policies as well as his failure to restore the Republic in name as well as fact. MacBride's party represented those Republicans who had refused to follow De Valera into Fianna Fáil but who now were disillusioned with Sinn Féin and IRA violence. They hoped to attract others from the ranks of Fianna Fáil who, for one reason or another, were dissatisfied with De Valera. MacBride called for the integration of all Ireland in an independent, democratic republic without any external associations save those truly chosen by the Irish nation, a system of social justice on Christian principles, the full international status of Ireland as a republic, and the restoration of spoken Irish as the predominant language of the country.[18]

The party was inaugurated in July, 1946, its founders including a former supporter of De Valera, the Dublin barrister Noel Hartnett, and the well-known independent deputy John McQuillan. It got its first chance at the polls in three by-elections in October, 1947. De Valera was aware that MacBride had attracted a number of former Fianna Fáil adherents and announced that unless his party won all three by-elections he would call for a general election. MacBride and one of his colleagues won two of the by-elections and the general election was held in February, 1948. Fianna Fáil retained much the largest representation of any party but its numbers were reduced by eight seats and the new parliamentary leader of Fine Gael, John A. Costello, was able to construct a coalition or interparty government of all other parties and independents.[19] MacBride joined the coalition and became Minister of External Affairs. Another member of his party, Dr.

Noel Browne, became Minister of Health. This represented the high point in the party's fortunes. Its subsequent failure and its reduction almost to the status of a one-man party may be traced to the party split that came about during the struggle over Dr. Browne's maternity and child welfare measure, treated elsewhere.[20] Another reason for the party's decline may be the fact that its simon-pure republicanism was adopted by J. A. Costello.

In 1954, the party ran 18 candidates and elected 2. In 1957, 12 candidates contested seats and again there were 2 victories. In 1961, the number of candidates had dwindled to 5 and only one, John Tully, was elected. MacBride was defeated in this election. In 1965, the party published its intention to quit national politics.

Despite its poor showing in the elections, Clann na Poblachta could claim to have had some influence upon national policies. Its insistence upon the formal designation of Ireland as a republic possibly influenced Mr. Costello. Of greater importance to the Irish people was its advocacy of improved public health programs, which were commenced under Dr. Browne and continued by subsequent governments. It was responsible also for the formulation of a forestry program which was accepted by the interparty government of which it was a part.

After the split with MacBride over the maternity and child welfare measure, Dr. Browne and some others withdrew and formed the National Progressive Democratic Party early in 1958. One NPD candidate was entered without success in a by-election in June, 1958. Three candidates stood in the 1961 general election and two were elected, Dr. Browne and John McQuillan.

The Irish Liberal Party is so small that it resolved to nominate no candidates at all at the next general election. The Liberal Party held meetings in December, 1968, and January, 1969, at which it decided to avoid electoral contests for the moment and elected as party chairman Mr. Kevin Clear, a Dublin publisher.

Other minor parties appear as the sponsors of candidates in every general election, only to disappear afterwards. Some of these are in reality not parties at all but the chosen designation of a single candidate who prefers a party label to the uninformative adjective, "independent." An example would be the single candidate who appeared under the label "Christian Democrat" in the 1961 General Elections but who disappeared from politics along with his "party" after his defeat. A party calling itself "Young Ireland" presented three candidates in one election but none was elected and the party was not revived.

Sinn Féin

The middle-class movement, originally moderate in its objectives, was formed by Arthur Griffith under the name of Sinn Féin and first began to be noticed about 1903; by the end of World War I, it had become the embodiment of outraged and violent Irish nationalism. As mentioned previously, it was the single major party in Southern Ireland and swept all before it, not without some resort to force and intimidation, in the Free State counties in the "partition" election of May, 1921. The subsequent split into pro- and anti-treaty sections, the civil war, and De Valera's founding of Fianna Fáil, left Sinn Féin as the designation only of a hard core of republican nationalists who would accept neither the Government of Northern Ireland nor the Free State as legitimate. After De Valera's resignation along with his followers, the remaining Sinn Féin members chose Miss Mary MacSwiney as their leader. She was the sister of an Irish hero-martyr, Terence Mac-Swiney, who had died in an English jail in 1920 as the result of a hunger strike. Miss MacSwiney herself was a civil war veteran and had been imprisoned by the Free State authorities.

Sinn Féin adherents regarded themselves now as forming the only party still loyal to the Republic of 1916 for which their comrades had died and for which they intended to continue to fight. In this, their views and intentions coincided with those of the IRA units that had battled with the Free State troops in the civil war and who remained ready and eager to use force to compel the Six Counties of northeast Ireland to rejoin the others in a genuine republic. Naturally, there was considerable coincidence of membership between Sinn Féin and IRA. The latter had, in fact, withdrawn its support from De Valera even before he created Fianna Fáil. This happened at an IRA convention held November 14,

1925. At this meeting the IRA formally renounced allegiance to "the government," meaning De Valera, Lemass, and Aiken. The IRA then elected its own army council to command it.

The objectives of Sinn Féin are outlined in the party's constitution: [21]

The Organisation is based on the following fundamental principles:

(a) That the allegiance of Irishmen and Irishwomen is due to the Sovereign Irish Republic proclaimed in 1916.

(b) That the sovereignty and unity of the Republic are inalienable and non-judicable.

The objects of Sinn Féin are:

(a) The complete overthrow of English Rule in Ireland.

(b) To bring the Proclamation of the Republic, Easter 1916, into effective operation and to maintain and consolidate the Government of the Republic, representative of the whole people of Ireland, based on that Proclamation.

(c) To establish in the Republic a reign of social justice based on Christian principles, by a just distribution and effective control of the Nation's wealth and resources, and to institute a system of government suited to the particular needs of the people.

(d) To promote the restoration of the Irish Language and Irish culture and the widest knowledge of Ireland's history; to make Irish citizens conscious and proud of their traditional and cultural heritage; and to educate the citizens of the Republic in their rights and responsibilities as citizens.

Means:

(a) Through Sinn Féin organizing the Irish people into a united and disciplined movement for the restoration of the Republic and the achievement of the above ideals.

(b) Assisting, as directed by the Árd Comhairle, all Organisations working for the same objects.

The party program includes, as its foremost demand, the "freeing of Ireland from the yoke of foreign occupation," but contains as well a number of social and economic objectives.[22] Believing that Ireland's economic subjection to Great Britain is due to the fact that Ireland remains in the Sterling area, Sinn Féin wants to break this connection, create a purely Irish currency, repatriate Irish foreign investments and, if necessary, forbid foreign investment in Ireland. Although it does not demand the outlawing of the English language, it recommends that all Irish become bilingual and that all public education be conducted in the Irish language, English to become the secondary language.[23]

It may be noted that the statements under the heading "means" can be interpreted to cover the alliance between Sinn Féin and the IRA intransigents who held that only force would settle the partition issue and who were responsible for the raids and bombings along the border, in Northern Ireland, and sometimes in England. More specifically, in another document issued by the general committee of the party, it was stated: "In the circumstances it appears that means other than constitutional ones will have to be adopted." [24] This pamphlet made a distinction between the various legislatures. Within the Twenty-Six Counties (the Republic of Ireland), Sinn Féin would enter candidates in local government elections and serve if elected; it would enter candidates in Oireachtas elections but serve only if the party were to win a majority. In the Six Counties (Northern Ireland) all twelve constituencies returning members to Westminster would be contested but elected Sinn Féin candidates would refuse to sit. Once a majority had been secured for Sinn Féin in the Twenty-Six Counties, the members of the Stormont Parliament would be invited to take seats in the Irish Republican Parliament. Those refusing to do so would be replaced by persons chosen at a constituency convention or otherwise.

All candidates accepting the Sinn Féin nomination must sign a pledge to abide by these rules, to accept orders from the party leadership, and to resign the seat if so ordered by the Árd Comhairle. The pledge form concludes with the ominous statement: "Any breach of this pledge will be considered as an overt act of treachery, and will be treated as such." [25]

The party constitution indicates that members must not only

accept the aims of Sinn Féin but pledge themselves not to vote or work for the election of any candidate who intends to take a seat in the existing parliaments in Dublin, Stormont, or Westminster. Applicants for membership may be rejected by the local party branch.

The electoral success of Sinn Féin candidates has not been impressive. In June, 1927, the party nominated 15 candidates of whom 5 secured election and, in accord with party policy, refused to take their seats. In any case, they were too few to have any effect upon the composition or policies of the Government. For some years after 1927 no Sinn Féin candidates were nominated. Subsequently the number of Sinn Féin candidates has varied greatly in various elections. In the general election to the fifteenth Dáil (May, 1954) only 2 seats were contested by the party. In March, 1957, at the general elections to the sixteenth Dáil, 19 Sinn Féiners were nominated and 4 succeeded in winning seats. Subsequently 5 by-elections to this Dáil were contested, all without success, and in October, 1961, 21 were candidates of Sinn Féin at the general elections to the seventeenth Dáil. None was elected. The next Sinn Féin candidate to contest a seat was in a Wicklow by-election in 1968. He was badly defeated.

It may also be noted that in Northern Ireland Sinn Féin succeeded in forcing the old Nationalist Party to withdraw from the electoral contest in both 1955 and 1957. The result was a considerable abstention by Nationalist voters and the victory of the Unionists in all twelve constituencies. Sinn Féin had won two contests in 1955, although the winners were declared ineligible to take their seats, both being in jail at the time. In 1959 the Sinn Féin vote fell to a fraction of its former numbers and Unionists won overwhelmingly.[26] The result therefore was to kill the Nationalist vote and strengthen the Unionists.

It would seem that the intransigence of Sinn Féin is strong enough to keep its members in the political battle despite hopeless odds and almost certain defeat. Even electoral victory is a hollow prize when the elected member must refuse to take his seat, succeeds merely in reducing the number of members in the Dáil by one, and cannot affect the composition or policies of the Government or even add a voice to the Opposition. The burden of contesting elections has been passed around in the party and rarely has the same Sinn Féin candidate appeared on the ballot in successive elections. It would appear that the Sinn Féin leadership is now reconsidering its fifty-year-old policy of abstention from sitting and debating in the Dáil. If this change of policy is made it might well increase the party's electoral appeal and Sinn Féin, with its far left program, might secure some parliamentary representation.

In line with the leftward trend noticeable in recent statements of both the ILP and Fine Gael, and consistent with the 1962 announcement by the IRA that it was abandoning the use of force against the Royal Ulster Constabulary, Sinn Féin would appear to be shifting its emphasis from revenge and irredentism to a policy of left-wing socialism. In January, 1969, at a meeting held in Jury's Hotel, Dublin, to commemorate the first (republican) Dáil, Thomas MacGiolla, President of Sinn Féin, declared the party's objective to be "a democratic, socialist republic" essentially similar to Connolly's ideal of state-owned enterprises cooperatively controlled by the workers. About three weeks later, at the inaugural meeting of the Republican Club of University College, Dublin, a representative of the IRA, Cathal Goulding, spoke on "The Revolutionary Role of the IRA Today." The IRA, said the speaker, is now a "revolutionary army of the Irish people" and has the task, as well, of teaching "republicanism." He alleged the Government and Civil Service to be the tool of the propertied class and that parliamentary action would not be enough to change this situation. A revolution is required, he said, and the IRA remains its military arm.[27]

Formal Party Organization

The larger Irish parties have similar constitutions and structural arrangements. At the grass-roots level is the branch, based usually on a polling district and consisting of the active partisans who live or work in the district. In numbers they may vary from twenty to a hundred or more. Over several branches is the district executive (Fine Gael) or cómhairle ceanntair (Fianna Fáil), which covers party activities in the county electoral area. This is made up of delegates from the branches, two in the case of Fianna Fáil and three in the Fine Gael. The latter party also includes any elected municipal officials who are party members. The cómhairle ceanntair summons conventions for the nomination of Fianna Fáil candidates in local government elections.

Branches have little more than a paper existence in some places, especially in the case of Fine Gael. Sometimes the only active group in a branch may be a few friends of the candidate.

Above the district organization is the constituency executive, the most important local party body. In Fianna Fáil this is made up of three delegates from each cómhairle ceanntair, all Fianna Fáil deputies from the constituency, the delegate to the national executive, and up to three co-opted members. Fine Gael includes as well any local government-elected officials of the party, senators who live in the constituency, two delegates from each district executive, and two members named by the national council. The constituency executive summons the convention for the choice of party candidates for the Oireachtas, and in Fine Gael for local government offices as well. The nominating conventions are composed of the constituency executive, delegates from each branch, and others chosen by the national council of the party. It is the constituency executive which oversees campaign strategy and bears the expense of campaigns with some assistance from the national headquarters, except as candidates defray their own election expenses.

The top body in both major parties is the annual convention, the árd-fheis. This is a very large body consisting of the national executive, all deputies and senators of the party, all constituency and district executives, and delegates from all the branches. It elects the party's national officers, approves the program advanced by the leaders, and legalizes any changes made in the party's constitution and by-laws. As a general rule, it does this without much discussion and argument. By reason of their size and composition, bodies of this kind are likely to give almost automatic approval to the proposals of the party leadership groups. The chief purpose of the convention is to present a public image of party solidarity and

enthusiasm, stimulate the devotion and energies of the local delegates, and provide a sounding board for the national leadership

Between meetings of the árd-fheis, party affairs at the national level are in the hands of the national council (Fine Gael)
and the national executive (Fianna Fáil). These bodies vary
slightly in composition. Both contain all the party's national officers: president, vice-president, general secretary, other officers,
and representatives of the county or constituency executives. Fine
Gael includes up to 10 additional members chosen by the party
president. Fianna Fáil adds 5 members co-opted by the national
executive and 15 members elected by the árd-fheis. This national
council or executive meets monthly or oftener, makes decisions
as to party policy and strategy, decides upon the way to conduct
the national aspects of an electoral campaign, and keeps an eye
upon the work of the constituency executives. In theory this body
or its standing committee may veto local decisions on candidates,
but, as already noted, the use of this power is conditioned by the
need to give weight to local preferences. Rarely, a locally popular
candidate may be rejected by party headquarters. Maurice O'Connell of Fine Gael was rejected as a party candidate in 1969 by
the standing committee, although he had already received a constituency nomination. In this case, O'Connell's public criticism of
his party leader, Liam Cosgrave, may have been the principal
reason for the committee's action. Although the choice of candidates is normally left to the local organization, the central authorities try to control the number of nominations to be made in a
particular constituency.

The Labour Party is set up much like the two major parties.
It does not try to have branches in every constituency but it is
organized in Northern Ireland as well as in the Republic and it
contests local and general elections in both. In Northern Ireland
it has recently had to compete for votes with two other groups
calling themselves Independent Labour and Irish Labour.

The basic ILP unit is the branch, as it is in the other parties.
A branch is formed with the approval of the national executive
body, the administrative council. It may consist of a group of citizens or a corporate member (trade union, cooperative, or other

organization in sympathy with the aims of the ILP). In all contested constituencies, a constituency council is formed with representation from all branches within the constituency. A prime duty of this council is the nomination of candidates, which is done by secret ballot and single transferable vote. Large constituencies may be split into two or more divisions, each with a divisional council to perform the duties of a constituency council for its division. To provide wider coordination of campaign activities, several neighboring constituencies may be organized into a region, as in the Dublin area.

The ILP Constitution confers final authority upon the annual, national conference. Its membership (850 in 1969) is elected by the branches, including affiliated unions, by secret ballot and single transferable vote. The principal task of the conference is to elect party officers and the administrative council. Nominations for all of these posts may be made only by the branches, including the affiliated unions and other associations, and are made in advance of the conference so that the names of the nominees may be circulated among the branches before the meeting. Branches may submit two resolutions for discussion at the conference and these are also circulated before the conference meets. This "grass roots" participation is deciding what the conference will discuss is claimed by the ILP to be unique among Irish parties. Party policies, however, are proposed by the administrative council.

The administrative council is the party's ruling body. It is made up of the party officers, including the parliamentary leader and deputy leader, six deputies or senators chosen by all ILP members of the Oireachtas, plus seventeen others elected by the national conference. The council meets every six weeks or oftener, makes policy decisions binding upon its parliamentary delegation, and has the authority under the party's constitution to prescribe the procedure for selecting candidates. Although the administrative council, together with all party officers, is elected and can be replaced by the annual conference, between conferences the council enjoys autocratic authority. A smaller group consisting of the party leader, some of the parliamentary members, and the staff of the headquarters office, meets weekly to settle minor matters.

Party Financing

All parties ask their individual members to pay a modest fee of a few shillings a year. Each branch pays an affiliation fee of about £2 per annum to national headquarters. Deputies and senators are expected to donate a portion of their parliamentary salary, £60 or more, to the party war chest. Of course wealthy supporters are approached for donations, but party officials are reticent in discussing this source of income. The branch contributions, although individually small, add up to a considerable sum. Fianna Fáil claims to have more than 1,500 branches, Fine Gael claims over 1,000, and the Labour Party has about 750.

All three parties conduct an annual fund drive. A principal feature of this is a church-gate collection made on a previously announced Sunday in most of the rural parishes. This has the advantage of speed and economy in covering the country because in rural Ireland virtually the total population of the community will be at church. The major parties collect several thousand pounds by these church-gate appeals. Ordinarily the bishops do not interfere with this procedure, but occasionally, when a bishop is sponsoring a drive for a church-building fund, he will forbid the political collections. In this event, the more laborious method of house-to-house visits by party volunteers will be used. This produces contributions but the money accumulates slowly because the volunteer canvasser, usually a friend and neighbor of the householder, must accept hospitality at every point of call and can cover only two or three places in an evening.

The Labour Party depends more upon affiliation fees from its branches and corporate members than do the two major parties. Its branches are supposed to submit £2 per annum and corporate members pay £12 or more, according to the number of members of the union or cooperative society. The various councils, constituency, divisional and regional, each pay a small fee to headquarters. The total ILP income from these sources in 1968 was about £5,000.[28] This does not represent the only available money for election expenses because some unions make direct contributions to the campaign funds of individual candidates.

Fianna Fáil enjoys the most substantial financial support and is able to employ expensive forms of publicity more extensively than the other parties. In order to stimulate donations from wealthy supporters, Fianna Fáil set up a fund-raising organization called "Taca" (meaning "aid") consisting of persons who contributed £100 or more per annum. Opposition speakers attacked this plan at once in the Dáil and elsewhere as the establishment of a "slush fund." It was charged that contributors would be entitled to receive special favors from Fianna Fáil governments. At the Fianna Fáil árd-fheis of January 28, 1969, it was announced that the party in 1968 had collected £37,873, an increase of £11,000 over 1967. At the same time it was announced that Taca was being reorganized to include small as well as large donors to the party funds and that the names of all and the amount of each donation would be published.

Branches of all parties use various money-raising devices for their local expenses. They sponsor entertainments and hold dances, card parties, and raffles.

Party Leadership

From the beginning until 1967, Fianna Fáil had only two leaders: Eamon de Valera and Seán Lemass. In 1967 Mr. Lemass retired and was succeeded by John M. (Jack) Lynch. Fine Gael, under its various names, has had several leaders. Two of these have headed the Government: William T. Cosgrave and John A. Costello. Of the five men who have held the office of president of the council in the Free State or taoiseach in the State of Ireland (Eire) or the Republic of Ireland, Cosgrave, Lemass, and Lynch did not have a university education. All five sprang from ordinary Irish folk, unconnected with either the native aristocracy or the wealthy middle class that furnished most of the leadership in the early history of the independence struggle. John A. Costello earned the degrees of B.A. and LL.B. at the National University. Eamon de Valera received the degree of B.S. in mathematics from the Royal University in 1904. He also took teacher training at Blackrock College and an additional year of mathematics at Trinity

College, Dublin. All but Costello and Lynch were involved in the 1916 Easter Rising. Mr. Costello established the record of bravery and patriotism indispensable for a politician of his generation by having worked with the illegal, revolutionary courts during the Anglo-Irish "Troubles" of 1920 and 1921.

Of the five prime ministers, Cosgrave and Lynch had served in local government before election to the Dáil. Cosgrave had served on the Dublin Corporation from 1913 to 1922 and in the Dáil from 1917 to 1944, when ill health forced his retirement. Costello and Lynch had practiced law and De Valera was a mathematics teacher. Lemass had no profession outside of politics.

Another party leader with a background similar to those of the other leaders of his generation was General Richard James Mulcahy. He had been chief of staff of the Irish Volunteers from 1918 to 1921, and a Sinn Féin M.P. In 1922 he was appointed commander in chief of the Free State army in 1922. He sat in the Dáil as a deputy from 1923 to 1944, when he was chosen president of Fine Gael. He had had ministerial posts as well, but despite this long parliamentary record and the presidency of his party he did not serve as taoiseach. He had made too many enemies by his severe measures against the IRA irregulars during the civil war.[29]

Another of the party leaders, Arthur Griffith, also lacked formal higher education. Apprenticed in his youth to a printer, he educated himself at the National Library. All these party leaders had in common the fact that they were of unimpeachable native Irish origin and of the Roman Catholic faith. The one seeming exception was Eamon de Valera, whose father was Spanish and whose birthplace was New York City. But he had been sent back to Ireland as a young child and had been raised by his maternal uncle, Patrick Coll, in County Limerick. He speaks with a plain, Irish accent and his identification with the independence struggle made him seem to many to be the very personification of Irish national aspirations.

In some respects, Seán Lemass represented a different type of leader. He might be considered a combination of the older, revolutionary type and the newer, parliamentary and administrative kind. His record of action in the fight for Irish independence is quite as impressive as that of the older leaders. At the age of sixteen he participated in the Easter Rising. He was an officer in the IRA in the 1919 to 1921 struggle with the British. He was a member of the Four Courts Garrison in 1922 and minister for defense in the Republican cabinet of 1923. He was jailed four times, twice by the British and twice by the Free State. He has had continuous parliamentary experience since 1924 and has occupied ministerial posts in all Fianna Fáil governments since 1932. In 1951 he became tanaiste as well as minister of commerce and in June, 1959, he succeeded his old chief as taoiseach and leader of Fianna Fáil.

Although he lacked the charisma of Eamon de Valera, he was an effective debater and speaker and the undisputed leader of his party. Despite dire predictions as to the future of Fianna Fáil without the personal magic and political shrewdness of De Valera, Lemass consolidated the party and kept it united under his leadership. He was a professional politician who had known no other career and who had risen steadily to leadership by unswerving party loyalty, devotion, and unstinted service to the party's leader as well as a real capacity for party management. The history of his party is essentially his own history. He was a founder-member and is said to have been the first to suggest its formation to De Valera. He was the bureaucratic and pragmatic kind of prime minister rather than the inspirational and ideological type. He had only moderate enthusiasm for De Valera's pet project, the revival of the Irish language. From the beginning his interests were mainly in the economic sphere. He inspired and developed Irish State enterprise and worked closely with Dr. Whitaker on the Economic Programme. It is said that his economic policies would have been more daring and radical had he not been restrained by the conservatism of his own party and the lack of a strong ILP delegation to support them.

His claim to a place in Irish history as an outstanding statesman will rest chiefly upon the success of his economic plans and policies. The grand climax of any taoiseach's career would be success in securing the reunification of Ireland. As a first step in this direction, by doing his best to establish improved relations with the Government of Northern Ireland, Seán Lemass made more progress than any of his predecessors.

When Lemass retired from the party leadership and the post of prime minister in November, 1966, his successor was the Finance Minister, Jack Lynch. Born in 1917 and so with no revolutionary background, his rise in politics was due entirely to his likable personality and his abilities. No doubt his early success in securing election to the Dáil was greatly facilitated by his fame as a hurler and a Gaelic football player for Cork County. He had won the all-Ireland medal in both games in several seasons. His education was of the usual sort: Christian Brothers' North Monastery College in Cork City followed by legal training at University College, Cork, and King's Inns, Dublin. His family background was the usual one of successful Irish politicians, neither rich nor very poor. His father kept a tailor shop and Jack had to pay for his legal education out of his own earnings as a junior civil servant. He had three years as a practicing barrister in the Munster courts which gave him valuable experience in public speaking and debating. It was at this point that Eamon de Valera met him at a Fianna Fáil meeting and persuaded him to embark upon a political career. His qualities soon led to ministerial appointments. During his tenure of the ministry of industry and commerce he established a remarkable record as a mediator in major labor disputes, settling every one that came before him after the labor court had failed. As minister of finance he was closely concerned with the Whitaker Report and its implementation. Besides his experience as a cabinet member he has served his government abroad as a vice-president of the Council of Europe and a member of the International Labor Office. His views on both foreign and domestic policies have always been in harmony with those of his predecessor.

If Seán Lemass exemplified the transition from freedom fighter to administrator and pragmatic politician, Lynch is the first taoiseach whose rise has been entirely parliamentary, owing nothing whatever to participation in the birth struggles of the Republic. As it happens, he is the first taoiseach to hail from Cork, a matter of great local pride.

James Mathew Dillon differed in several respects from other

leaders of the two major parties. Born in 1902, he was too young to have been an active participant in the Easter Rising. It is most unlikely that he would have done so had he been older. Unlike the other leaders he is not of humble origin although of a pure native, Catholic family. He is the fourth son of John Dillon, M.P., who succeeded John Redmond as leader of the Irish Parliamentary Party at Westminster. His mother was the daughter of Lord Justice Sir James Mathew. He graduated from University College, Dublin, and studied business administration in London, New York, and Chicago. He also studied for the bar and has both mercantile and farming interests in County Mayo, but sat in the Dáil as a deputy from county Monaghan. A political moderate, he was a co-founder of the Centre Party in 1933. After its fusion with Fine Gael, he was elected a vice-president of that party. Although he resigned from Fine Gael in 1942 and was elected as an independent from 1942 to 1952, he remained one of the most active and vocal opponents of Fianna Fáil governments. In 1952 he rejoined Fine Gael and in 1959 was chosen leader of the Fine Gael Parliamentary Party. In February, 1960, the next Fine Gael árd-fheis elected him president of Fine Gael.

Dillon is an able and witty debater and speaker with long parliamentary experience. He, like Lemass, represents the kind of party leader who arrived at his position of leadership by the parliamentary route rather than by his extraparliamentary career and reputation.

The newer leadership is exemplified also by Liam Cosgrave, who had extensive parliamentary experience before election to party leadership. The eldest son of William T. Cosgrave, he was born in 1920. He was educated at the Christian Brothers School, Synge Street, Dublin (a celebrated school), and at Castleknock College, a Vincentian institution, where he prepared for a legal career. He is a farmer as well as a barrister. In the first interparty coalition he was given a parliamentary secretaryship, a junior ministerial post, and later became minister for industry and commerce. In the second interparty government he was minister for external affairs. As noted earlier, he succeeded James M. Dillon as leader of Fine Gael and president of the party in 1965.

Gerard Sweetman of Fine Gael may serve to exemplify the rarest type of Irish political leader, the conservative of Unionist background. Although he has never been party leader or taoiseach, he has held the important cabinet post of finance minister. He was chief whip of Fine Gael when James M. Dillon was the party leader and in 1966 he was made director of organization for the party and chairman of the standing committee on candidates. In sharp contrast with most other prominent Irish politicians, he was a Unionist in his youth and a loyal "West Briton." He comes of a "Castle Catholic" family and his professional occupations are those of solicitor and company director. His educational background differs from that of the average T.D.—his university preparatory training was received at Beaumont, the fashionable Roman Catholic English public school, and his university degree at Trinity College, Dublin. His influential position in Fine Gael is derived from twenty years of parliamentary experience and his outstanding shrewdness and skill in debate.

The new ILP leader, Brendan Corish, was born in 1918 and had the usual primary and secondary education at the Christian Brothers School in Wexford. As with Liam Cosgrave, his revolutionary record necessarily came through his family rather than his own background. Dick Corish, his father, was a labor revolutionary who fought alongside Connolly and Larkin in the Wexford disputes of 1911, when there were bloody encounters between union workmen and police. Brendan Corish became a county civil servant and in customary fashion, when his father died, inherited his father's seat in the Dáil in a 1937 by-election. From 1954 to 1957 he was minister for social welfare. He served as secretary of the Wexford branch of the local government officials' union and for a year was county secretary of the rural workers' federation, but his career has been essentially a parliamentary one rather than that of a trades union official.

Notes

1. See M. Ayearst, "Some Characteristics of West Indian Political Parties," *Social and Economic Studies*, III, No. 2 (September, 1954)

186–196, and *The British West Indies, the Search for Self-Government* (London and New York, 1960), Ch. IX.

2. See J. Dunsmore Clarkson, *Labour and Nationalism in Ireland* (New York, 1925), Ch. V.

3. See P. O. O'Cathasaigh, *The Story of the Irish Citizen Army* (Dublin and London, 1919).

4. Clarkson, *op. cit.*, p. 288.

5. The best biography is Desmond Ryan, *James Connolly* (Dublin and London, 1924). A brief, memorial biography appeared in *Labour*, May, 1959.

6. See his *The Axe to the Root* (Dublin, 1921).

7. It may be noted, however, that Labour polled few ballots in Dublin where neutralist feeling was strong.

8. Statements based on interviews with active politicians, particularly members of the ILP.

9. In the 1961 general election Labour candidates were successful in Cork City, Dublin N. W., and in the county constituencies of Carlow-Kilkenny, mid-Cork, N. E. Cork, S. W. Cork, N. Kerry, Kildare, E. Limerick, Meath, N. Tipperary, S. Tipperary, Waterford, Wexford, and Wicklow. In 1965 Labour elected 6 Dublin candidates, 5 from the city and one from the county. At this election the ILP tied its best previous record of 22 deputies, one being the nonvoting chairman of the Dáil.

10. *The Labour Party, Constitution (as approved by the National Conference 18th April, 1952)*, II: Principles and Objects. Item 1.

11. *Ibid.*, Item 7 (f).

12.   "Lacking even so imprecise an objective as Socialism, Labour has had no goal, no target, no sincere spokesman, and no public. . . . Whatever thunder it might have possessed has been stolen by Fine Gael and, far more conspicuously, by Fianna Fáil" (Editorial, *Irish Times*, July 23, 1959).

13. *Labour's Way* (Dublin, n.d.) [1957].

14. See *The Labour Party, Official statement relating to the disaffiliation from the Labour Party of the Irish Transport and General Workers' Union* . . . (Dublin, 1944). In 1967 the IT & GWU again became affiliated with the ILP.

15. Noted by Chubb in D. E. Butler (ed.), *op. cit.*, p. 205.

16. See the *Irish Times*, December 20, 1968, p. 4, for a transcript of the speech.

17. See editorial, the *Irish Times*, January 8, 1969.

18. See *Clann na Polachta Constitution*.

19. The official leader of Fine Gael was General Richard Mulcahy but he still had a number of enemies because of his civil war activities and Costello was chosen to lead the coalition.

20. *Infra*, pp. 220–222.

21. *Sinn Féin Constitution* (as approved by the Árd-Fheis, November, 1957) [Dublin, n.d.].

22. *Sinn Féin, Social and Economic Programme* (pamphlet, n.d.).
23. *Ibid.*, p. 12. Gearóid Ó Cuinneagáin, editor of *Aiséirí*, a monthly ex-
    pressing sympathy with the IRA, complained (*Aiséirí*, mean Fomhair,
    [September] 1959) that he was denied the right to vote in Dublin be-
    cause he refused to use English. He complained, further, that the
    paper's telephone bill was sent in English and asserted that it would
    not be paid until submitted in Irish. An article in the same issue urged
    that only Irish be used in the schools as a method of discouraging
    emigration. Most of this periodical is written in English.
24. *Sinn Féin National Unity and Independence Programme issued by the
    Árd Comhairle Sinn Féin, Dublin* (n.d.).
25. *Ibid.*
26. Sinn Féin poll in Mid-Ulster, 1955: 29,737; 1959: 14,170; in Fermanagh
    and Tyrone, 1955: 30,529; 1959: 7,348. See "Nationalist vote collapses,"
    The Guardian, October 12, 1959.
27. See the *Irish Times*, January 21 and February 14, 1969.
28. See Brendan Halligan, "The Political Machine," *Hibernia*, XXXIII,
    No. 5 (February 28–March 13, 1969). The author is General Secretary
    of the ILP.
29. Whereas the British authorities had executed sixteen Irish patriots in
    1916, including Sir Roger Casement, the Free State authorities executed
    seventy-seven IRA irregulars. See D. Marcardle, *op. cit.*, pp. 984, 985.

Eamon de Valera.

Seán T. O'Kelly.

Leinster House, Dublin.

James M. Dillon, T.D.

John M. Lynch.

William T. Cosgrave.

Liam Cosgrave.

Fianna Fáil candidate Stafford makes good use of his delivery vans in the general election, June 1969.

Some election posters do not last long: the present-day equivalent of "white-washing."

Maggie Diranne, one of the stars in Flaherty's film *Man of Aran*, encounters a canvasser outside the National School polling place.

A Fianna Fáil speaker makes his way to the platform.

A lamp post is used by the three major parties.

Brendan Crimon, Fianna Fáil candidate in Meath (June 1969) electioneering for the farm vote.

Voting in West Galway in the general election, June 1969.

VIII

NOMINATIONS, CAMPAIGNS, AND ELECTIONS

The legal requirements for nomination of Dáil deputies are very similar to those for British members of Parliament. All that is required for eligibility is that the candidate have reached the age of twenty-one, be a citizen, and not be disqualified by law.

To be nominated, he or she must be nominated by a registered elector and seconded by another and by eight additional registered electors. A deposit of £100 is required which is returned to the candidate if, during the count, he receives votes to the number of at least one-third of the quota.[1]

Almost anyone willing to risk the deposit can secure nomination under this system. To obtain the nomination of a major party requires the approval of a constituency organization of that party, and confirmation, usually automatic, by a central committee.

Nominations by the major parties are made by constituency conventions made up of representatives from all the party branches in the constituency. Their work is more complicated than it would be under the single-member system because they usually have to pick more than one candidate and because they have to decide how many candidates to pick. They are advised on this point by party headquarters. It is not customary to nominate a slate of five candidates in a five-member district. The optimum number is that which reflects most accurately the proportion of the vote which the party will receive at the polls.[2] Additional candidates would only dissipate the energies of the party workers, divert some first choice votes to losing candidates, and risk lost deposits. Furthermore, especially in a large rural constituency, it is important to pick candidates from different parts of the area. Although not required by law, it is rare that any but local men are chosen because an outsider, unless he be of national prominence, would stand a poor chance against a popular local figure. This is particularly the case because voters tend to look upon their T.D. as very much their local representative in Dublin. They expect him not only to consider the needs of the constituency as a whole but to be ready and willing to shepherd individual constituents in their dealings with government authorities. The candidates tend to campaign principally in their own section of the constituency. Each asks for first-choice votes although in joint efforts such as a leaflet put out by the whole party list it is usual to appeal for a vote for all candidates "in the order of your choice." It is true, nevertheless, that they remain rivals for first-choice votes. This is very much the case in three-member constituencies where the two main parties are likely each to nominate two candidates. At least one of these is certain to be defeated and so the competition for first-choice ballots is keen. Of course the parties expect their candidates to work together as a team and display party loyalty. They may take action against candidates who are too emphatically personal in campaign tactics. An article by "Backbencher" in the *Irish Times* (June 15, 1968, p. 10) gives details of the expulsion from Fine Gael of one Matt Finnegan for "selfish" electioneering.

The central party headquarters, normally quiet between campaigns, becomes active and busy just before the campaign begins. Headquarters representatives go to the constituency conventions and attend the meetings and discussions that precede them to try to influence the choice of candidates satisfactory to the party and to keep the number down to a realistic figure. Because of the aid available from headquarters in the case of the two major parties, headquarters influence on candidacies may be considerable. In other cases, where the local constituency must bear the full cost of the campaign, headquarters influence may be negligible. In any event, the local man who has succeeded in building a loyal following among the voters by his services to them in Dublin, even if he be of little other use to the party, is in a very strong position to secure renomination. Quite often, his entrance to national office has come by way of local government where he has served on a municipal or county council and has become favorably known to many voters. It is obvious that the individual's local connections and reputation are all-important. Party affiliation is not enough to guarantee votes, especially as the voters can satisfy their party loyalty by voting for a party candidate they approve and giving subsequent choices to Independents or candidates of another party.

Professor Chubb mentions a case of the failure of the national headquarters of the Labour Party to control the voters locally. An outgoing Labour member for Carlow-Kilkenny was not renominated by the constituency convention in 1957. His name, however, was added to the Labour Party list by the central office. This meant three Labour candidates in a five-member district. The one added by the central office received the lowest number of first-choice votes and was badly beaten.[3]

Parties cannot afford to ignore the local popularity of candidates. The ideal candidate is one who is well known, well liked and, if he has had previous service in elected office, has proved to be accessible and useful to his constituents—all of which characteristics are nonpartisan. One of Chubb's informants mentioned these desiderata for a candidate: that he have a record of service to individual voters; that he have a record of bravery and participation in the struggle for Irish independence or, at the least, enthusiasm for Irish independence if too young to have been involved in the 1916 Rising; that he be a renowned player of Gaelic football. Chubb quotes a County Waterford paper, *The Dungarvan Leader*, as giving editorial approval to a candidate because of his activity in the independence struggle, his celebrity as a Gaelic football player, and his record of county council service in which he fought for his own section of the county. The paper went on to disparage the deputies "whom we do not see only when election time comes around." [4]

There are few women deputies—the parties seldom select
women candidates. This is due, it is said, to the relative unpopularity of women candidates with the female portion of the electorate. Feminism is not a characteristic of Irish women. However,
relationship to a popular deputy who has died in office can overcome this handicap. By-elections, in fact, are very often contested
by the widow or other near relative of the former member. "Between 1944 and 1961 out of thirty-seven by-elections, ten were
fought by near relatives of the previous member; and out of the
six fought between 1961 and 1964, *all* were successfully contested
by widows, brothers or sons of the deceased deputies. . . ." [5]

In general, relationship to a popular or heroic figure can be
an important factor in attracting votes. It was believed that the
success of one of the Sinn Féin candidates in the 1957 election was
due in large part to the fact that he was the brother of an IRA
man who had recently been killed in a border raid. In his manifesto for a by-election in Northeast Dublin in April, 1956, Patrick
Byrne stressed two points: that he was the son of the popular
Alderman Alfred Byrne and that, as his father's assistant, he had
become familiar with the daily problems of the constituents—
"Housing, Pensions, Health Benefits, Unemployment and a thousand and one individual troubles. . . ." Byrne ran as an independent, interparty candidate but with the blessing of the taoiseach,
Costello. He was successful, and in the March, 1957, general elec-
tion was one of the three Fine Gael candidates for Northeast
Dublin.

Not all parties nominate candidates in all constituencies.
Where there is no party organization and few supporters there
is no advantage in sacrificing the election deposit. In the case of
minor parties, there may be nominations in only a scattering of
places where victory would seem to be possible. As a rule, with
minor parties, the central office can contribute no financial support
and so cannot control nominations, which remain entirely at the
disposal of the local organization. Independent candidates have
their personal organizations consisting of a few friends who volunteer to help.

Some independent candidates are always elected. Under the

PR system the voter in a multimember constituency can vote for an independent and still vote for the top candidates of his favorite party. Encouraged by the existence of PR, a number of ex-Unionists and former adherents of the old Nationalist Party stood as independents in the 1923 election. Most of these eventually faded from the political scene or joined the Cosgrave party. Later independent candidates tended to be disgruntled ex-members of a major party who took a more precise ideological position or totally nonideological candidates who traded upon their local popularity or their services to their constituents.

The number of independents nominated and elected varies considerably from one election to another. The largest number, sixteen, were elected in 1923. Nine were returned in 1957 and six in the seventeenth Dáil (1961). If we consider as independents not only those who stood for office under this simple designation or that of Independent Labour, Independent Farmer, or Independent Republican, but also the successful candidates of Clann na Talmhan and the splinter parties, Clann na Poblachta and the National Democratic Party, the figures are somewhat larger: twelve in 1957 and eleven in 1961.

There are usually a few eccentric candidates who stand as independents. Professor Chubb mentions one such who secured election from 1937 to 1951. This was Thomas Burke, a County Clare farmer who campaigned entirely upon his reputation as a skilled bonesetter who supplied his surgical services without charge to his constituents. He had no policy program whatever and appears to have been inactive in the Dáil, but asked for and received the support of the voters as a form of payment for his free attendance upon all County Clare inhabitants with broken bones.[6]

Many candidates use election agents after the English fashion. These agents see to the printing and distribution of the candidate's campaign manifesto and other literature, which is always published under the agent's name. They arrange meetings, issue press releases and so forth. Unlike the modern English election agent, who is usually a full-time employee of the constituency party organization, the Irish election agent is often a solicitor employed only for the duration of the campaign, as used to be the case in England. Sometimes he is a senator of the candidate's party. Very often the several candidates of a party in a constituency will employ a single election agent to work in their behalf.

Campaigns in Ireland nowadays are orderly, even rather dull affairs. The dullness may be due to the fact that they amount to a struggle for office between the two major parties—Fianna Fáil, and Fine Gael plus its allies—and that there is no great, rousing issue dividing the parties. There is substantial, overall agreement as to what needs to be done and the chief difference is simply the question of who is to be given the chance to do it. Attempts to build up a campaign on the issues tend to resolve themselves into quibbles over minor matters or broad generalities. This may be another reason for the tendency of candidates to stress their personal service to the electorate as much as they do their party loyalty. One candidate, Ritchie Ryan, standing for Fine Gael in Southwest Dublin in July, 1959, and a member of the party's national council and standing committee, still thought it well to include this statement in his manifesto: "Ritchie Ryan is a loyal supporter of Fine Gael policy but he is no 'Yes man' and never hesitates to make constructive criticism whenever he believes he should."

In the 1957 election neither of the major parties had an election manifesto for the party as a whole, although its various printed materials contained generalities as to program and attacks upon the opposition. No single document gave a precise and detailed party platform. The reason for this omission may well be that both major parties hope to attract voters with a wide variety of interests. Too precise a delineation of policies would certainly offend some potential supporters and embarrass the party candidates in certain constituencies. Indeed, many candidates prefer to conduct their campaigns on local issues as much as possible and not to be tied to detailed statements of policy issued from Dublin headquarters. Fine Gael issued a single-sheet, two-page document in 1948 for the general election called "What Fine Gael Stands For, General Election, 1948, Heads of Policy." It was devoted largely to generalities, with a few specific proposals such as a reduction of beer and tobacco taxes and an inquiry into the compulsory use of Irish as a medium of instruction. In 1957 the Labour Party issued a statement calling for a planned economy and the repatriation of Irish capital invested abroad. Sinn Féin, of course, demanded the immediate annexation of the Six Counties of Northern Ireland. Fianna Fáil called for the overthrow of the unstable Fine Gael coalition and a return to strong, one-party government in its preelection "throw-away" in newspaper format, called "Let's Go Ahead Again." Fianna Fáil, the party organization best supplied with funds, made the largest use of election posters and bought the greatest amount of newspaper advertising space in local papers.

Every candidate, or slate of candidates, issues a campaign letter paid for by the candidates or the constituency organization. The law provides that a copy of this letter may be sent postage free to every registered voter. Most candidates take advantage of this opportunity but some do not because they cannot afford the expense of addressing the letters. These printed appeals are nearly all of a pattern. Consisting of a single sheet or of a folded sheet to make four pages, they display a half-tone photograph of the candidate or candidates and an appeal to the voters. This begins with a brief biography of each candidate, including any connection with the fight for independence and any relationship to celebrated or heroic personages. Previous public service at local or national level, or any philanthropic service, is mentioned. The candidate's interest in and identification with the locality is stressed in many cases. If the candidate is a supporter of the government party he urges that it be allowed "to finish the job." If he is an opposition candidate, he attacks the government record and tries to show how it has harmed the public. In the case of the four-page appeals, the inside pages are devoted as a rule to a defense of government policies or attacks upon them. Only in something under ten percent of such letters, of a sample examined, were these inside pages devoted to an appeal by the candidate as a person. The back page sometimes continues the political argument but more often repeats the name or names of the candidates in boldface type and leaves a space for the elector's name and address. The single-sheet appeals are more often used in rural constituencies where the candidates and their constituency backers are likely to be poorly supplied with funds. Many of these omit the half-tone photograph, an expense often unnecessary in rural areas where most voters are familiar with the candidate's appearance. Many of these appeals concentrate entirely, or nearly so, upon agricultural policy arguments. Only the few Sinn Féin candidates use Gaelic to any extent in their election literature and posters.

All party officials agree that numerous public meetings are a thing of the past. Nowadays, in the tepid atmosphere of an Irish election, they do not draw crowds. Church-gate meetings are still held in rural parishes. The advantage of such meetings is that a ready-made audience is already assembled and many who would not go out of their way to listen to a party speaker will remain a few minutes after mass to hear what he has to say. As the parishioners file out of church they may find a car nearby with a speaker already standing on the trunk (or "boot") ready to make his appeal. The audience assembles along the churchyard wall and listens quietly. When two or more candidates of different parties show up at the same church on the same Sunday, it has become customary to match coins to see who will speak first and for the orators to confine themselves to fifteen-minute speeches. Nowadays there is little or no heckling at these meetings and the public is inclined to give all candidates a fair hearing and to applaud politely at the conclusion of the speeches. The speakers are often local candidates but may be party volunteers from headquarters. Larger meetings with leading party figures as speakers are held in the cities and more important towns. De Valera always campaigned with a series of meetings, the equivalent of an American "whistle-stop" campaign tour. He was driven around from town to town, and at the outskirts of each chosen town his car would be met and escorted into the market place or other suitable space by a brass band and the local party members as a guard of honor. Several speakers would precede De Valera, whose speech would provide the climax of the meeting. After a round of handshaking the leader would be driven to the next town on the route. In the 1957 election he was driven almost 2,000 miles and spoke several times a day. A tradition in the West of Ireland is to welcome the party leader with a torchlight procession, the torches consisting of lumps of turf dipped in kerosene and held aloft on sticks.

Despite the tendency of party officials to decry the importance of public meetings, the whirlwind campaign tour by the party chief is a fixture and cannot be dropped without offending many partisans. Another necessity is the election-eve mass meeting in Dublin. The favorite spot for such meetings is the broad avenue of O'Connell Street in front of the General Post Office with its memories of the heroes of 1916. The government of the moment can always secure this for its own meeting, as Fine Gael did in 1957, by making the reservation first and then fixing the election for the following day. At the mass meeting, all the party's chief figures appear and speak.

Campaigns are financed both centrally and locally. The national party headquarters issues a general, nationwide appeal while the local organizations confine themselves to the constituency campaign. Fianna Fáil spends more than the other parties upon printed materials, posters, newspaper advertisements and other costly publicity. The Labour Party has a meager war chest and its candidates can expect little in the way of election materials from the central office.

Candidates are expected to meet as much of their own campaign expenses as they can afford. Fianna Fáil helps out by remitting to the constituency organizations forty percent of all the money they have collected locally for the national party, and the Labour Party gives each of its candidates a small subvention toward his campaign fund. It is not unknown for a candidate to make a personal appeal to a rich constituent. It is well understood, without exchange of promises, that a generous response to this appeal obligates the candidate to do what he can for the donor should the opportunity occur. Fianna Fáil also helps its candidates by insuring their election deposits. This party's expertise in forecasting the precise portion of the vote it will receive is indicated by the fact that out of one hundred and twelve deposits insured by Fianna Fáil in the 1957 general election, only three were lost.

All parties depend heavily upon volunteers to do most of the campaign work. The two major parties enjoy a big advantage over the smaller parties and independent candidates in recruiting volunteers—the Labour Party could always use many more volunteers than it can obtain. In the 1957 election it was unable even to station party watchers at most of the polling places. A Labour Party official, upon what basis it is impossible to say, estimated that superior party organization, advertising, and an ample supply of volunteers may have swelled the vote polled by the two major parties by as much as fifteen percent.

Radio is not as important in Irish political campaigns as it is in larger countries in which fewer voters have a chance to see and hear the candidates and party leaders in person. Nevertheless it is used and in 1957 Radio Éireann assigned the prime hour of 10 P.M. to a series of 16 ten-minute speeches by representatives of various parties. As of April, 1964, there were 543,685 licences for radio or television or both. About 230,000 were combined licences for both services. It is estimated that about 90 percent of all Irish households have a radio while 30 percent of the rural and 60 percent of the urban households have television receivers.[7] The heaviest concentration is in Leinster, including Dublin County. In 1963, radio newscasts accounted for about 18 percent of broadcast time; something under one-quarter of these were given in the Irish language. Television devoted almost one-quarter of its programs to news, public affairs, and religious events and an additional 5 percent to imported documentaries and public affairs programs.[8]

The first general election in which television was used for campaign purposes was that of April 7, 1965. Fourteen ten-minute telecasts were assigned between March 18 and April 4. It was agreed that the Government would present the final telecast and that this would be aired on the Friday before election day. Fianna Fáil had seven spots, Fine Gael had five, and Labour had two. One other telecast was offered to any other party or candidate but this was not claimed. The principal was established that any party with a minimum of seven members in the Dáil should have television time made available to it and so should any party with fewer deputies but nominating at least 15 candidates. If they chose, the parties using television were allowed to split their ten-minute telecasts into 2 five-minute appeals but this was rarely done. In contrast to American custom, the political telecasts were given without charge to parties or candidates and, by law, the Radio Telefís Éireann is forbidden to sell political advertising on a commercial basis, or time in addition to the assigned spots. If parties wish to use film, however, they have to prepare and edit the film at their own expense.

In the case of by-elections the policy is that most are of local concern only and the candidates do not require network exposure. In certain cases, however, political broadcasts are allowed and equal time is given to all candidates.[9]

Posters are still widely used by the two major parties. In the 1965 campaign both used them extensively. In the presidential election campaign Mr. T. F. O'Higgins, the Fine Gael candidate, made an old-fashioned, countrywide sweep with Mrs. O'Higgins, speaking in many places.

The local press is inclined to be editorially impartial as regards the parties, although a popular local candidate may receive endorsement on personal rather than partisan grounds. Evidently such impartiality is due to the fact that the readers are sure to include adherents of all parties whom the editor is careful not to offend. According to Professor Chubb, 4 out of 5 of the more than 60 local newspapers maintained an attitude of neutrality in the 1957 elections.[10] This is an additional reason for newspaper advertising by candidates—to ensure that their meetings and speeches are given due notice in the press.

In former times, volunteer partisans were accustomed to go about with a pail of whitewash and paint election appeals and slogans on any convenient wall or fence. Very often these would be defaced or changed by a political opponent. "Whitewashing" has become fairly rare. Professor Chubb mentions an amuisng example of an old appeal that appeared on a wall near Dublin to "vote for . . ." to which had been added; "and Ireland's dead will rise and curse you." [11] Loudspeakers mounted on trucks are widely employed by candidates nowadays, especially for last-minute appeals in big towns and cities. Music is seldom used except for the brass bands that escort the party leaders in the principal towns.

The law limits campaign expenditures of candidates in borough (urban) contests to four pence per voter and to six pence per voter by a team of candidates if they campaign as a team. In county (rural) constituencies these sums may be increased to five pence and seven pence, halfpenny, respectively. Few candidates spent more than a fraction of this amount according to the sworn returns declared to the returning officers.[12] While such returns may not include, in fact, every penny spent by candidates and their supporters on an election, it appears likely that there is no serious violation of the law and that corruption is not widespread. Few candidates have the means to spend lavishly on campaigns. So far as fraud is employed, it is charged by most commentators against Fianna Fáil. The famous clean sweep made by Sinn Féin, led by De Valera in 1921, when this party gained 124 seats to 4 for the Unionists in the Twenty-six Counties of the present Irish Republic, was accomplished by means of widespread fraud and intimidation.[13] At that moment in Irish history, such tactics were considered laudable and patriotic, justified as political warfare. This tradition has not been entirely forgotten or abandoned.

The method commonly used to increase a party's vote fraudulently is personation. Every Irish voter is sent a postcard indicating his polling place. Party enthusiasts can sometimes induce indifferent nonvoters to surrender these postcards. Such a card, presented at the polling place, is often taken as sufficient proof of identity and personation is thus a simple matter, especially in urban constituencies. It is unusual for parties, even the major ones, to have scrutineers at all the polling places in a district. Sometimes there will be none at all at a particular place and in such cases the personators will have no fear of being challenged, as the poll clerks rarely do so. Where party watchers are present and have reason to suspect personation, they will sometimes challenge voters at random. As a rule, personators are afraid to perjure themselves. The door-to-door canvass is a useful way of learning what voter has just died or gone abroad and therefore whom it is safe to personate.

As already noted, the disorder and violence that punctuated the elections of the civil war period and the following years are a thing of the past.[14] Heckling, when it occurs, is usually good-natured. The election-eve mass meetings in Dublin sometimes provide occasion for more boisterous heckling and even scuffling but no longer are there organized attempts by partisan gangs to break up the meetings of the opposing party as in 1922.

The Election

Voting is by the single transferable vote in places determined by the returning officer, usually in the national school nearest to the voter's residence. There are no absentee ballots allowed except for members of the armed forces. After his name is checked off the list of electors, the voter is given a paper ballot listing alphabetically the names of all candidates, their addresses and occupations. There is no information as to party affiliation. The number of candidates on the ballot may vary from six to fifteen or more depending upon the size of the constituency. The ballot is marked in a booth and to be valid must have no marks other than numbers opposite the names of the candidates. At least one candidate must be chosen and numbered "1." The voter may then proceed to number other choices in sequence. He may not pick a first and, omitting a second choice, indicate a third. The ballot becomes untransferable at the point where the gap in the sequence occurs.

The counting is done for each constituency in a central spot chosen by the returning officer, who inspects the ballot boxes for tampering and oversees the shuffling together of all ballots. Each ballot is then examined and invalid ones discarded. Invalid ballots include those with marks other than numbers or those lacking the identifying mark of the returning officer placed on the outside of the ballot before it is handed to the voter. Valid ballots are then piled according to first choices and each pile is counted. The total of all piles enables the returning officer to determine the quota. This is the number of valid votes divided by the number of seats plus one, to which quotient, one is added.

If there is a long list of candidates it may well happen that none receives the quota for election in first-choice ballots or one barely makes the quota with only a few votes to spare. In this case, the candidate with fewest choices is out of the race and his ballots are transferred to the candidates given second choice on them. This happened after the first count in twelve cases in the 1961 election. If, on the other hand, one or more candidates has received first choice ballots in excess of the quota he is declared elected. All of their ballots are resorted into piles of second choices (unless the second choice has already been elected, in which case the next available unelected choice is used). This resorting is done to avoid the element of chance in the distribution of second choices which might operate if only those ballots were used that happened to be added last to the successful candidate's pile. The second choices are then distributed according to this formula: the surplus ballots of the winner are divided by the number of transferable votes received by him and this gives the fraction of the surplus to be assigned to each second-choice candidate. So, if a winner has received 20,000 first choices on transferable ballots and the quota is 10,000 the fraction to be redistributed the first time around will be $\frac{10,000}{20,000} = \frac{1}{2}$. Assuming that the second choices have gone to candidates X (6,000), Y (5,000), and Z (9,000), half of these will be given to each. X will get 3,000 more votes, which are physically removed from the pigeonhole and added to his pile, Y will get 2,500 more, and Z will get 4,500 more. Assuming that Z needs only 4,000 votes to make the quota, the extra 500 he does not need are distributed according to third choice. If the name of one already elected appears on a ballot as the choice for the current distribution, it is passed over and the next choice is used instead. After the surplus ballots of the first candidate to be elected have been distributed, those of the next one to win are also distributed and so forth. If after all have been assigned there are still places to be filled, the candidate with the smallest number of ballots is declared by the returning officer to be defeated and his votes are all redistributed according to the second choice indicated on them. It is not unusual, if there are many candidates, for a situation to arise in which the non-eliminated candidates equal in number the places remaining to be filled even though one or two of them may not yet have reached the quota. In this case, there is no more counting and they are declared elected.[15]

An example of the actual count is provided by that in a Wicklow by-election reported in the *Irish Times* of March 16, 1968 (p. 11). The electorate numbered 36,658. The valid poll came to 26,293 ballots. Only two members were to be returned so the quota came to 13,147. There were five counts taken with these results:

NAME AND PARTY OF CANDIDATE	FIRST COUNT	SECOND COUNT	THIRD COUNT	FOURTH COUNT	FIFTH COUNT	RESULTS
Nancy O'Neill (Fianna Fáil)	9,788	+41	+116	+398	+1,707 =	12,050 *elected*
Godfrey Timmins (Fine Gael)	8,035	+54	+191	+443	+3,868 =	12,596 *elected*
Liam Kavanagh (Labour)	5,761	+35	+ 96	+905		= eliminated after 4th count
Seamus Costello (Sinn Féin)	2,009	+15	+ 57			= eliminated after 3rd count
Kevin McLeavy (Liberal)	509	+17				= eliminated after 2nd count
James T. Tallon (Independent)	191					= eliminated after 1st count

It will be noted that in this case neither winner actually reached the quota—there were 1,222 nontransferable votes because that number of voters failed to indicate preferences for all candidates.

Recent Irish elections have been tame affairs. In 1957 Thomas P. Ronan, *The New York Times* Dublin correspondent, wrote, "A casual visitor to Dublin today would scarcely know that a general election campaign was taking place." [16] As Basil Chubb observed, "Irish elections in these days are usually very dull and this one was no exception." [17] The same general atmosphere of public indifference was true of the October, 1961, general election when both major parties advocated entering the European Common Market. Every voter is aware that no great issues divide the two principal parties and that neither of them can, at the moment, do anything concrete to end the partition of Ireland—the one issue that could arouse popular enthusiasm. This is one reason, perhaps the principal reason, why local popularity rather than party affiliation is often the explanation of a candidate's success.

Apart from the candidates who owe their electoral appeal to local popularity, the voting strength of the major parties is remarkably stable. The floating vote is small in Irish elections. It would appear that voters choose a party and remain loyal to it. Younger members of a family tend to accept the party loyalties of their elders. One factor in this voting pattern may be the importance to the individual, and the cohesion, of the primary family, especially in rural Ireland. Family influence upon voting behavior is powerful even in societies such as the United States, in which family life takes up a smaller proportion of the individual's daily routine and the younger members are likely to leave home and form other ties at an earlier age than is the case in Ireland, except for the young people who emigrate and do not become Irish voters. Family influence is doubtless the most important single factor in the party loyalties of Irish voters.[18] An example of such persistent and hereditary party loyalty can be observed in the rural South, where Labour Party candidates have been elected ever since the days of the Land and Labour League of the late nineteenth century.

Once elected, the new T.D. becomes entitled to an expense allowance. Originally £30 per month, this allowance has been increased several times. In June, 1968, the Dáil increased the allowance from £624 to £2,500 per annum. Although the allowance is considered to be an indemnity for expenses and for time taken from the deputy's regular employment, rather than a salary, it is often the deputy's sole or chief source of income. Since 1938 special salaries have been paid to the leaders of the two leading opposition parties. Of course the ministers receive salaries. The June, 1968, increases included a rise in the taoiseach's annual pay from £3,300 to £5,000. Other ministers' salaries rose to £3,500, and parliamentary secretaries' to £2,250. Deputies are also given vouchers entitling them to first-class railway travel between their homes, constituencies, and Dublin when this travel is required by their duties as deputy. If they use their own cars they are given a mileage allowance instead.

It used to be maintained that the occupation most likely to lead to a candidacy and election to the Dáil was that of publican. The publican is always well known in his community. His business brings him into frequent and friendly contact with most of the adult males in his neighborhood and he is often in a position to leave the routine conduct of his business to family or employees and take the necessary time for electioneering. Certainly this was the case in the days of the old Parliamentary Party of Parnell and his successors. It has been much less true since the establishment of the Free State. As might be expected, a record of participation in revolutionary activity was almost a prerequisite to election in 1922 and after. It has remained a consideration to this day even though time has removed many of the heroes of the struggle for independence and young men have become important who were born long after the fight was over. Even so, as late as 1948, 63 T.D.'s, or 43 percent of the total membership of the Dáil could claim this distinction.[19]

In general, it can be stated that many deputies serve for long periods, that they are nearly all residents and, in many cases, natives of the constituency from which they are returned. About one-fifth of the members have had a university or professional education. This is well above the national average but much lower than that of the British House of Commons in which, in 1959, over half of the entire membership had had university training.[20] The number of deputies with a secondary school education varies between 50 and about 60 percent of all, and the rest, with only a primary school education, compose 40 to 45 percent of the total.

The relatively underdeveloped economy of Ireland is reflected in the considerable number of enterprising and successful men who have more than one occupation. A heavily industrialized economy is likely to produce a greater proportion of individuals with single and highly specialized skills and employment. It is not astonishing, therefore, to find that many deputies combine two or more occupations. To own and operate both a farm and a shop is common. It appears obvious that a farmer-shopkeeper will be in an advantageous position to become widely acquainted with his rural constituency. It is often difficult to decide the category in which a particular deputy belongs. Lawyers, whether barristers or solicitors, often have important interests outside of their profession, and so do physicians. Farming is represented in close approximation to its incidence among the total population. About 38 percent of the deputies in 1955 were farmers, many of whom had other occupations as well. This compares with about 32 percent of the working population of Ireland who are employed on the land. Business and professional men are more numerous in the Dáil than in the general population. Together they constitute about 40 percent of the deputies. Working class members, excluding farmers, are few in number. There were only 16 deputies in this category in 1955 although there were also 8 trades union officers.[21] Retired persons and housewives numbered 9 in this same year and 9 deputies had no known occupation. For these 18 persons it is possible that the annual expense allowance provided the principal income.

One reason for the high incidence of professional and self-employed individuals among the deputies can be found in the fact that it is possible for such to continue their normal occupations in most cases and not suffer a diminution of income. For them, a political career does not mean a financial sacrifice.

The weakness of the Labour Party is reflected in the small number of trades unionists and employees in the Dáil. An examination of all election candidates as compared with those who are elected leads to the conclusion that urban voters prefer the more educated and more successful business and professional candidates who, to be sure, are likely to be more skilled in the arts of persuasion than are the working-class candidates or that the best potential candidates among the working class are unlikely to stand for election because of the drop in income that would be entailed if they had to leave their jobs.[22]

Certainly the Irish electorate does not display communal class voting behavior. It is conceivable that there is a disposition on the part of the voters to prefer candidates who seem to have leadership qualifications over those who are merely typical of the average working man.

Fianna Fáil in 1955 had almost twice as many farmer deputies as had Fine Gael, whereas the latter had twice as many professional men. They were about equal as regards business men. The largest block of working-class deputies were Fianna Fáil members. There were 9 such, whereas the Labour Party had only 4 in addition to 1 farmer, 1 business man, 8 trades union officials, 3 housewives or retired persons, and 2 deputies without recorded occupations.

Notes

1. The legal provisions relating to nominations and elections are found in the (1937) Constitution of Éire, Article 16, and by a series of statutes, the basic ones being the Electoral Act, 1923, and the Prevention of Electoral Abuses Act, 1923.
2. In the 1961 general election, Fianna Fáil nominated 4 candidates in 7 of the 9 five-member constituencies and 3 candidates in 2 districts. Fine Gael nominated 4 candidates in 4 of these constituencies, 3 in 4, and 2 in 1. Of the 34 Fianna Fáil candidates, 22 were successful, and of the 30 Fine Gael candidates, 16 won seats.
3. Butler (ed.), *op. cit.*, p. 197.
4. *Ibid.*, pp. 202, 203.
5. Coogan, *op. cit.*, pp. 140, 141.
6. Butler (ed.), *op. cit.*, pp. 135, 136.
7. Irish Consulate, *Documents on Ireland*, No. 16, May, 1964.
8. *Statistical Abstract of Ireland* (1964).
9. Information from Radio Telefís Éireann.
10. Butler (ed.), *op. cit.*, p. 205. In the 1961 general election not a single multimember constituency returned a solid party slate.
11. *Ibid.*, p. 206 n.
12. *Ibid.*, p. 204.
13. See McCracken, *op. cit.*, pp. 74, 75, who mentions a number of incidents of intimidation, armed violence, and fraud, as reported in the *Irish Times*.
14. As when, according to a journalist, the election director for Cumann na nGaedheal, Edward Lawler, passed out brass knuckles to his election workers. See Coogan, *op. cit.*, p. 68.
15. McCracken, *op. cit.*, p. 69, quotes the *Irish Times*, June 15, 1927, to the effect that 48 deputies were elected without reaching the quota in that June, 1927, election. *The official Election Results and Transfer of Votes in General Election (October, 1961)* indicates that 29 deputies

were so elected at that election. McCracken, *op. cit.*, pp. 67–72, gives
a complete description of the Irish transferable vote system, which is
also described in James Hogan, *Election and Representation* (Cork,
1945); J. F. S. Ross, *The Irish Electoral System* (London, 1959); and
M. Lawless, "The Dáil Electoral System," *Administration*, V, No. 1,
57–74.
16. Dispatch to *The New York Times*, March, 1957.
17. Butler (ed.), *op. cit.*, p. 183.
18. See McCloskey and Dahlgren, "Primary group influence on party
    loyalty," APSR, LIII, No. 3 (September, 1959), 757–76. These political
    scientists concluded that "the family is the key reference group which
    transmits, indoctrinates and sustains the political loyalties of its mem-
    bers."
19. McCracken, *op. cit.*, table, p. 89. This work has a series of tables, pp.
    86–99, analyzing the composition of the Dáil in various ways from 1922
    to 1948.
20. According to D. E. Butler and Richard Rose, *British General Election
    of 1959* (London, 1960), 218 of the 365 Conservative and 101 of the
    258 Labour M.P.'s had attended a university.
21. See analysis and table by a journalist in "Dáil Deputies: Their Other
    Lives," *Irish Times*, June 14, 1955.
22. According to the analysis in the *Irish Times* mentioned in the pre-
    ceding footnote, 6 out of every 10 farmers, businessmen, and profes-
    sionals who are nominated are elected, whereas fewer than 3 out of
    every 10 employees who secure nomination are successful at the polls.

IX

NONPARTY INFLUENCES AND PRESSURE GROUPS

The pre-Union Parliament of Ireland had a simple task. Its members represented and considered it their duty to represent the landed interest. Its electorate was dominated or easily managed by the landlords. In any case, the members of the Irish House of Commons were of the Old Whig persuasion, to use Professor Beer's term.[1] They felt no obligation at all to consult their constituents on matters of policy. The Irish Parliament, indeed, had a much simpler task than its British counterpart because the latter had a more complicated collection of interests to evaluate and reconcile.

The Free State Parliament at the start of its existence was embroiled in a civil war. Everything had to be subordinated to winning the war, reestablishing civic order, and creating a political system that would be legitimate in the view of the great majority of the Irish people. Once this was accomplished, it had to try, as must all freely elected legislatures, to act as arbitrator and conciliator between the conflicting interests of its society. The claims and desires of various segments of that society had to be examined and reconciled as far as possible with those of other segments. As a twentieth-century representative democracy, the Irish political system was based upon the assumption that the State must provide welfare services, low-cost housing, and other services. It was generally agreed that the Government has the duty to concern itself with the distribution of the national income so as to produce a just division.

Under such circumstances there is every reason for those who share a particular interest to bring pressure to bear upon government in whatever way may be most effective and to create formal organizations for this purpose if such do not already exist. Trades unions, farmers' associations, chambers of commerce, manufacturers' associations, and other groups are vitally concerned with tax and tariff schedules, the establishment of government enterprises, and other economic policies.

Labor

At first glance it would seem that organized Irish labor should be one of the most powerful of all pressure groups in securing favorable government action on policies desired by the Trades Union Council. Early in the history of labor organizations in Ireland, as indicated above,[2] Irish trades unionists chose the British rather than the American approach. They formed a labor party and took to the hustings in the attempt to elect a delegation of deputies numerous enough to influence legislative action directly rather than, as in the United States, to avoid identification with any party and to use their voting strength to reward the friends of labor regardless of party affiliation and to employ lobbying tactics at the legislature. The choice made in Ireland was due, no doubt, to the socialist ideology of early labor leaders and to the relative success of the British Labour Party. In Ireland, however, the ILP enjoyed only a modest success and the rank-and-file union members have never given it anything approaching general support. The only hope Irish labor could have of exerting much influence on policies would be by the election of a delegation holding the balance of power in a divided Dáil. The major party leaders are aware of the amount of working-class support they can expect to receive and ordinarily do not feel obliged to pay much attention to the views of ILP leaders. Indeed, although leaders of both major parties have always given lip service to the needs and aspirations of the working class, none has been responsive to specific requests by the leaders of organized labor. Johnson's emphatic demand for government action to improve wages and attack the problem of unemployment made on the floor of the Dáil in January, 1922, was answered by President Griffith with an assurance that he understood the problem and would appoint a committee to "try and deal with this question." [3] It would not appear that any committee was appointed or any other action taken. Subsequently, members of the national executive of the Labour Party twice met with President Griffith and four of his ministers and made specific requests, most of which were either refused or ignored.[4] This was at a time when labor and its leaders had something of a moral claim to recognition and influence because of the part they had taken in the struggle for independence. Labor had no better luck with De Valera. In fact, the major parties could afford to ignore the requests of the labor leaders because the latter had a meager political following. Both major parties were unimpressed by labor's economic arguments and were not inclined to accept labor's policies on their merits.

Although the ILP had participated in several governments, first supporting Fianna Fáil in 1932, 1937, and 1943 and then the Fine Gael interparty coalitions of 1948 to 1951 and 1954 to 1957, the result of such cooperation had been most disappointing. Labor had been unable to exert any significant influence over policies. No doubt this was an important factor in the decision taken by the Labour Party Conference in 1957 to the effect that "the Labour Party will not again take part in an Inter-Party Government but will remain in opposition until it receives a parliamentary majority."

It is tempting to speculate upon the amount of influence Irish labor might have wielded had its leaders chosen the American pattern. The electoral system in Ireland would have militated against the labor vote being as influential in affecting elections as it would be under the single-member-district, plurality election system. In any case, the socialist bent of the early Irish labor leaders, not strongly supported by most union members, made cooperation with nonsocialist parties difficult. As noted in Chapter VII, internecine feuds plagued the ILP and tended to confirm trades union members in their continued allegiance to one of the major parties. But having chosen the electoral route to power, Irish labor leaders deprived themselves of the alternative of pressures upon government enforced by the ability to swing the labor vote to the party more favorably inclined toward the acceptance of labor's demands.

Farmers

Ireland's economy has long been primarily agricultural and one might expect the Irish farmers to be able to exert a predominating influence upon any policy in which they were interested. Davitt's Land League proved how powerful this influence could be when the farmers presented a united front. But the land reforms turned Ireland into a country of small proprietors and thenceforward Irish farmers in general began to display the social and economic conservatism as well as the narrow parochialism of rural property-holders. Like the rest of Irish society they were split over the treaty issue and continued to support one or other of the two major parties formed over this issue. Farmers' parties, discussed above,[5] have never been able to become more than minor, essentially satellite political parties.

As one might expect, there are a large number of agricultural organizations and societies in Ireland. Many of these are concerned with a precise specialty and not with the farm interest in general. At times they oppose each other's proposals in the interest of their own particular group.[6]

The most important general agricultural society is the National Farmers' Association. It was an outgrowth of Macra na Feirme (Scions of the Soil), which had been founded in 1945 and was particularly interested in the improvement of farming techniques. The National Farmers' Association absorbed Macra na Feirme and other smaller farm associations when it was created in 1955. By 1959 it had 770 branches, each consisting of from 30 to 50 farmers in a neighborhood. The local branches hold monthly meetings. They choose representatives to a county branch and the national council is chosen from the executives of the county branches. The national council in turn picks the national executive, which is the effective leadership group of the NFA. It meets every two weeks or oftener. It appoints subcommittees, each concerned with a specific product—beef cattle, sheep, pigs, and so forth. The chairmen are in constant touch with the Department of Agriculture.

The national council and the executive committee keep in touch with agricultural developments abroad and try to assess their effects on Irish agriculture. They also meet with industrial, banking, and trade union officials to acquaint them with the farmers' views. It is claimed that such a conference with bankers in 1958 was responsible for easing the farm credit situation.

The executive committee does a good deal of educational work as well, sends speakers to meetings of farmers, and sponsors agricultural courses for farmers' sons.

It is listened to with respect by most ministers of agriculture although it cannot claim to influence all government policies in this field. Other pressures too are brought to bear on government, such as those of the transport and exporting interests, which are not always in accord with the views of the NFA.

The NFA publishes a yearbook containing a report as to the accomplishments of the past year and a summary of policies for future action. It usually contains a statement in praise of the association by the minister of agriculture. The 1962 yearbook was devoted to "world agriculture and farmers' organizations" and contained articles on agriculture in twenty-one countries throughout the world. This is characteristic of the educational aspect of the NFA, which tries to be much more than a self-interested pressure group, and to educate Irish farmers about their role as citizens in Irish and international society.

Since 1961 the NFA has had an Oireachtas Committee which has the duty of reviewing all proposed bills that affect agriculture. The breadth of its concern in public affairs is demonstrated by its action in 1964 urging the Government to place more restrictions upon the alienation of Irish land to Germans. The Chairman and

Secretary of this committee visited London to study the methods of the British National Farmers' Union's Parliamentary Committee. The Oireachtas Committee reports to the NFA membership on legislation before the Dáil or Senate that may affect farmers and acts as a lobby to keep T.D.'s and senators informed about the NFA viewpoint. The claims of Irish farmers to a fair share of the national income in a period of rising prices and wage increases were outlined in a document on farm income drawn up by NFA officials and presented to the Government. This policy was first endorsed by the national council of the NFA and then at the annual convention, attended by over two thousand delegates.

A pressure tactic used recently for the first time by the NFA was the approval by the national council of mass protest demonstrations by farmers against rising rates (local taxes). There was also discussion of a possible farm commodity strike—the refusal to sell specified produce which would at once affect city consumers.[7]

It has been difficult to organize Irish farmers. They have been suspicious of associations which they fear may be manipulated by a few men for selfish ends. Not since the Land League days have the farmers been truly united. However, the NFA policy as regards farm income seemed to arouse general enthusiasm because it proposed farm subsidies on a variable scale, the smaller farms to receive proportionately higher subsidies. As ninety percent of all Irish farms are small holdings, this policy was popular with the great majority of farmers.

The NFA has been relatively successful in influencing government policies. Certainly it has been more successful than the farmers' parties and more effective than the Trades Union Council in the latter's attempts to obtain a positive response to the demands of organized labor.

But the NFA is not unchallenged. The Ministry of Agriculture set up the National Agricultural Council to enlighten the minister as to the views of the farmers. This was denounced at once by the NFA as a "tool of the Minister" rather than an independent and genuine representative of the farmers. When the Beet Growers' Association (the oldest of the individual product associations) accepted two seats on the NAC in 1966, the NFA sponsored a rival body, the Irish Sugar Beet and Vegetable Producers' Association. This new organization attracted a number of members in some areas. The government-owned Irish Sugar Company found itself in an embarrassing position. It came to the conclusion that, for 1968, it could not negotiate sugar beet prices with either body. Later, the two associations agreed to hold an election for officers of the BGA under BGA rules, but with all beet growers, members or not, eligible to vote. This agreement resulted in an electorate of more than 22,000 and both the ISBVPA and the BGA electioneered vigorously.[8]

The influential position of the NFA and the lengths to which the Government will go to meet its wishes are exemplified by the agreement of the taoiseach to meet with T. J. Maher, President of the NFA, and hold conversations "preliminary to early consultation" on the third Programme for Economic Expansion, and, at Mr. Maher's insistence, to exclude Mr. Blaney, the Minister of Agriculture from these conversations.[9]

The Civil Service

All special interest groups sometimes find it more effective to approach the permanent administrators in a department, rather than the political head, the minister. The minister, not conversant with many of the day-to-day aspects of his department's work, must very often rely upon the advice of the permanent Civil Service in making policy decisions.

So far there have been no important scandals in the Civil Service and there is no evidence that the Civil Service has been corrupted by favor-seekers. The Cosgrave Government deserves the credit for maintaining the tradition of a nonpartisan Civil Service recruited by examinations administered by independent civil service commissions at both the local and the national level. This practice has forestalled the development of a partisan spoils system in most areas of the public service.[10]

The worst that can be said about the Civil Service is that its officials, as is the case in other countries, sometimes become routine and hidebound in their attitudes and that, being human, they are subject to error. During World War II an enterprising black-marketeer discovered that Great Britain imposed no customs duty on mincemeat and that the official definition of mincemeat was "a mixture of sugar and fruit." He bought great quantities of Irish sugar at the low, controlled price, had it mixed dry with Greek currants, and sent it to England as "mincemeat." There he screened off the currants, sold the sugar on the black market, and shipped the currants back to Ireland to repeat the procedure. As a result of this individual's dealings, the Irish Sugar Company (a statutory body) had to buy foreign sugar at high prices to replenish its stocks. Within a few months the cost to the company, and therefore to the Irish taxpayer, was about £200,000. This operation had been undertaken with the approval of a civil servant who imagined that he was stimulating Irish industry, and the directors of the Irish Sugar Company had to appeal to higher levels of the Government to stop the flow of Irish "mincemeat" to England.

A significant example of the influence which a civil servant may have upon key policies is provided by the Whitaker Report.[11] In December, 1967, Thomas K. Whitaker, Secretary of the Department of Finance and Head of the Civil Service, suggested to his minister that he be authorized to prepare and present a report containing a scheme for an integrated program of national economic development. The completed report pointed out the weak spots in the Irish economy, the need to anticipate unemployment, methods whereby savings might be increased, and so forth. The report became the basis for the first official Programme for Economic Expansion, inaugurated late in 1958. Whether or not this was a prime factor in Ireland's immediate economic advance, the fact remains that the Gross National Product began to climb at a rate about twice that of the years before 1958.

The Catholic Church

It has long been noted by sociologists and political scientists that institutionalized human associations tend to acquire social power and to increase its extent.[12] This is true of all sorts of associations, whatever the specific reason for their original formation. It is true of business corporations, universities, criminal gangs, and churches. Under special circumstances an ostensibly nonpolitical association may assume political control of an area whether it becomes identified formally with the Government of that area or remains the actual power-holder behind a facade of the traditional institutions of government. A power-wielding association of this kind is clearly to be distinguished from a pressure group in aims and methods. "Incipient feudalism" is a permanent threat to state supremacy. This threat is handled in totalitarian states by the strict control of all associations from churches to sport clubs. In states organized on the principle of limited government, a sphere of freedom from state control for both individuals and associations is a necessary accompaniment of the pluralistic society. At the same time, if a particular association is virtually identical in membership with the nation itself, there is always the possibility that this association may supersede the official government, especially if the association has claims to divine authority. This is the basic reason for the church-state conflict in many countries, for the medieval contest between pope and emperor, and the resolution of the conflict by the coalescence of the two associations and the priest-king institution in some societies. Another solution is found in those societies with a variety of religions and general acceptance of the proposition that religion is a matter of individual decision having no connection with national identification or political loyalty. This is a relatively recent concept, a product of the Reformation which broke the unity of the Christian Church and subsequently of the individualism and skepticism of the Enlightenment. Even in societies with many different religious denominations and a tradition of religious liberty, churches, when their adherents are numerous, can and do exert influence on government policy by pressure-group tactics.

Ireland was virtually exempt from the ideological ferment caused by the Renaissance, the Reformation, and the Enlightenment. The Roman Catholic Church was long the only important association and institution that the Irish people could regard as truly Irish and truly theirs. It would be an oversimplification to say that to be Irish was to be Roman Catholic. Nearly all the early leaders in the struggle for Irish freedom were Protestants: Tone, Emmett, Parnell. These Irish patriots inspired fanatical loyalty among the Catholic masses. At the same time, for most Irish people, their church gave them a sense of community, social identity, national dignity, and patriotism. This was the case even though the hierarchy and the clergy in general often did not support individual patriots and their efforts. This identification of religion and patriotism inspired a modern critic to write: "I am only interested in a literature which would immortalise that fusion of religion and patriotism which gave to our Irish consciousness a rare quality not to be found among—say—Italian, French or Spanish Catholics." [13]

As Arland Ussher has written:

> Thus in Ireland—and in Ireland alone, perhaps, of Catholic nations—the priesthood have continuously been united in sentiment with the people rather than with the gentry or the Government; in their clergy the Irish have had that rare thing, a popular aristocracy or elite of learning, a class to speak for them and suffer with them.[14]

This is an understandable situation in view of the alien race and religion of the gentry and the Government before 1921 and the fact that the clergy, including the hierarchy, sprang from ordinary Irish folk.

One would expect the Roman Catholic Church to constitute an important locus of power within Irish society, to exert strong influence upon the policies of government, and possibly to have, at times, a controlling influence.

Many Protestants in Northern Ireland firmly believe this to be the case and advance it as their principal argument against union with the Republic. IRA outrages, of course, strengthened this belief even though the IRA was proscribed in the Republic and was condemned by the clergy. Many Protestant Ulstermen foresaw union with the Republic as meaning the suppression of their religion and various kinds of discrimination practiced against them by the overwhelming Catholic majority. Although there is little in the history of the IFS and the Republic to lend credence to this fear, it is conceivable that an all-Ireland state might see the rise of religious political communalism to the disadvantage of effective representative government. The Ulster Protestants, judging by their past behavior, would be likely to adhere to religious communalism in politics and this might inspire a counter-communalism.

To understand the relation of the Catholic Church to political life in the Republic of Ireland it is helpful to look at some aspects of the hundred and sixty-odd years of Irish history since the Act of Union, 1800. At the beginning of this period the Church had only two aims: first and most important, to secure and retain the freedom to perform its duties, teach its doctrines, and insure the continuance of its faith among the Irish people; second, to discourage, to the best of its ability, the tendencies toward violence and social revolution which not only involved sinful acts but might lead in the end, as they had in France quite recently, to anticlericalism and damage to the Church and its authority.

The undeviating devotion of the clergy and hierarchy to these goals explains the fact that the Church did not, as an institution, play an important part in the struggle for Irish independence nor provide many leaders for Irish nationalist movements. Indeed, it might be described as nonpolitical as far as Irish politics were concerned in the early part of the nineteenth century. It seemed to the hierarchy that the best way to accomplish its ends was to convince the British authorities that there was no longer any trace of Jacobite subversion among Irish Catholics and that their loyalty to the Crown and the Protestant Succession entitled them to full membership in the British nation. In January, 1799, the Catholic archbishops and bishops passed a resolution approving the requirement of a British loyalty test to be applied to Roman Catholic bishops before their appointment to Irish sees—in effect, a Crown veto over such appointments.[15]

It may be noted, however, that individual priests took a part, and sometimes an important part, in virtually every rising against the British connection. For instance, one of the leaders of the Rebellion of 1798 was a Wexford curate, Father John Murphy, who was active despite the fact that this rising was inspired by the French Revolution and its republican principles.[16]

The Act of Union, by which the Protestant- and landlord-dominated Irish legislature was abolished and which gave Irish representation at Westminster, had the approval of most of the Catholic hierarchy. This approval was given because of the assurance given by Prime Minister Pitt that Catholic Emancipation would be an immediate consequence of the Union. When the king's obstinate refusal to agree prevented Pitt from making good on his promise, Anglo-Irish relations were again embittered.[17] It was under these circumstances that Daniel O'Connell founded his Catholic Association, the history of which as outlined in Chapter I need not be repeated here.

It was natural that the Catholic clergy should be deeply concerned about the disestablishment of the Church of Ireland. This raised some difficult theological problems as well as the legal and social questions about the disposal of ecclesiastical property.[18] In the outcome, the Irish Church decided in favor of that liberal objective (anathema to the Pope at the time) of a "free church in a free society." As the elections of 1868 approached, the episcopate as well as the parish clergy electioneered vigorously for Gladstonian Liberals, with such vigor, in fact, that undue influence was charged. Bishop Gillooly of Sligo announced in the pulpit that any who voted for the Tory candidate "would be considered rotten branches and should be lopped off," and that they would have to "make reparations." At Drogheda a mob led by a priest was said to have stoned Tory voters. As a result, this election was invalidated.[19]

Clerical electoral activity could hardly go beyond this, but disestablishment, duly passed in 1869, did not have the effect of inducing the clergy to withdraw from politics. To the contrary, they now felt relieved of certain legal restraints, such as inspection of their activities by government officials, and had greater freedom to speak their minds on everything, including politics. They openly embraced the cause of Irish nationalism and soon became the political as much as the spiritual leaders in their parishes. In their political aspects many priests could be compared only to political "bosses." Better able to raise money than anyone else, the priest tended to become so indispensable to the party that he had the most influential voice in party counsels and could often name the candidate. This leadership was natural enough. Usually the priest was the most educated and respected native Irish Nationalist in the parish. In rural districts, especially, his views would be in complete harmony with those of the small-holders who made up the bulk of the population, who were pious Catholics, ardent Nationalists, and conservative in their ideas about property. During the years when Parnell dominated the Irish political scene with strong clerical support, many priests assumed the dominating position formerly held by the landlord and simply ordered the voters to support a particular candidate. Some priests believed it to be their duty to provide political leadership. One Maynooth professor taught that a priest in charge of an ignorant congregation should instruct them in politics and that the parishioners would have a moral duty to vote as instructed. Not all Maynooth professors agreed with this view.[20]

As noted previously, the clergy sometimes did more than advise their congregation. Some threatened with spiritual penalties those who failed to heed their instructions. In 1872 a number of Galway clergy had thus intimidated those who were inclined to vote for the Unionist candidate and in this electioneering had the backing of the bishops. The defeated Unionist filed a petition charging undue influence and as a result the Bishop of Clonfert was brought to trial under the Corrupt Practices Act of 1854 but acquitted for lack of evidence.[21] The judge who investigated the charges found ample evidence of undue influence and issued a scathing denunciation of clerical interference in politics that produced a vigorous reaction among Catholic clergy and laity in Ireland.

The latter part of the nineteenth century was a period of great activity for the Catholic Church in Ireland. Many convents, churches, and schools were built at this time. Education was a matter of vital interest to the Church. In the view of the clergy it was not a matter of political or public concern but a matter for family and Church control. National schools, therefore, represented a danger to the faith so long as they were under government regulation. At this time they made no distinction between Protestant and Catholic students. Bible passages read in school were chosen carefully by the Protestant Archbishop of Dublin to avoid anything likely to have a sectarian interpretation. The Catholic bishops regarded this as a subtle attempt to introduce ecumenism and even proselytization.[22] As the earlier discussion of Irish education has shown, this battle was eventually won by the Catholic Church.

The reaction of the Catholic Church to the Galway undue influence cases was to caution the clergy against the behavior which had led to the inquiry and court action. This had the effect of moderating clerical political activity but not of stopping it. This was, after all, the "era of clericalism" when the Catholic Church was "the dominant political power except in Northeast Ulster" for a period of some twenty-five years.[23]

Also, in 1872, a change was made in the election procedure. An Act of Parliament provided for the use of the secret ballot in place of the public, voice vote that had been used hitherto. Unquestionably this undercut the ability of the landlords to dictate the votes of their tenants. Probably it did not much affect clerical influence, which relied upon spiritual rather than economic sanctions. One priest is said to have threatened to use the confessional if necessary to find out how his parishioners had voted.[24] Clerical activity at elections was less obtrusive after the passage of the ballot act. One reason for this was the fact that the act had greatly increased the number of polling places from four to about twenty in each county, on the average. This made it much more difficult for a priest to shepherd his flock at the polls. Clerical control of nominations also diminished when the Nationalist Party, instead of accepting nominations from county groups, chose its candidates at a national caucus of the party held in Dublin.

As already mentioned in Chapter I, when the clergy of all ranks threw their full weight behind the condemnation of Parnell and his supporters after the divorce scandal, there is no doubt that they played a major role in the destruction of the parliamentary party as Parnell had built it. Their subsequent denunciation of the Fenians also diminished Fenian influence, especially in the rural parishes.

After the Irish Free State had become well established the clergy no longer had the same reasons as before to be active in politics. They had generally supported the Free State Government during the civil war and had no fault to find with the legislation passed by that government regarding divorce, contraception, and the censorship of immoral publications. De Valera was disliked because of his anti-treaty stand and the civil war, so that for some years thereafter Cosgrave's party received many more clerical votes than did Fianna Fáil. Eventually it became evident that Fianna Fáil was not revolutionary and that both major parties, almost totally Catholic in membership, were equally unlikely to sponsor policies offensive to the Church. There remained no good reason, certain no reason in theology or morality, to favor one party over the other or engage in partisan activities.

In his study of Irish parties in the Free State period, Professor Moss had little to say about the Catholic Church. He wrote: "The Roman Catholic Church, as such, does not participate in politics except when, occasionally, the bishops condemn activities which they feel have an immoral character." [25]

As a generalization, this statement is still correct as regards party politics. As time passed, the party allegiances formed during the struggle over the treaty became traditional. Some are even older, such as the Labour Party strength in certain southern constituencies, which dates back to the days of the Land and Labour League. These party allegiances are firmly, even obstinately held and widely distributed, so that there is no parish in Ireland without faithful supporters of two or more parties. No Irish politician since Parnell could command such fervent personal loyalty as Eamon de Valera. No other had such a measure of charisma, to use Max Weber's coinage. A Connaught farmer is quoted as having said: "If he pulled the bed out from under me, I'd still vote for Dev." Nevertheless, even in his home county of Clare, De Valera could never secure the election of the entire Fianna Fáil list of candidates. Any priest who used the pulpit to electioneer for one party over others would be certain to offend some of his parishioners and probably receive a reprimand from his bishop.

The priest, of course, is often an influential person in the community and it is safe to assume that when his advice is sought privately on political matters, he will give it, but he will do so as a citizen with no claim to speak for the Church. How often this is done and how influential it may be, it is impossible to say. Presumably only those who are perplexed are likely to turn to the priest for advice.[26]

The use of "church-gate" meetings on Sunday by all parties for electioneering and fund raising has been mentioned already. The clergy do not forbid or interfere with these meetings unless the bishop has denied the privilege of holding them to all parties and candidates because of a church-building or other fund-raising campaign of his own or for some other nonpolitical reason. Here again, clerical neutrality prevails.

The concern and involvement of the Church with secular education at all levels has been treated previously.[27] As noted, there are virtually no truly nondenominational schools in Ireland. A result is the segregation of the non-Catholic from the Catholic population, not only during their formative years as primary school children, but also during their secondary and college education, for the most part. As Arland Ussher, scion of an ancient Ascendancy family, has written about the non-Catholic Irish citizen: "The life of his country is an intricate pattern of fasts and festivals, pilgramages and retreats, in which he has no part." He feels himself to belong to an alien society, an outsider as far as the great majority of his fellow citizens are concerned. Nor is it easy for him to discuss fundamental, philosophical questions with his Catholic friends because their views are so completely molded by religious dogma.[28]

A seeming paradox is that in this most Catholic of countries there has never been a clerical political party after the pattern of such parties as the Italian Christian Democratic Party or its predecessor, *Il Partito Popolare*. The nearest approach to such a party was the Irish Christian Front of 1936. This was a militant

Catholic lay organization founded by Patrick Belton, a veteran of the Easter Rising. Belton had a varied political career but finally allied himself with General O'Duffy. The Irish Christian Front was essentially an auxiliary of O'Duffy's Blue Shirt forces. It may be that the absence of any anticlerical party as antagonist was one reason for the failure of the Front to develop into a political party. It supported certain candidates but did not nominate any under its own name and faded from the scene along with the Blue Shirts.

Another seeming paradox is clerical neutrality as regards Protestant candidates for election to the Oireachtas. There have always been some Protestant members in both houses of parliament in both Free State and Republic. In 1953 there were four Protestants in the Dáil, one of whom was a minister in the Fianna Fáil cabinet. No Protestant could possibly be elected if there was a religious communal voting pattern among the electorate. Spokesmen for the major parties refrain from any reference to a candidate's religion or any statement likely to reinforce Orange prejudice against the Republic. Neither clergy or laity any longer have reason to fear Protestant political power.

Church neutrality in the party struggle does not imply neutrality in any question affecting what the clergy consider to be matters of faith or morality. The notoriously broad literary and theatrical censorship is administered by government agencies but along lines satisfactory to the clergy. The Censorship of Publications Act (1929) authorizes the seizure and suppression of indecent or obscene publications, including those advocating abortion or artificial methods of birth control. It is generally believed that this law was drafted with clerical assistance. The act set up an unpaid censorship board of five members to advise the minister of justice as to works it believes should be prohibited from public sale. An appeal against such a ban may be made to the minister by the editor, publisher, author, or five members of the Oireachtas. The board, for its part, seems to rely mainly upon alert citizens to draw its attention to books that should be suppressed. The Irish Censorship Board has often been ridiculed for banning works by many of the most celebrated and respected British and American authors, but in so doing it appears to reflect the views of a substantial part of the Irish public. Banned books of quality, however, are usually obtainable "under the counter," so those who decry the censorship and those who support it are both satisfied. Among the authors whose works have been condemned as "obscene and indecent" are George Bernard Shaw, Charles Morgan, Thomas Mann, Erich Maria Remarque, André Malraux, Robert Graves, Ernest Hemmingway, Aldous Huxley, Somerset Maugham, Storm Jameson, Graham Greene, and a great many others of international reputation.[29]

The Censorship Board is not concerned with the cinema. The post of film censor was created in 1925. The censor, unlike the board, is a civil servant. An appeals board was set up to review his decisions and is said to be more permissive than the censor.[30]

Pre-censorship of books is exercised effectively by the Library Association of Ireland, which has an advisory committee on book selection. This lists new books as "good" or "objectionable." Most libraries follow these recommendations faithfully. Public libraries are watched carefully to see that they contain no books considered objectionable by the clergy. In 1931, a Trinity College professor was appointed librarian in County Mayo and this appointment was attacked vigorously by Catholic Action. The Government at first refused to heed the attack but, after threat of a tax strike, gave in and canceled the appointment.[31]

Many countries offer examples of self-appointed guardians of community mores in the form of voluntary associations ready to display extreme patriotism and zeal in attacking other organizations or individuals who are suspected of being less than devoted to the same principles as are the patriots. In Ireland there are many Catholic lay societies, such as Catholic Action, the Catholic Women's Federations, the Catholic Boy Scouts, and numerous others who are always on the alert and ready to mobilize community disapproval and pressures against persons who seem to be acting in defiance of rules of behavior approved by the clergy. It is unnecessary for the Church or its official representatives to intervene when the "universal and pervasive" pressures of these lay organizations are so effective.[32]

The most noteworthy recent instance of clerical intervention in connection with an important government policy had to do with the bill introduced by Dr. Noel Browne as Minister of Health in the Costello Government of 1948. Dr. Browne's bill proposed to set up a national maternity and child welfare scheme under which expectant mothers, mothers of small children, and the children themselves would be given medical advice and care at government expense without a means test. Because of the constitutional provision forbidding a religious test for government employment, some of the doctors and nurses working in such a scheme would have been non-Catholics. The Bishop of Ferns, as Secretary to the Hierarchy, wrote a letter to Mr. Costello, the taoiseach, noting that such a bill might be regarded as an invasion by the State of the sphere properly belonging to the family and the Church. It was pointed out that health "education," given sometimes by non-Catholics, might involve matters of morality, and that the views of the doctors and nurses might well differ from those of the Church. The bishops denied the State's right to have its employees give any instruction regarding sex relations, chastity, or marriage. Further, the bishops objected to the scheme on the ground that it would destroy the personal, confidential relationship between physician and patient, might destroy private medical practice, and would set up a "costly, bureaucratic scheme of nationalized medical service."

It is obvious that the above arguments fall into separate categories. One is purely Catholic and the others are nonreligious, political, and economic and echo the objections advanced by the Irish Medical Association.

Dr. Browne had a meeting with Archbishop McQuaid of Dublin, after which he believed that he had met the hierarchy's objections to the educational features of the bill. The attack on the measure was continued, however, conceivably because of the influence of the Irish Medical Association.

Subsequently the Government fell over this issue and its ranks were badly divided. The next Government, headed by De Valera, who had avoided involvement in the debates over the Browne bill, introduced a modified version of the maternity bill. Cardinal D'Alton, the Primate, sent a letter to the newspapers condemning this measure but after an interview with De Valera withdrew his letter before publication and the bill passed without trouble.

This incident is not a clear case of clerical power to veto government policies. The hierarchy itself was not totally united on the issue. The Jesuits were ignored. That is, their advice on the doctrinal aspects of the bill was not sought by the Archbishop. It is claimed that Cardinal D'Alton's withdrawal of his letter was induced by De Valera's threat to publish another letter from the Archbishop of Dublin in which the new bill was approved. Personalities were involved as well. Dr. Browne was guilty of intemperate remarks. Archbishop McQuaid was pompous and pontifical. Dr. Browne and Mr. Costello appeared to misunderstand each other. In spite of the Archbishop's assertions that all the bishops were behind him, Dr. Browne received assurance that his concessions in connection with the educational aspects of his scheme had induced some to withdraw their opposition, and some of the lower clergy supported the plan. Certainly the Irish Medical Association exerted strong pressure to defeat the Browne bill. It is conceivable that Costello need not have given in so easily and might have succeeded in getting an amended bill as De Valera did a little later.

Many of the voting public did not follow Archbishop Mc-Quaid. Dr. Browne and some other independent deputies who supported his bill retained their seats at the subsequent general election even though clerical influence was used against them.

It is interesting to note that many Protestant voters, most of whom have a Unionist background, have tended in recent elections to vote for Fianna Fáil candidates. They deserted Fine Gael because of Costello's introduction of the Republic and his withdrawal of Ireland from the Commonwealth of Nations and also because of his relative subservience to the Catholic prelacy as compared with the supposed greater resistance of the Fianna Fáil leaders to clerical pressure.

It is obvious that no Irish political party can afford to advocate policies that are contrary to the Church's views concerning education, the family, or moral questions generally. Nor can a politician who hopes for a successful political career, especially

within one of the two mass parties, afford to flout Catholic opinion in such matters. This clerical preventive veto, backed by a
pious laity, is not less effective for being unobtrusive.

Within his diocese, the bishop has what amounts in practice
to an absolute veto over some activities which are legal but of
which he disapproves. For example, a number of bishops imposed
a ban upon Saturday night dances as likely to interfere with attendance at mass and, because of late suppers, with eligibility for
communion on Sunday morning. These bans were effective in
closing the dance halls even though they might legally have remained open. Eventually the bans were lifted in one diocese after
another. The last bishop to do so, in June, 1968, was Dr. Michael
Browne, Bishop of Galway, who observed that dancing was a more
wholesome activity than an evening spent in a public house bar.
In removing the ban Dr. Browne issued a statement reading in part,
"the rule . . . was faithfully observed by the people *and by the
dance hall proprietors*. I wish to express my sincere thanks to them
for this local observance which has been most faithfully kept all
the years since I became bishop." [33]

In other matters, such as state capitalism and state control of
transport, turf fuel production, and so forth, the bishops are silent.
There is very seldom any need to employ lay associations under
clerical guidance, such as Catholic Action, to represent the Church
in politics. In fact, the members of Catholic Action and the
Knights of Columbus are as divided in party loyalties as are other
Irishmen. Their main concern with politics is in securing patronage
for their members. Not much patronage is available and most of
this is at the disposal of individual ministers and others rather than
the party organizations.

The effective veto over policies concerning moral or religious
matters is not accompanied by any substantial power to impose
policies upon the Government. In 1945 a social insurance plan
proposed by Bishop Dignan was rejected by the Minister for
Local Government. It is said that other suggestions by the bishops
have been ignored.[34] In any case the clergy in general have tended
to be conservative in the social and economic fields rather than to
promote or suggest changes. The hatred and fear of "Godless

Communism" has been transferred, in part, to what they regard as its sister doctrine of socialism. A socialist member of the Irish Labour Party remarked to the author: "Socialism is a dirty word in Ireland." There can be little doubt that this attitude, fostered by the clergy in both secular and religious education, has influenced predominant opinion in Ireland subtly but powerfully to maintain the conservatism of the major parties and even the Labour Party and to militate against the successful development of a socialist party. But times change, even in Ireland. Important elements of the Roman Catholic Church are no longer opposed to policies once considered socialist. Large sections of the Irish economy are State owned and operated as a consequence of pragmatic decisions by the Government without any reference to socialism. It may be that additional policies of a socialist nature may be introduced under the label of Fine Gael's "Just Society" or by a revitalized Labour Party.

It is possible that the puritanism, the anti-intellectualism (manifested in the attitude of the Maynooth-educated bishops toward the more sophisticated Jesuits), and the moral and social dogmatic rigidity of the bulk of the Irish clergy, may be traced to the peculiar history of the Roman Catholic Church in Ireland. The Church was the militant arm, not only of the faith but also, in a sense, of the Irish nation. Prudence might require submission to the British occupation but this meant not surrender but a compromise which would allow the clergy to continue to defend and propagate the faith. Toleration of heresy could never be condoned and in its embattled position the Church would be most unlikely to develop the quality of tolerance toward dissent. The clergy, including the parish priests, had to become community leaders, willy nilly. In their role as social and political leaders, they tended to carry over an attitude of suspicion toward all non-Catholic ideas and influences.[35]

It is interesting to note that the Roman Catholic Church in French Canada had an experience similar to that of Ireland in finding itself the only important national institution of a conquered people who had to submit to alien rule. The French Canadian clergy assumed a dominating political role. They used every means at their command to maintain their control of education, to foster the identity of the French Canadian nationality and the French language, and to crush political movements they believed to be receptive to alien, non-Catholic influences.[36]

Notes

1. Samuel H. Beer, *British Politics in the Collectivist Age* (New York, 1965), pp. 9 ff.
2. *Supra,* p. 151.
3. Clarkson, *op. cit.,* pp. 440, 441.
4. *Ibid.,* pp. 447, 448.
5. *Supra,* pp. 161, 162.
6. Examples are: Irish Sugar Beet Growers' Association, Ltd., Irish Beef Canners' Advisory Association, Irish Beef Cattle Traders' and Stock-Owners' Association, Irish Fresh Meat Exporters' Society, Irish Short-horn Breeders' Association, Kerry Cattle Herd Book Committee. Others concern themselves with milk production and marketing, pig breeding, poultry, sheep, and so forth. There are more than fifty organizations of this character.
7. See the *Irish Times,* September 21, 1965, p. 5.
8. See the *Irish Times,* June 20, 1968, p. 16.
9. See the *Irish Times,* January 17, 1969.
10. Postmasterships, however, are patronage appointments. An entertaining account of a prolonged squabble over the appointment of a village postmaster is recounted in Lawrence Earl, *The Battle of Baltinglass* (New York, 1953).
11. *Economic Development* (Dublin: Stationery Office, November, 1958), Pr. 4803.
12. By "social power" is meant control over the actions of individuals, enforced by means of sanctions of some kind, not necessarily legal.
13. Liam Maher, in *Hibernia,* 23, 9 (September, 1959), pp. 5, 12. Mr. Maher would seem to be wishing for something that does not, in fact, exist. Much modern writing in Irish concerns nature and love rather than religion or patriotism. Religious literature is concerned with religion alone. Plays and novels with patriotic themes deal with religion only as part of the daily life. As Conor Cruise O'Brien has pointed out, the relationship between religion and patriotism is highly complex and sometimes religious and patriotic sentiments operate at cross purposes. See Conor Cruise O'Brien, "The Parnellism of Seán O'Faoláin in *Maria Cross* (Oxford University Press, 1952).
14. Arland Ussher, *The Face and Mind of Ireland* (New York, 1950), p. 110. A somewhat fanciful explanation is given by Seán O'Faoláin in *The Irish: A Character Study* (New York, 1949), p. 82. He claims that the "indissoluble merger" of the Roman Catholic faith and Irish

patriotism dates from the return to Ireland in 1579 of Sir James Fitzmaurice who brought a papal bull deposing Queen Elizabeth from the throne of both England and Ireland. Thenceforward British Government had no legitimacy in the view of Irish Roman Catholics.

15. Sir James O'Connor, *History of Ireland, 1798–1924* (London, 1925), pp. 1, 56, 57, quoting Wyse, *History of Catholic Emancipation*, II, App. xvii.
16. J. A. Froude, *The English in Ireland*, III, 404, 438.
17. ". . . the refusal to solve the Catholic question at the time of the Union and to endow the Catholic clergy was the greatest political blunder ever committed by a British Government in its dealings with the Irish people" (E. Strauss, *Irish Nationalism and British Democracy* [London, 1951], p. 91).
18. E. R. Norman, *The Catholic Church and Ireland in the Age of Rebellion, 1859–1873* (Ithaca, N. Y., 1965) Ch. 7, "Moves Towards Disestablishment, 1866-8."
19. *Ibid.*, p. 349.
20. McDowell, *op. cit.*, p. 32, referring to *Report of Her Majesty's Commission appointed to inquire into the management and government of the College of Maynooth, evidence*, 36 H.C. 1854–55 (1896, I).
21. Norman, *op. cit.*, pp. 427, 428.
22. *Ibid.*, Ch. 2, "A First Phase: Rome and Education."
23. Strauss, *op. cit.*, Ch. XXI, "The Era of Clericalism."
24. Norman, *op. cit.*, p. 429, n. 4.
25. Warner Moss, *Political Parties in the Irish Free State* (New York, 1933), p. 31 n.
26. This paragraph is based upon personal observation and statements by Irish informants of all parties.
27. *Supra*, pp. 87 ff.
28. Ussher, *op. cit.*, pp. 103, 105.
29. Ussher, *op. cit.*, p. 131. It should be noted that the Censorship Board in recent years has been far more tolerant than formerly.
30. Coogan, *op. cit.*, p. 170.
31. This incident is recounted in Paul Blanshard, *The Irish and Catholic Power* (London, 1954), pp. 110 ff.
32. Seán O'Faoláin, *op. cit.*, p. 153.
33. *Irish Times*, June 3, 1968, p. 1 (author's italics).
34. Seán O'Faoláin, *op. cit.*, p. 149.
35. Even interdenominational movements that had nothing to do with religion were frowned upon. When the Tenant League was formed in 1850 to work for parliamentary action and reform of the laws concerning tenancy, its founders tried to get joint action of Ulster Presbyterians and Southern Catholics and sought the sponsorship of Presbyterian ministers and Catholic curates. They had some success until the bishops forbade such interdenominational cooperation. The League died in 1854 (Strauss, *op. cit.*, p. 148).
36. See M. Ayearst, "The *Parti Rouge* and the Clergy," *Canadian Historical Review*, December, 1934, pp. 390–405.

GLOSSARY OF IRISH
WORDS AND PHRASES

WORDS AND PHRASES	APPROXIMATE PRONUNCIATION	MEANING
Árd-fheis	awrd-esh	Annual conference of a political party (literal meaning: high council)
Ceann Cómhairle	kyown kohwórla	Chairman (of Dáil or Senate)
Clann na Poblachta	clown na publokta	Republican Party
Clann na Talmhan	clown na tholoón	Farmers' Party
Cumann na nGaedheal	cumman na ngale	League of Gaels
Dáil Éireann	dawl áyrann	Chamber of Deputies (literal meaning: assembly of Ireland)
Éire	áyra	Ireland
Fianna Fáil	feéana foil (or fahl)	Soldiers of Destiny
Fine Gael	finna gale	League of Gaels
Leas-Cheann Comhairle	lasskyownkohwórla	Deputy Chairman

Oireachtas	irókthas	Parliament
Poblacht na hÉireann	publokt na háyran	Republic of Ireland
Saorstat Éireann	sare-stawt áyran	Irish Free State
Seanád Éireann	shanád áyran	Senate of Ireland
Sinn Féin	shin fane	Ourselves
Taoiseach	teeshock	Prime minister (literal meaning: chief)
Tanaiste	táwnishta	Deputy prime minister (literal meaning: heir designate to the chiefship)
Teachta Dala	chóckta dawla	Deputy, member of Dáil
Uachtarán	oochtaroin	President (of the Republic)

SELECTIVE BIBLIOGRAPHY

General

Bence-Jones, Mark. *The Remarkable Irish*. New York, 1966.

Connery, Donald S. *The Irish*. London, 1968.

Curtis, L. P., Jr. *Anglo-Saxons and Celts; A Study of Anti-Irish Prejudice in Victorian England*. New York, 1968.

Donaldson, Loraine. *Development Planning in Ireland*. New York, 1966.

Freeman, T. W. *Ireland, A General and Regional Geography*, 3rd edn. London, 1965.

Ussher, Arland. *The Face and Mind of Ireland*. New York, 1950.

Biographies

Abels, Jules. *The Parnell Tragedy*. New York, 1966.

Beaslai, P. *Michael Collins and the Making of the New Ireland*. London, 1926.

Bromage, Mary C. *De Valera and the March of a Nation*. New York, 1956.

Butler, Matthew. *Eamon de Valera—A Biographical Sketch*. Waterford, 1932.

Colum, Padraic. *Arthur Griffith*. Dublin, 1959.

Greaves, C. D. *The Life and Times of James Connolly*. London, 1961.
Hurst, Michael. *Parnell and Irish Nationalism*. London, 1968.
Larkin, Emmet. *James Larkin, Irish Labour Leader, 1876–1947*. London, 1965.
Lyons, F. S. L. *The Fall of Parnell, 1890–91*. London, 1960.
McManus, M. J. *Eamon de Valera*. Dublin, 1944.
O'Brien, R. B. *The Life of Charles Stewart Parnell, 1846–1891*, 2 vols. London, 1898.
O'Faoláin, Seán. *De Valera*. Dublin, 1933.
O'Neill, Tomas P. and An t-Athair Pádraic O Fiannachta, *De Valera*, Vol. I. Dublin, 1968 (first of three volumes of the authorized biography).
Skeffington, F. Sheehy. *Michael Davitt: Revolutionary, Agitator and Labour Leader*. London, 1908.
Van Vorhis, Jacqueline. *Constance de Markievicz*. Amherst, Mass., 1967.
White, Terence de Vere. *Kevin O'Higgins*. London, 1948.

Irish Free State

Bromage, A. W. "Constitutional Development in Saorstat Eireann and the Constitution of Eire," *American Political Science Review*, 31, 842–61, 1050–70 (1937).
Douglas, J. G. *President de Valera and the Senate*. Dublin, 1936.
Figgis, Darrell. *The Irish Constitution Explained*. Dublin, 1922.
Gwynn, D. R. *The Irish Free State, 1922–1927*. London, 1928.
Harkness, D. W. *The Restless Dominion*. Dublin, 1969.
Kennedy, Hugh. "The Character and Sources of the Constitution of the Irish Free State," *Journal of the American Bar Association*, XIV (1928), 437–45.
Kohn, Leo. *The Constitution of the Irish Free State*. London, 1932.
Mansergh, Nicholas. *The Irish Free State, Its Government and Politics*. London, 1934.
Moss, Warner. *Political Parties in the Irish Free State*. New York, 1933.
O'Briain, Barra. *The Irish Constitution*. Dublin, 1929.
O'Sullivan, D. *The Irish Free State and its Senate*. London, 1940.

The De Valera (1937) Constitution

Barrington, D. "The Irish Constitution," *Irish Monthly*, February, 1952–March, 1953.

Chubb, Basil. "Cabinet Government in Ireland," *Political Studies*, III (1955), 256–74.

———. "Vocational Representation in the Irish Senate," *Political Studies*, II (1954), 97–111.

Kelly, John Maurice. *Fundamental Rights in the Irish Law and Constitution*. Dublin, 1961.

The Partition Issue

Gallagher, Frank. *The Indivisible Island: The History of the Partition of Ireland*. London, 1957.

Green, Alice Stopford. *Ourselves Alone in Ulster*. London, 1918.

Gwynn, Denis. *The History of Partition (1921–1925)*. Dublin, 1950.

Harrison, Henry. *The Neutrality of Ireland*. London, 1942.

Sibbett, R. M. *Orangism in Ireland, and throughout the Empire*, 2 vols. Belfast [1914].

Political History

Beckett, J. C. *A Short History of Ireland*. London and New York, 1952.

———. *Protestant Dissent in Ireland, 1687–1780*. London, 1948.

———. *The Making of Modern Ireland, 1603–1923*. New York, 1966.

Bergin, J. J. *The History of the Ancient Order of Hibernians*. Dublin, 1910.

Caulfield, Max. *The Easter Rebellion*. New York, 1963.

Clarkson, J. D. *Labour and Nationalism in Ireland*. New York, 1925.

Coogan, T. P. *Ireland Since the Rising*. London and New York, 1966.

Curtis, E. *A History of Ireland*, 6th edn. London, 1951.

Curtis, L. P., Jr. *Coercion and Conciliation in Ireland, 1880–1892.* Princeton, 1963.

Fox, R. M. *Labour in the National Struggle.* Dublin, 1946.

———. *Green Banners, The Story of the Irish Struggle, 1916–1925.* London, 1938.

Froude, J. A. *The English in Ireland in the Eighteenth Century,* 3 vols. London, 1881.

Gooch, G. P. *Great Britain and Ireland, 1792–1815,* Cambridge Modern History, I, 627–708.

Good, J. W. *Irish Unionism.* Dublin, 1920.

Gwynn, D. R. *Young Ireland and 1848.* Cork, 1949.

Hayden, M. and G. Moonan. *A Short History of the Irish People.* Dublin, 1921.

Henry, R. M. *The Evolution of Sinn Féin.* Dublin, 1920.

Hobson, Bulmer. *A Short History of the Irish Volunteers.* Dublin, 1918.

Hogan, David. *Four Glorious Years.* Dublin, 1953.

Knowlan, K. B. *The Politics of Repeal; A Study in the Relations between Great Britain and Ireland, 1841–50.* London, 1965.

McCaffrey, Lawrence J. *The Irish Question, 1800–1922.* Lexington, Kentucky, 1969.

Moody, T. W. and F. X. Martin (eds.). *The Course of Irish History,* New York, n.d. [1968].

Norman, E. R. *The Catholic Church and Ireland in the Age of Rebellion, 1859–1873.* Ithaca, N. Y., 1965.

O'Brien, Conor Cruise. *Parnell and his Party, 1880–1890.* Oxford, 1957.

O'Brien, George. *The Economic History of Ireland in the Eighteenth Century,* 3 vols. London, 1881.

O'Connor, Sir J. *The History Ireland, 1798–1924,* 2 vols. London, 1928.

O'Donnell, F. H. *The History of the Irish Parliamentary Party,* 2 vols. London, 1910.

O'Leary, John. *Recollections of Fenians and Fenianism,* 2 vols. Dublin, 1969 (originally published 1896).

Phillips, W. A. *The Revolution in Ireland, 1906–1923,* 2nd edn. London, 1926.

Rogers, Revd. Patrick. *The Irish Volunteers and Catholic Emancipation, 1778–1793.* London, 1934.

Ross, J. F. S. *The Irish Electoral System.* London, 1959.

Ryan, Desmond. *The Rising, The Complete Story of Easter Week*, 3rd edn. Dublin, 1957.

Ryan, W. P. *The Irish Labour Movement.* Dublin, 1919.

Strauss, E. *Irish Nationalism and British Democracy.* London, 1951.

Whyte, J. H. *The Independent Irish Party, 1850–1859.* Oxford, 1958.

Woodham-Smith, Cecil. *The Great Hunger, Ireland, 1845–1849.* London and New York, 1962.

INDEX